16. Reporting on Scientific Matters 345
Technical Reporting • The Processing • Short Write-ups • Writings on Medicine • Reporter's Credibility • The Applicability

17. Reporting on Economic Matters 375
Model Reports

18. Reports on Development 385
No Propaganda

Bibliography 397

Preface

In Modern world, Journalism is one discipline, which attracts people like any thing, but, it is equally challenging and drastic in cases. Particularly, under the new world order and in current global scenario, its value has increased manifold.

Apart from being a glorious profession, Journalism, today is a full-fledged subject, mastery of which leads one to a successful career and an all powerful status in society.

As a discipline, Journalism requires proper training and a comprehensive course, if possible. Although, there is no defined qualification for appointment as a journalist, in any capacity, in any media organisation, yet it is always better to be properly qualified and well-equipped with all essential knowledge.

Of course, there are books on Journalism but not in a great number. And, if one goes selective, then only a few books would rest in hand, as there is still a dearth for exclusive and exhaustive books on several streams of Journalism.

This series of books on Journalism is an effort to fill the abovesaid vaccum only. Here are books on all subjects and topics, related to Journalism. The undersigned is confident enough that this humble endeavour would prove to be worthy on the basis of its merits and receive a warm acceptance by students of journalism, scholars and the working journalists, as well.

—Editor

1

Introduction

The editor and the publisher of a newspaper are responsible for whatever is printed in it. In many Indian newspapers the editor and publisher is the same person. In such papers editor is also the proprietor and manager.

But where the editor and the publisher are different people, the editor looks after the editorial content, that is, anything except advertising. An advertising manager looks after the advertising.

The publisher, general manager or managing editor or executive director look after the management of the paper.

A number of assistant editors assist the editor in looking after editorial and feature pages. The news content of the paper is looked after by the news editor under whose guidance a number of sub-editors and reporters work.

In India the entry into the profession of journalism is normally as a trainee journalist who is later absorbed as a reporter or a sub-editor.

The job of a reporter is to gather news and write it for his organisation. The Sub-editor makes it fit to print. Reporters go out in the field while sub-editors work at the 'news desk' where all the news that comes is selected, edited, each news story is given a suitable headline and its place in the newspaper is decided. Reporters can become senior reporters, correspondents, senior correspondents, chief reporter, special correspondent and foreign correspondent. Sub-editors are promoted to the positions of senior sub-editor, chief sub-editor, deputy news editor and news editor. But the basic job of a reporter remains news gathering and filing the report or "copy" to the news desk. Similarly, the basic job of the sub-editor also remains the same; to "sub" copy, to make it fit to print which includes collecting, selecting, arranging, reducing, translating and adapting for publication, according to the importance of the copy. Sub-editor is also called copy editor as what he edits is called copy. Whatever is filed by reporters, special correspondents etc., is copy for him, whatever comes to the news desk from wire services (news agencies like PTI and UNI) is also copy.

But reporting and editing sides are not water-tight compartments. Reporters can exchange places with sub-editors. In many newspapers it is a routine. A sub-editor is sent on a reporting assignment many a time. He is also asked to write news items from the handouts that land up in the newspaper office when reporters are away.

To be a good reporter or a good sub-editor what one needs is common sense and command over language. These two requirements in fact summarise the qualities newsmen should have as other qualities flow from these two and the basic human values.

It is customary to describe desired qualities of a reporter and sub-editor separately, but as both of them deal with the same commodity, news, and their basic job is to communicate effectively many of these qualities have to be common.

News sense is the basic quality of newsmen. Every reporter

has to have news sense or nose for news–to distinguish news from non-news. He should be able to compare various news values and decide where to begin his story and should not miss important details.

News sense is essential for a sub-editor also. He is the first reader of a reporter's copy, and if the reporter has made a mistake he has to correct it. A bad copy may have the most important element of the story buried in the fourth paragraph. It will be left to the sub-editor's nose for news to bring that to the first paragraph.

A reporter should have clarity of mind and expression. A person who is himself confused cannot tell a story to others. Only clarity of mind is not enough unless it is accompanied by clarity of expression. Without clarity of expression, clarity of mind has no meaning.

A sub-editor is the judge of clarity of the copy. A good sub-editor will never allow a copy to escape him unless the meaning is crystal clear. He has every right to make life miserable for a reporter who is not clear and does not write in simple language.

Reporters and sub-editors should aim at objectivity while dealing with a story. They should not allow their personal bias or ideas to creep into a story. They should not take sides but try to cover all the different viewpoints to achieve balance in the story.

A reporter should strive for accuracy. He should check and re-check his facts till he is satisfied that he has them accurate. In this respect he should not take any chance. as accuracy is directly proportional to the credibility of a reporter and his newspaper.

The role of a sub-editor is to check for accuracy. It is particularly important when background is involved. In the case of dates and names the reporter may rely on his memory but the sub-editor must check them from reference material available in the newspaper office. When there is a doubt he should leave it out—this is the golden rule of journalism. It is better not to say a thing than to say it wrong.

A reporter should always be alert while dealing with his subjects. Many major news breaks in the past were possible because of the alertness of reporters. Scoops don't walk into newspaper offices—alert reporters catch them in air and pursue them.

A sub-editor has to be alert while working on news-desk. Lack of alertness of a sub-editor can be seen by readers in the morning for he will be leaving or introducing mistakes for everybody to see.

In today's world speed matters everywhere. A person who cannot work fast cannot be a good reporter. While maintaining all other desirable qualities a reporter should strive to work faster. He should think fast, decide fast and write or type fast for he has to meet deadlines or may have to go to another assignment.

A sub-editor also has to work with speed. He cannot sit with a copy for long. He has to do swiftly whatever is required of him for a lot more copies are waiting for him.

A slow sub-editor is a curse at the news desk and is treated with contempt. Such people are misfits in the profession.

Reporters and sub-editors often work in trying circumstances. They have to remain calm and composed in the most exciting and tragic circumstances. In many situations they have to be calm—devoid of hysterical actions or utterances–and apply appropriate mental and physical effort to write or edit the story.

Reporters and sub-editors are human beings. They have emotions but they have to stifle them in the face of disturbing influences—they have to develop resistance to excitability. Being in the field, reporters face many such occasions when they have to control their emotions.

Sub-editors should develop a temperament to work under pressure of deadlines. They should not lose their cool if they are behind the clock for calm minds can work faster.

Reporters and sub-editors should have an unsatiable curiosity. For reporters it is useful in developing lust for facts that may lead to better stories. This characteristic will keep on improving a sub-editor for, with every passing day, a curious sub-editor will have a better background to do his job the next day. Reporters and sub-editors should read as much as possible to constantly improve their awareness level.

Scepticism is another necessary quality which a reporter and a sub-editor should cultivate. They should not take anything for granted. They should have an unwavering posture of doubt until faced with undeniable proof.

Reporters should be more vigilant for many forces constantly try to use them, and, through them, their paper. Many people try to plant on reporters a wrong story for their own ends. Many a time reporters fall into such traps in good faith. They should have enough scepticism to avoid such plots.

Sub-editors should also be careful for some clever politicians, public relations men and product advertisers keep on trying to take them for a ride. They should not allow anything to go in news columns that should actually go as advertisement. They should not fail to check even reporters' copy for such foul play.

Punctuality is a good habit. For reporters it is a must for if they are not punctual they may miss something for which they may have to depend on secondary sources. It is always better to be punctual and then wait, than to reach late and ask others—a rival may misinform you or hide some important information.

At the desk too punctuality pays. If a sub-editor is punctual he will be treated with respect by his co-workers. If he is late he will irritate them and spoil the working atmosphere. Besides, he may have to face the problem of backlog of copy which he will have to clear under the pressure of deadline.

Patience is a quality which helps a reporter in a big way for almost daily he has to test his patience, the voluntary self-control or restraint that helps one to endure waiting, provocation, injustice, suffering or any of the unpleasant vicissitudes of time and life. Most of the time a reporter waits for someone or something and patience gives him the willingness to wait without becoming disgruntled or anxious. Many a time he has to tolerate other people's shortcomings and has to remain unperturbed by someone else's slowness or other quirks.

Patience also helps sub-editors as they work long hours in trying conditions. They have to put up with many annoying situations everyday vis-a-vis reporters, proof-readers or printers.

Imagination, a basic mental faculty helps reporters in writing better stories that retain the reader's interest. For a sub-editor this creative faculty is very useful as he can add sparkle to somebody else's copy and make it lively. Besides, imaginative headlines attract the reader and improve the quality of a newspaper.

An intelligent envisioning of the future helps, newsmen in general. The quality helps them in identifying processes and people who will be important in future. Reporters can watch such processes and cultivate people who may become important news sources in the future.

It helps reporters and sub-editors in determining the importance of an event. A reporter with foresight can think ahead and prepare for eventualities. With a little forethought sub-editors can plan their work so as to avoid tension and it results in better functioning of the desk.

One can achieve a degree of proficiency in sub-editing or reporting by systematic effort and self-control. In this sense self-discipline suggests dedication and firm commitment. It helps in journalism as in any other field.

Integrity is a virtue in itself and implies undeviating honesty and strict adherence to a stern code of ethics. This human quality is important for journalists. It is more important for reporters for they are more exposed to temptations as compared to sub-editors.

Fearlessness and Frankness help reporters in asking unpleasant questions and taking risks to find out the truth. Nobody gives a story on a platter. The reporter will have to probe, question, authenticate and exercise his power of deduction to get a good story.

A reporter should be tactful. He should have the ability to handle sensitive people and situations gracefully without causing hurt or angry feelings. He should be considerate of others and should be careful not to embarrass, upset or offend them. A reporter should have a flexible and sociable personality and should have a nature that relishes variety of experiences. He should have an understanding of human behaviour and emotions. This will help him in developing contacts that are so essential for news gathering.

A reporter who works in the field should have an outgoing nature with initiative and drive. These qualities will help him get acquainted with news sources and get stories from them. A meek, retiring or shy person is not fit for reporting. Reporters need a fair amount of assertiveness and aggressiveness to be successful in their career.

A reporter should be mobile. He should enjoy moving around and should not hesitate travelling distances to get stories when required. He should go to his news sources as often as possible for such constant contacts help him get news. A mobile reporter is seldom caught napping when a major story breaks.

Reporters and sub-editors should be diligent. Their jobs require painstaking exertion of intense care and effort, alertness and dedication to the task and wary watchfulness. They have to make extremely fine distinctions while writing or editing copy. A sub-editor should insist on perfection and should love his job for he can make or mar the newspaper.

These qualities are basically qualities of good and efficient human beings who make good and efficient sub-editors and reporters. All other things being equal, reporters need additional qualities to deal effectively with all sorts of people they meet in the field. Sub-editors should have better command over language as they improve what reporters write.

2

The Fundamentals

The heroes of journalism are reporters. What they do is find things out. They go in first, amid the chaos of now, battering at closed doors, sometimes taking risks, and capture the beginnings of the truth. And if they do not do that, who will? Editors' Commentators? There is only one alternative to reporters: accepting the authorised version, the one the businesses, bureaucrats and politicians choose to give us. After all, without reporters, what would commentators know.

The Heroes

Reporters are, like almost all heroes, flawed. As a group, they have a more soiled reputation than most; for enough of them routinely exaggerate, simplify and contort the truth to have made parts of the trade a by-word for calculated dishonesty. Not for nothing do screen writers and dramatists, in search of a booable villain, regularly opt for a tabloid reporter. It saves time. They don't have to spend pages establishing a lack of morals, the mere announcement of the character's line of work is enough for audiences to grasp that this person is going to wheedle and deceive. Then there are the lazy — those who opt for spoon feeding and the facile, rather than the hard, painstaking, often exposed job of getting it as right as they can. There is, to be sure, a lot of calculated malice and shoddy workmanship in the history of journalism.

But there is a lot that is heroic, and far, far more of it than most media critiques and journalism schools would have the beginner believe. There is John Tyas's exposure for *The Times* of British atrocities against demonstrators in Manchester in 1819; William Howard Russell's accounts of the bungling of the British army in the Crimea; William Leng's exposure in the *Sheffield Telegraph* of corruption and violence in that city (he was threatened so often that he kept a loaded revolver on his desk and had a police escort home every night); Emily Crawford, who incessantly risked her life to report the 1871 Paris Commune for the *Daily News* and then scooped the world at the subsequent Versailles Conference; Nellie Bly, who feigned mental illness to get inside an asylum and wrote a series for the *New York World* that described the terrors and cruelties she found and which led to improved conditions; W.T. Stead's exposure in the *Pall Mall Gazette* of child prostitution; and Ida Tarbell's articles in *McClure's* that documented the corruption and intimidation of the Standard Oil Company 1902–1904 and prepared the way for the dissolution of the firm.

Then there is Emilie Marshall, who broke several all-male preserves in becoming the first woman reporter in the House of Commons' press gallery and the first woman staff reporter on both the *Daily Mail* and *Daily Express;* John Reed's reporting of the Russian Revolution; the unmasking of the violently racist Ku Klux Klan by Roland Thomas of the *New York World;* Ilya Ehrenburg's reporting for *Red Star* that first revealed the Nazi extermination camps; John Hersey and Wilfred Burchett's reporting from Hiroshima that disproved the official lie that there was no such thing as radiation sickness; the courageous opposition of the *Observer* and *Manchester Guardian* to the Suez invasion of 1956; the relentless pursuit of high-level security breaches by the whole British press in the early 1960s, the uncovering by Seymour

Hersch, then a young freelance, of the full horrors of the My Lai massacre in 1968; the *Sunday Times'* campaign for the limbless victims of the drug thalidomide; Carl Bernstein and Bob Woodward's Watergate investigation in the *Washington Post* that proved a US President to be a corrupt liar; and Robert Fisk's refusal to swallow the NATO line (or, for that matter, anyone's line) in reporting the Kosovo conflict in the *Independent* in 1999.

There are also those whose names are read fleetingly, but rarely remembered; the ones whose efforts to inform their communities are met, not with an obstructive official or evasive answer, but with intimidation or worse. Every year, thousands of reporters are arrested or threatened, hundreds imprisoned, and scores killed. In its most extreme form, this is what Peruvian journalist Sonia Goldenburg has called 'censorship by death'. In 1982 nine journalists were killed around the world. In 1994 no fewer than 103 journalists died for getting too close to the truth. By the turn of the twentieth century, each month saw 40 journalists threatened, 20 arrested, 90 in jail and three killed. Each one of them is a definitive answer to those, both inside and outside the business, who think that journalism is a branch of marketing that organises and exaggerates trivia. After all, no authority would bother obstructing, jailing or murdering people for that.

Finally, there are the tens of thousands of other, often local, journalists whose lot is nothing more glamorous or heroic than discovering the most complete version of what happened in their areas and reporting it. They don't expect gold or glory, and there is no particular reason why they should get it. But they are, nevertheless, an antidote, socially and professionally, to those who have traded in their credibility for a high salary or easy life.

Aims and Objectives

And all these good reporters share something. They may keep it well hidden under the journalists' obligatory, hard-bitten mask, but the immortals, the persecuted and the unsung all share a belief in what the job is about. This is, above all things, to question; and, by so doing, then to:

- Discover and publish information that replaces rumour and speculation.
- Resist or evade government controls.
- Inform, and so empower, voters.
- Subvert those whose authority relies on a lack of public information.
- Scrutinise the action and inaction of governments, elected representatives and public services.
- Scrutinise businesses, their treatment of workers and customers, and the quality of their products.
- Comfort the afflicted and afflict the comfortable, providing a voice for those who cannot normally be heard in public.
- Hold up a mirror to society, reflecting its virtues and vices and also debunking its cherished myths.
- Ensure that justice is done, is seen to be done and investigations carried out where this is not so.
- Promote the free exchange of ideas, especially by providing a platform for those with philosophies alternative to the prevailing ones.

If you can read that list without the hairs on the back of your neck beginning to stand up, then maybe journalism is not for you.

To meet the aims listed above on a regular basis is a tough assignment. The idea, common among those outside journalism, that what a reporter needs more than anything is the ability to write well is not even the half of it. Literary ability is only part of the job, and often not the largest part. Neither is good reporting a matter of acquiring a little bag of tricks and tools, out of which the appropriate one is selected according to circumstance. What is needed to succeed as a reporter are the right attitudes and character.

The most important equipment reporters have is that which is carried around between their ears. Some of these attitudes are instinctive, others are learnt quickly, but most are built up through years of experience – by researching and writing, re-researching and re-writing hundreds and hundreds of stories.

You need a keen news sense and for three reasons. First, in the positive sense of knowing what makes a good story and the ability to find the essential news point in a mass of dross. Second, in the negative sense of not wasting time by pursuing stories that will never amount to much. Often you have to ask yourself: 'What is the best this story can be? What is the strongest news point it will have if one gets all the information I need?' And sometimes the answer is that it will not be much of a tale. So drop it. The third reason is that if you don't have a news sense, or have it but don't use it, you will miss things and make a fool of yourself. Take the case of Duncombe Jewell, a reporter for the Daily Mail in its early days. He was sent to cover the launch of HMS Albion at the Thames Ironworks in London and in due course returned to the office with a piece of purple prose that was, in his own words, 'the nearest thing to a Turner sunset that you could get in manuscript'. As he handed it in, news reached the paper that 30 people had drowned at the launching. His news editor was beside himself with anger. 'Well,' said Jewell, 'I did see some people bobbing about in the water as I came away but...'

As a news editor, passion and precision is the one attribute which is valued more than any other in reporters. Could one rely on their work and trust their accuracy? As a reporter you also speedily appreciate that your reputation for accuracy and not exaggerating, either in print or beforehand, is a valuable commodity. Lose it, and it will be very difficult to regain.

Precision means three things. First, the obvious one of recording and writing accurately what people tell you. Second, taking care that however accurate each little part of your story, the whole thing is true to the spirit and atmosphere of the situation or events — which means adding background and context. Third, not falling into the dangerous and widespread habit of saying, 'Well if that happened and the other happened, then this other thing must be true.' You should not wish but report your stories into print. If there are any gaps in a sequence of events that you are reporting, find out precisely what is missing: don't think that if A happened, then something else and then C, then the missing part must be B. It may not be.

Making assumptions applies to all assumptions — either of logic, identity, fact or motives. The great problem with assumptions is that most of them turn out to be correct; that is what makes them so dangerous and tempting. Play safe, report only what you know, not what you think you know. That way you will avoid being inaccurate, dishonest and misleading — or sacked.

There was a famous occasion when a freelance photographer gave a British mass-market newspaper a picture of Prince Charles putting his arms around a lady who was not his wife at a time when he was known to be unhappily married. The paper published the picture under a headline that suggested a romantic relationship, because the editors assumed that was what was taking place. They were wrong. Unknown to them, the picture was taken at the funeral of the woman's child, who had died of leukaemia at the age of four. The Prince was doing what any of us might have done in a similar situation — he was comforting the distressed mother. However rudimentary you may imagine your ignorance to be, if you don't know, ask; if you don't understand, request an explanation. Don't worry if anyone laughs at you. The really stupid reporters are the ones who pretend to know, who sit there nodding throughout an interview they only partly understand and who then try to write the story — and find that they can't. The place to show your ignorance is when questioning people, not on paper in your subsequent story.

An essential general attitude for reporters, indeed all

journalists, is to be suspicious of all sources. Why is this person telling me this? What is their motive? And are they really in a position to know what they claim to know?

You cannot be expected to shed all your cherished beliefs, but you should never allow them consciously to affect your work. Reporters should accurately relate what happened, not strain everything through the sieve of their own prejudices, cultured and intelligent though they imagine these to be.

This invocation applies to newly minted prejudices as well as old ones. Don't let the opinions you form early on in the research prematurely colour your judgement of the story. A great sin of some reporters, particularly those often asked to write colour and atmosphere pieces, is that they will write the intro in their heads on the way to an interview. Their intro may be smart, it may be a beautiful piece of writing, but the chances are that it will say more about them than their subject.

Reporters are subject to what editors want. By all means argue with them, shout at them and try to sweet-talk them, but, in the end, you have to accept their decision — or go and work elsewhere. That is professionalism. So, too, is the acceptance of the discipline of the schedule of your paper. A lot of reporters think it is somehow a mark of a literary talent in full flower to be late and over length. It is not. It is the sign of an unreliable amateur. So too is the reporter who, when out on a story, fails to call into the office regularly. You can often, however, use the paper's needs to your advantage, getting prominence for your stories by calculating when in your paper's production cycle they are most in need of early stories or ones illustrated by pictures, graphics, sidebars, etc. — and delivering them.

Unless people read your story, you might as well be muttering it to yourself in a darkened room. They will read it if you consider them — when you write, but especially when you research. What will readers want to know? What do they need explained? And what will bring this story home to them? Find anecdotes, show how the events will impact on readers' lives, or impact on other lives; use examples that will be relevant to their own experience; above all, where possible, tell the story in terms of real people.

Sooner or later the new reporter experiences the dawning realisation that the rest of the world is not run for the convenience of newspapers. Stories happen at bad times and in awkward places, telephones are not always available or working; and, if you are out of the city or country, you can be running out of money, time, food, drink and energy. You need a strong desire to beat whatever circumstances are strewn in your path, get to the story and then file as fast as possible. To be like Ed Cody of the *Washington Post.* Mort Rosenblum's excellent book *Who Stole the News,* tells the story of how Cody was in Paris one night in December 1988 when word reached him that a Pan Am jumbo jet had crashed on Lockerbie, a little town in Scotland. It was 8.20 p.m. and the last flight to Britain that evening had already left. Cody found a charter operator, persuaded his foreign editor in the United States to authorise the cost and, a few hours later, the reporter was in Glasgow. Lockerbie was 60 miles south and by that time had been sealed off by police roadblocks. Miraculously, Cody found a cab driver who was from the town and, with his local knowledge and contacts, Cody made it to the scene. The driver even had a friend who owned a pub, which he opened up so that the reporter could call Washington to file his story.

The crash, in which all 259 passengers and 11 people on the ground died, was one of the biggest stories of the 1980s. Cody's excellent job on it was possible because he had the will to win. He may also have had a paper prepared to pay $6,000 for a charter aircraft, but, on most occasions, a reporter's desire to get to the story will not cost as much and it will always bring rewards.

Newspapers want their reporters to file the earliest and fullest account of a story that they can get. A little healthy, or even unhealthy, competition to be first is part of the reality — and fun— of the job. And it serves readers well, just so long as not too many corners are cut.

Beating the rival agency, for instance, was uppermost in the minds of the Associated Press (AP) and United Press International (UPI) photographers who were assigned to take pictures of the Dalai Lama as he fled Tibet in 1959. Both chartered planes and organised relays of motorcyclists so that they could get their pictures from the Chinese borders to the nearest transmitter in India. When the Dalai Lama emerged from his aircraft, the photographers leapt forward, took their pictures and ran to their already-revving planes. After a break-neck race in the air and on the ground, UPI won.

The AP man was devastated. He went back to his hotel room and sat there, full of recrimination about what might have been and the shame of being beaten. Then he received a cable from his office: 'Opposition's Dalai Lama has long shaggy hair. Yours bald. How please %'The AP man cabled back: 'Because my Dalai right Dalai.' In his desperation to be first, the UPI man had photographed the interpreter.

Acceptable rivalry has its limits, however, and they were surely reached — and considerably exceeded — by the former *New York Post* journalist Steve Dunleavy who as a young man worked as a reporter when his father was with the opposition paper. Both were assigned the same story and he was so keen to be first to the scene that he immobilised his father's car by slashing its tyres.

All around the world governments are getting ever more sophisticated in their management of news, tightly controlling what information they distribute and who gets it. In some places access to these channels even involves reporters joining a kind of informal 'club', with rules about what constitutes 'responsible' behaviour and the threat of exclusion from the official information for those who stray. This is unhealthy, as is the habit of reporters sometimes to cooperate with each other, sharing quotes and phone numbers. But good reporters should always be prepared to strike out on their own when necessary, to go where no one else is going, and — when it does not work out — take the flak. They are ready to spurn predigested meals from the official spoon because they know there is something far tastier to be found if only they go foraging for themselves.

Almost any intelligent human being can, with sufficient application, learn how to be a competent reporter. But to rise above that, to be good or great, you must have real talent and flair for either research, or writing, or both. And you should have the right kind of character; for if there is one thing that separates outstanding reporters from the ordinary, it is this.

If one was to select one piece of reporting that in its quality and impact represents the best of journalism, one could do a lot worse than go back a century and a quarter to a Central Europe riven by nationalist claims and systematic violence. In what follows, any resemblance to contemporary events in that part of the world is almost certainly not a coincidence. The story started with allegations of atrocities, the simultaneous lying of several governments, censorship and a dying empire. It drew in Turkey. Russia, Britain and a nascent Bulgaria, continued with heroism and a war, and concluded with nothing less than the creation of several new nations in the re-drawing of the map of Europe. And what drew all these disparate strands together was a former St. Petersburg correspondent, an Irish-American called Januarius Aloysius MacGahan.

Even by the adventurous standards of his day, MacGahan was a thrill-seeker of the first order. In an age when men in an international hurry used the horse and the steamship, MacGahan in five hasty years reported from the Paris Commune (where he was imprisoned), the court of St. Petersburg, Central Asia, Cuba, the Arctic, the Caucasus and the Pyrenees. Famously distinguished for his impartiality and sharp eye, MacGahan was also never one to shirk a challenge. In 1875 he sailed through the Arctic's ice-choked waters in a wooden boat and two years earlier he defied a Russian embargo on reporters to make a remarkable ride over the Central Asian steppes. His goal was to catch up with a Russian military expedition on its way to Turkestan. Cossacks bent on his destruction pursued him for nearly 1,000 miles but after 29 days, accompanied by two attendants, sometimes forced to wade knee-deep in sand and several times lost, he reached the camp. His towering reputation for reliability and bravery reached new peaks.

By the summer of 1876, this 32-year-old reporter was in London with his Russian-born wife, Barbara, and a young son. He was planning a third book and some rest. But his relaxation was short-lived. The *Daily News*, a prominent liberal London paper, contacted him. They had an urgent assignment.

The *News* was in some trouble. A day or so before, on 23 June, they had published a story from their man in Constantinople, Sir Edwin Pears, based on rumours of terrible atrocities in southern Bulgaria by Turkish forces against the Christian population. The British Foreign Office was furious. So too was the pro-Turkish Prime Minister, Benjamin Disraeli. Describing the reports as 'coffee-house babble', he flatly denied them and openly charged the paper with misreporting and with, that old standard whine of the politicians, 'irresponsibility'. The Turks, who had imposed a total censorship on events, denied the whole thing.

It was now up to the *News* to prove their charges, or humiliatingly to climb down. So they sent for MacGahan and commissioned him to go to Bulgaria and try to discover the truth. By early July he was on his way; by the middle of the month he was there, investigating and interviewing hundreds of survivors. What he found was beyond even his hardened imagining: the frenzied and wholesale butchery of some 12,000 Bulgarian men, women and children.

In the first of his dispatches, published by the *News* on 28 July, MacGahan wrote: 'I think I came in a fair and impartial frame of mind ... I fear I am no longer impartial, and I am certainly no longer cool...'. His most telling account was from the village of Batak. Despite his own remarks about impartiality, it is a model of how the controlled reporting of facts, rather than emotions, is the most effective form of journalism:

> The hillsides were covered with little fields of wheat and rye that were golden with ripeness. But although the harvest was ripe, and over ripe ... there were no sign of reapers trying to save them. The fields were as deserted as the little valley, and the harvest was rotting in the soil.

... At last we came to a little plateau on the hillside ... We rode toward this, with the intention of crossing it, but all suddenly drew rein with an exclamation of horror, for right before us, almost beneath our horses' feet, was a sight that made us shudder. It was a heap of skulls intermingled with bones from all parts of the human body, skeletons, nearly entire, rotting clothing, human hair, and putrid flesh lying there in one foul heap, around which the grass was growing luxuriantly.

... In the midst of this heap I could distinguish one slight skeleton form still enclosed in a chemise, the skull wrapped about with a coloured handkerchief, and the bony ankles encased in the embroidered footless stockings worn by the Bulgarian girls.

... On the other side of the way were the skeletons of two children lying side by side partly covered with stones, and with frightful sabre cuts in their little skulls... As we approached the middle of the town, bones, skeletons, and skulls became more numerous. There was not a house beneath the ruins of which we did not perceive human remains, and the street besides was strewn with them... The church was not a very large one, and it was surrounded by a low stone wall, enclosing a small churchyard about fifty yards wide by seventy-five long. At first we perceive nothing in particular,... but upon inspection we discover that what appeared to be a mass of stones and rubbish was in reality an immense heap of human bodies covered over with a thin layer of stones.

... We were told there were three thousand people lying here in this little churchyard alone ... There were little curly heads there in that festering mass, crushed down by heavy stones; little feet not as long as your finger on which the flesh was dried hard by the ardent heat before it had time to decompose; little baby hands stretched out as if for help; babes that had died wondering at the bright gleam of sabres and the red hands of the fierce-eyed men who wielded them; children who had died shrinking with fright and terror; young girls who had died weeping and sobbing and begging for mercy; mothers who died trying to shield their little ones with their own weak bodies, all lying there together, festering in one horrid mass.

They were silent enough now. There are no tears nor cries, no weeping, no shrieks of terror, nor prayers for mercy. The harvests are rotting in the fields, and the reapers are rotting here in the churchyard.

MacGahan's reports (which were reprinted across the world and later published as a booklet in many languages) instantly detonated a chain reaction of enormous proportions. Amid the worldwide indignation that followed, the British government was forced to concede the truth, pressure for military intervention built up and, in the spring of 1877, Russia launched a war against Turkey.

80 correspondents arrived to cover the Russian side but such were the rigours of the campaign that by its end less than a year later, only four of the original reporters were still in the field. MacGahan, of course, was among them. He had gone off to war with one foot in plaster, after injuring it in a fall. He ignored this and two further accidents which seriously crippled him, and carried on reporting, watching the fighting from a gun carriage. Six months and two treaties later, the nations of Bulgaria, Serbia, Montenegro and Romania had come into being, Russia was enlarged and the British had Cyprus.

MacGahan, however, was not alive to report it. A few weeks after the end of the war he went to Constantinople to nurse his friend, Francis Greene, through typhoid fever. Greene survived, but MacGahan caught it himself and on 9 June 18 he died, aged 34. The Bulgarians, who had already christened him 'The Liberator', buried him in Pera, masses were said for his soul in St. Petersburg and he was mourned in London, Paris and America. In Sofia a statue was erected to him and for years afterwards his death was commemorated with an annual requiem at Tirnova.

Five years later his body was brought by an American warship to New York, where it lay in state in City Hall, and thence was taken to its final resting place in New Lexington, Ohio. His wife, who had been the Russian correspondent of the *New York Herald*, crossed the ocean with her husband's body and became the American correspondent for the Moscow paper, *Russkaya Viedmosti*. Later that year an official inquiry confirmed, in the cool calm of hindsight, everything that MacGahan had written from the chaotic killing fields of Bulgaria. Universal journalism is nothing new.

3

Art of Reporting

The news is the timely report of events, facts, and opinions and interests a significant number of people. It is a new piece of information about a significant and recent event that affects the audience and is of interest to them. The definition of a news item is dependent on :

(a) the size of the community,

(b) the periodicity of the publication,

(c) the social character and economic base of the community,

(d) the focus of attention of community.

Jhon Bogart pointed out that unusual events fall under the purview of the news. Later, Joseph Pulitzer, publisher of New York World defined news as "original, distinctive, dramatic, romantic, thrilling, unique, curious, quaint, humorous, odd and apt-to-be-talked about". Walter William, the founder of the first school of Journalism, defined news as, "News in its broadest sense, is that which is of interest to the readers-the public....."

The former-managing editor of the New York Times said that the news was "..... anything you can find out today that you didn't know before."

Thus, the news is Perishable; of interest to a large number of people; of unusual events and happenings; what is new to the public; an event put forward by a reporter.

Hard News and Soft News : These are the two main categories in which the news is mainly divided.

Hard News is mostly event-centered. It is a narration of an event. The Hard news items are centered on, "what, when, where and why".

No doubt, the major thrust of a daily newspaper is the hard news. The main task of the dailies is to provide information to the readers. Mere accounts of events however do not satisfy the readers. They would like to enter beneath the upper crust of hard news. This type of news is called soft news. Thus, soft news goes beyond what has happened. It analyses, interprets and draws logical conclusions. It is becoming a very important segment of the daily newspaper.

The Contents

Timeliness : News must be timely and new. It loses interest if it is already known.

Nearness : People are more interested in what happens under their nose. They are more concerned in the occurrence of an immediate impact on them.

Conflict : People gather in a street if and when there is a fight. Conflicts of all kinds are part of life and make good copy.

Prominence : What happens to important persons makes news. The value of the news increases with the prominence of the person involved. What the prominent people say, is also grist for a reporter's mill, particularly if they make some announcements which have an impact on the common people.

Government Action : The passing of a law or other orders concerning general people, cabinet meetings, parliament and assembly sessions, notifications about new rules and regulations are news worthy.

Development Projects and Issues : This is not news about government action, activities, though sometimes it will also qualify to be covered. The intention of a high yield variety rice and its success in changing the lifestyle of a community will be of interest to people who will financially benefit from it.

Weather and Sports : Both the weather and sports have great news value. Also entire page is devoted to sports in many newspapers.

Follow-up : The news item become very interesting for the general public when the issues are followed and updated. It is important to remember that follow-up of news events will keep the interest of the readers alive.

News Values : News values differ from community to community, country to country. News values are also different for developing and developed countries. For the industrialized and individualised societies of developed countries, communally provocative speeches and incidents may be reported word for word, blow by blow. But the same treatment would be suicidal in a developing country. One should take all possible care in reporting such developments keeping in mind the volatile nature of the audience and the reach of one's publication. One must follow some journalistic ethics and at times some self-censorship. Freedom of the press is not a licence to damage or destroy any one's reputation.

Fundamental Qualities

Accuracy : Accuracy is basic to any news item. When you fail in accuracy, you lose credibility. Cross check your facts and information. Check figures, names and facts. Make sure that the meaning is not changed and the statements are not quoted out of context. Exclude rumours or gossip from your report.

Balance : To be balanced in reporting, is as important as being accurate. While writing about a controversy, both sides of the story should be given. A story may appear to be 'imbalanced' and thus biased, if it has too much of government views, or tends to give too much of foreign news which has little relevance to readers.

Objectivity : Your opinion should not be mixed in the story. Report only facts and other peoples opinions. You should be a disinterested observer, reporting events without taking sides.

Clarity : Your introductory sentence should be short and in active voice to the maximum extent possible. The ideal length of each para may be 3-4 lines containing one-to-three small sentences to facilitate easy comprehension.

Impact : Whenever you do a news report, consider the impact your story should have. Will it induce some changes somewhere for the better? Develop a "nose for news", particularly news that will make an impact.

News Sources : A reporter, to be successful, should have a variety of reliable and highly placed contacts. There are some of the useful 'sources' for his information. Among the news sources, some are available to all reporters, such as public meetings, monitoring of radio and television programmes, press conferences, news briefing, seminars and other functions. But the contacts are sources of exclusive information for the reporter. They may be in the government, public or private sector business or just anywhere. Some of the contacts may like to be quoted for the story as it gives them publicity. In case of a critical story, they may not risk their neck. In that case, the story may have to be distributed to 'sources' only. It is the responsibility of a reporter to ensure the truthfulness of a report. In such cases, it will be advisable to keep some documents or audio tape to prove your story.

In the business of collecting the news, particularly of critical and investigative nature confrontation with the government is inevitable. A journalist chronicles daily events, places facts before the public, and tries to communicate that he considers truth. This may not suit the politician all the time, hence confrontation may occur. In case, a confrontation becomes inevitable, a reporter should face it. He should also treat his sources as 'sacred'. There may be pressure on the journalist from the government and the judiciary at times to disclose the sources. Protecting one's source is a cardinal principle of journalism.

News Reporting : Here is a description about news reporting and the main components of a news report-the body and the lead.

The Lead : The lead should contain the essence of the story. It should give the reader an idea of what the story is about and help the copy desk to pick a suitable headline for the story. A good lead should arouse the reader's curiosity and force him on to read the rest of the story. It should be precise and made up of short, simple sentences. The lead should answer the five W's- Who, What, Where, When and why and How.

The Body : While the lead should arouse the reader's interest, the body should sustain it. The body should flow smoothly and logically from the lead. The body should be as complete and as tight as possible and should provide all the relevant information within the shortest space possible.

The essence of good journalistic writing is brevity and simplicity. Do not use a complex or long word where a short word would do.

Various Types

Objective Reporting : A reporter is essentially a short story teller and he should tell the story in an objective and truthful manner, without lacing it with personal opinions or subjective comments. He should be fair and impartial and present both sides of the story. Complete objectivity is a mere concept. The reporter is a human being and he has certain ideas, feelings, attitudes, opinions and prejudices. However, a good reporter should try to rise above them and tell the facts as he has collected them in his search for truth. Objective reporting is, of course, not synonymous with dullness. It means fair and impartial reporting that is free from personal bias or prejudice.

Interpretative Reporting : It combines facts with interpretation. It delves into reasons and meanings of a development. His the interpretative reporter's task to give the information along with an interpretation of its significance. In doing so he uses his knowledge and experience to give the reader an idea of the background of an event and explain the consequences it could led to. Besides his own knowledge and research in the subject, he often has to rely on the opinions of specialists to do a good job. Interpretative reporting goes behind the news, brings out the hidden significance of an event and separates truth from falsehood.

Investigative Reporting : It is difficult to define the term 'investigative' journalism. In one way, of course, investigative journalism is a redundant concept, since all stories require some kind of investigation on the part of the reporter. However, the investigative reporter is expected to dig deeply beyond the facts stated in the hard news. Though we may face difficulty in defining the term, we can not ignore the concept of investigative journalism. Investigative reporting has made great leaps in western countries. In India, it is still in its infancy. Attempts at investigative reporting, to quote one eminent Indian editor, arc like drilling for oil. A fair amount of wastage of effort has to be taken for granted. But when the oil is discovered and becomes marketable, the sense of achievement is usually more than in any other sector of journalistic enterprise. In India, investigative reporting started making a mark after the end of internal emergency in 1977. With governments becoming increasingly secretive and corruption spreading its tentacles far and wide, the need for investigative reporting can not be over emphasized.

Investigative reporting requires hard and sustained work. The investigative reporter should be combination of a crusader, super detective and blood bound and should have the necessary time and finance to carry out his work. The best thing of Investigative Reporting is that which keeps the public interest in mind. It may highlight an injustice, expose corrupt practices or unmask dishonest politicians and bureaucrats.

But experience shows that unless an investigative reporter or a crusading reporter gets the support of the judiciary, the executive or the legislative, can not bring his reports to logical ends.

Crime Reporting : There is tremendous public interest in crime stories and no newspaper can afford to ignore them without damage to its circulation and credibility. Crime is a part of life and it is newspaper's duty to inform the readers of what crimes are going on in their city, state or country.

Crime reporting is a highly responsible and specialised job. The reporter should not only have the ability to shift the grain from the chaff, and the truth from lies, he should also have good contacts in the police and other departments of the administration as well as working knowledge of the penal codes and law on libel and other relevant matters. Besides, he must observe a code of honour. He should not suppress news of public interest. Nor should he seek to settle personal scores with police officers or lawyers or judges. And he must be careful that in the course of this work, he doesn't necessarily invade a citizen's privacy. The crime reporter must never violate standards of decency and good taste.

Crime as News : There are several types of crime news-murders, fires, accidents, burglaries, fraud, blackmail, kidnapping etc.

Fires : The reporter must get his facts correct about the essential elements of a fire story-the number of persons killed or injured, the extent of damage, to property, the loss of valuables. He should question eye-witnesses about any act of bravery or cowardice. All these are essential ingredients of a fire story.

Homicides : In cases of a major murder, the reporter should rush to the scene as soon as possible and gather all the relevant facts. Their dependence on police information often hampers their search for truth.

In reporting dowry deaths or alleged dowry deaths, the reporter should refrain from levelling uncorroborated statements by one party or the other.

Accidents : Most accidents are reported on the basis of police bulletins or information supplied by police spokesmen. However, wherever possible the crime reporter must rush to the scene of a major accident to give authenticity to his story.

The Qualities : A journalist must possess and uphold certain noble qualities in order to be professional. Integrity of character, commitment to the truth and a reasoning power of mind are essential to any reporter. These qualities also contribute to the credibility of the reporting organization. Besides, a journalist has to be truly responsible. A journalist is responsible to the audience as much as to the news organization. Again a journalist is always responsible to the sources who reveal information. A reporter must also have a healthy respect for news values.

The Responsibilities : It is said that a reporter is both eyes and ears of a news organization. It is not possible to strictly prescribe qualifications which a good reporter must possess. However, novice reporters must train themselves informally for the job so that they would be able to discharge their responsibilities with confidence, courage and competence. To be a successful reporter and to accomplish your job competently, you must be able to perceive, predict, calculate and plan your action appropriately in anticipation of a news event.

Significant Elements

A Nose for News : The reporter is the most important functionary of a newspaper. So one must know what constitutes news in order to be able to gather news. A reporter's job of discovering the news has been simplified in one, way and rendered difficult in another sense, in this age of information. While there are the usual press notes on which news reports can be based, there are other sources of information on a variety-of news event. But quite often, most of the material before a news reporter may just be a publicity matter. Therefore, as a reporter, one must check the material and squeeze the news that would interest one's reader. A sharp sense of observation may also help one to gather amusing sidelights of interest to one's readers. This alertness will help one to discover contradictions and problems.

Outgoing Nature : Professional journalists are never arm chair writers. Introverts normally make poor reporters. Reporters have to move about meeting people, making their acquaintance and winning their confidence. This would help them to establish contacts, which in turn helps in writing well-investigated reports. This is the era of investigative reporting and readers are keenly interested to know what is going on behind the scenes. To get that kind of stories, one has no alternative but to be outgoing. One has to develop an affable temperament and an easygoing nature.

Ability to Establish Contacts and Develop Sources : An outgoing nature is the basic quality to establish contact and develop sources. You must have the ability to win the confidence and respect of those who may be potential sources of news. During the course of your regular duties, people may voluntarily offer you information.

Alternatively, this might not be the case when you are working on an investigative story. People may hesitate to talk on sensitive matters. They may like to reveal, yet are afraid to in case it were to affect them adversely. It may be quite difficult to win their trust. While you are establishing contact, there may be some among them who may want to plant information on you to serve their vested interests. Such information may consist of half-truths and even lies. So, you must have other independent contacts through whom you can verify the information. What matters is the alertness and ability to pursue your sources to get the right lead.

Ability to be an Unprejudiced Observer : The reporter must be an unprejudiced observer of events, one who presents the facts to the reader in a balanced, objective manner. It has been said that reporters mix comment with fact and so their reports are quite subjective. The reporters should not allow personal opinions at any place in the copy. One must be able to throw light on unclear aspects if any, of the news event. At the same time, the news reporter must endeavour to write a report which is only a statement of facts.

Thus, the first thing is to source your copy properly, to assure the reader that what you are passing on as news, is not your opinion. Even when you are not able to quote the sources, you must ensure that the story is balanced, by giving adequate coverage to all the sides of the subject. You should also ensure that the information you are presenting is true, which can be done by counter checking.

But remaining an unprejudiced observer does not mean adopting what is known in American journalistic parlance as 'man from the Mars' stance, i.e., seeing each event afresh, unconnected to any previous expectations or future possibilities and passing them on untouched by interpretation. In many cases, this would mean an irresponsible attitude, a refusal to make the reader understand the event in its proper context and realise its significance.

Clarity of Expression : Your command, as a reporter, over the language must be such that you can explain even the most complicated issues in simple terms to any general reader. In addition to specialised subjects such as science and technology, even government press notes are written in complicated language, burying the news point. You must be able to simplify it and bring out the news point.

Team Spirit : Except for routine coverages which can be handled by one person, many investigative stories have to be handled by a team. You must be able to work as a member of such a team. And you must pool your talents, sources and contacts into the team and work under a leader. In the course of time, you may rise to head such a team. Working under a team discipline will certainly be of help to you later.

Ability to Cope with Pressure : With investigative journalism seeking to bring out scandals and exposures, there is bound to be pressure on journalists to keep someone's wrong doings hidden from public view. The 'pressure' on journalists is exerted in the hope of preventing exposure. The concerned journalist may also be bribed with attractive favours in return for silence on the matter.

The pressure could be used to make you change the news or 'kill' a story. This constitutes censorship. Pressure could also be applied with the hope of inducing journalist to volunteer the change or omission which is then equal to self-censorship.

There are three ways of coping with pressure: fighting it, giving in or anticipating the pressure and taking preventive measures.

Preventive measures to fight pressure could be legal steps, like seeking a court stay on any law or ordinance that could affect the freedom of the press.

Other Responsibilities : The reporting profession is unlike any other profession. At times, some slight carelessness in doing one's duty, can cause incalculable harmful repercussions, both for the news organization and society. A slight laziness in cross checking certain facts could endanger the credibility of the news organization.

Responsibility towards the News Organization : As a reporter, you have to follow the character, style and policy of your newspaper or magazine or news agency. There are conservative papers which may prefer to stick to routine coverage, not bothering about investigation of scandals. In such papers, you have to stick to their policy even if it cramps your style. But in a news organization with a more dynamic approach to news, you must develop the skills of an investigator. Whatever you do as a reporter will affect the newspaper and its reputation. So you must take pains to ensure accuracy and objectivity in your stories.

Responsibility towards the Sources : Your sources are sacred. Your credibility in their eyes could be a major factor in your performance as a newsperson. There are sources with whom you will have to take great pains to establish your credibility to make them open up towards you. You will have to assure them that no harm will come to them, and if they so desire, you must keep their identity a secret.

Responsibility towards the Reader and Society : As a news reporter, you have a duty to provide accurate, unbiased and objective information to the reader. Every effort must be made to ensure that the news is accurate, free from prejudices and that all sides of the news event are presented fairly.

To maintain your credibility with the reader you have a duty not to accept things or favours or pursue any activity that might compromise your integrity.

However, in these days, publicity seekers including those in private business, organize press conferences and conduct tours with attractive gifts and other incentives. While private firms depend mainly on advertising for publicity, they sometimes want their activities to be carried as news items since news carries greater credibility than advertisements. News reports are written by newspapers who are supposed to be independent and objective.

Interviewing Skills : A very authentic way of gathering facts, figures and opinions on various issues is to interview the persons concerned. The interview is a very useful input for all the media-print and electronic. It depends on how one would like to use an interview. It may be used as a programme to make the audience/reader get information/facts from the source directly. The interview can form the basis of an article, a feature or a commentary.

How to Prepare for an Interview : The most important part of the interview is to know your subject as completely as possible. It is imperative for you to not only fully research the information you want from your subject, but also the person behind it. You should also have all the essential background information on the interviewee which will help you to build an instant rapport with the interviewee.

Research : It is most important to research your subject matter. It could be a subject in which you neither have any interest nor adequate knowledge. But once you are fully armed with the basic and important information acquired through books, newspapers, journals or magazines articles, you will be much more comfortable and should be successful in your venture.

You must know your subject matter as well as the person whom you intend to talk to about the subject matter.

Editing Interviews for Use : Two fundamental factors are to be remembered by all journalists-First, all interviews are subject to editing. So there is no harm in culling more information than you can use. The information that you need to buttress an argument or to refuse another or to make a point, can be used at the appropriate place. The rest can be stored for use in future.

Second, no statement made in the interview is allowed to be used out of context. If the authority interviewed does not generalise it, the reporter or, sub-editor is debarred from generalising it.

Strategy : It is important to establish contact with the interviewee much in advance of the interview. More often than not, where important interviewees are concerned, there is a channel you will have to go through. It could be the private secretary or the members of the family referred to as the "protector of the interviewee".

So, the first thing to do is to establish a rapport with the protector. To get to your subject-matter or the person, you must be able to play to the gallery to defeat all the obstacles imposed by the "protectors".

What You Want from the Interview : If the first thing is to establish contact and to build up a rapport, the most important part of the preparation is to decide what you want to get out of the interview. May be you want substantiation of a fact you have discussed; or the refutation of something; or may be you want the interviewer's views on some, proposition you or someone else is making.

It is vital for an interviewer to decide what he wants out of the interview. It is not a fishing expedition in which you net whatever you get. It is a hunt where you go after a target and get it.

Also one has to keep his senses on full alert and the antenna unfurled to each nuggets of news which have a knack of falling from the lips of the interviewee at the most unexpected moments.

Preparing Yourself : It is important and essential to make a deep study of the individual you plan to interview. Paying attention to his minute, apparently insignificant, matters really helps in conducing the interview smoothly. You must build a personal rapport to begin with, so you may start the interview comfortably.

Physical Preparation : If it is a television interview, then you need the cameraman, sound recordist, lighting technician and sound technician.

The other way in which the interview is to be held in a studio, then arrangements should be made accordingly in the studio. For the radio studio interview, a good recording machine is required, a lip microphone is used which prevents extraneous sound from getting injected into the microphone.

How to Get an Interview : Getting an interview can often be difficult, because the interviewer is generally viewed with suspicion. The interviewer labours between two competing factors. One, the public has the right to know and you are the tool employed to gather the information. Two, from the legal point of view nobody can be forced into talking hence, the job can be tiresome and at times, very frustrating.

It is very important that one's own participation in the interview is secondary. One must let the interviewee do most of the talking. To make this happen smoothly, a number of skills have to be deployed like :

(a) There is the direct approach-to telephone and tell the interviewee what you want.

(b) *The End Round:* A secretary in a business or government office will generally try, and give you the 'brush off'. The attempt of the interviewer should be to try and make the secretary one's friend.

(c) When faced with repeated failure, find out the person's hide-out and with an overdose of apology, just barge in.

(d) *Sit in:* It pays to just 'sit and wait' till the subject of interview shows up in spite of secretaries saying that 'the boss has no time to see you'.

(e) *The Appeal:* As soon as you get the glimpse of the reluctant interviewee, make your appeal as quickly and strongly as possible.

(f) *Be Courteous and Polite:* Tell the interviewee that there are two sides to every story, and we want to know yours. Thus, you arouse the interviewee's curiosity and attention. In many cases, it pays to tell the interviewee of the other side.

Do's and Dont's for an Interview

(a) Be operational on time for the interview. This is very important. It shows the importance of the interviewee and that he has not been taken for granted. In a nut shell, you must be ready right on time to start the interview.

(b) Outline your reasons for being there, unless you are working on something very sensitive.

(c) Start the interview with a broad question. This helps you to size up the person and also collect your thoughts. It also helps to receive information you may not have anticipated.

(d) Do not interrupt until the interviewee has relaxed. Avoid making the interviewee uncomfortable at the outset. It would be of little value.

(e) Let him speak at length on his favourite topic/achievement/feat. You will get nuggets of information. The irrelevant facts can always be edited out.

(f) Grunt and chuckle occasionally.

(g) Stick to your subject.

(h) Avoid commenting except to egg him on to top more. Let the interviewee do most of the talking.

(i) Do not end the interview till you have the basics-how does he spell his name, official title, age etc. Preferably get the details in advance from his staff and then get it confirmed by him.

(j) Be understanding. Do not be insensitive. Make the interviewee feel important. Keep the interviewee at ease.

Interviewing Skills : Advance preparation for the interview by way of well-thought out questions and a thorough consideration of approach is very helpful. One need not fear that the final outcome will sound stilted with no natural spontaneity. Usually the reverse is true.

Taking Notes : Taking notes is an essential part of interviewing. Some take down everything, even irrelevant and redundant remarks. Take down only what is important. People sometimes stop talking when you start writing and so taking down only the important remarks may not be possible. And you don't always know what is relevant until you have written it all down and reviewed it.

(i) Write as fast as you can.

(ii) Keep hand and mind together, listen to key phrases. A tape recorder helps you to review the interview *in toto*. It is a must for a question and answer story.

Conducting An Interview : Know your subject. Read the person's eyes and mannerisms since these offer a reliable clue on how an interview is to be handled. Since the interview rarely goes as planned, therefore the interviewer requires a lot of instinct.

How to Establish Rapport with the Interviewee

(a) In many small and big ways, try to make your interviewee feel nice, cheerful and important.

(b) Outline your reasons for being there. Bring the interviewee up-to-date on what you are looking for.

(c) Start with a broad question. This helps you to see the person and collect your thoughts. It also gives you an opportunity to receive information which you may not have anticipated.

(d) Stick to the subject. Do not ramble or chit-chat. Neither is it advisable to beat around the bush. So go ahead and simply ask your questions straight-away.

(e) Doodling or writing down a lot of useless matter in your notebook can be helpful. Those who have important information to transmit, like to feel they are being recorded. You might be asked to show what you have taken down. For all that, jotting down points helps you to prepare the transcription of the interview-session for publication.

(f) Listen. Listen. Listen. Not only does this make the

interviewee feel good and wise, but it also helps you to control the interview. An interviewer might start speaking with good intentions and slowly digress. You can bring him back to point. "You were saying something about the time you were in college, prison, etc. When was that?" And you are back on the track.

(g) Be understanding. Nobody likes insensibility. The interviewee is often quite nervous while discussing his/her wrong doings, sin or tragedy. Help him/her to relax. If your mind goes blank, just say, "Excuse me. I forgot where we were and what I need to ask".

4

Practical Reporting

For success, a journalist must posses and uphold certain noble qualities in order to be professional. Integrity of character, commitment to the truth and reasoning power of mind are essential to any reporter. These qualities also contribute to the credibility of the reporting organization. Besides, a journalist has to be truly responsible. This responsibility extends to different groups of people at the same time. A journalist is responsible to the audience as much as to the news organization. Again, a journalist is always responsible to the source(s) who reveal information. Should the need arise, a reporter has to submit to a source who may request anonymity. A reporter must also have a healthy respect for news values. A journalist must inculcate other positive features besides clear perception. For instance, one must have specific skills to elicit information in a question-answer session.

Role of the Reporter

It is said that a reporter is both eyes and ears of a news organization. It is not possible to strictly prescribe qualifications which a good reporter must Posses. However, novice reporters must train themselves informally for the job so that they would be able to discharge their responsibilities with confidence, courage,and competence. In order to quality the role of a reporter you must prepare yourself in many ways.

It helps to be well-read, and you can do full justice to your reporting beat. You must equip yourself adequately with all aspects of your beat. If you are covering the civic body proceedings, you must be fully knowledgeable about several laws and rules under which the proceedings are regulated. In addition, you must know its various functions, areas of operations and jurisdiction. You should cultivate wide contacts with all kinds of sources in your beat, some times even outside your area of activity. As a reporter, you should be able to find out information; you should have a bent of mind for research. You should be a perfect talker, you should possess inexhaustible patience and the ability to get along with any kind of people in difficult situations. To be a successful reporter and to accomplish your job competently, you must be able to perceive, calculate, predict and plan your action appropriately in anticipation of a news event. The sole aim of good news reporting should be writing with a certain amount of responsibility to oneself, to an organisation, to society and to humanity at large. You must use your pen consciously, carefully and should bear full credit (or discredit) for what you say: "Just as an unclaimed torrent of water submerges the whole countryside and devastates crops, even so, an uncontrolled pen serves but to destroy." Besides, as you must write everyday, you should write to build your own image, as well as the image of your institution. You have a responsibility towards your city, state, region, country, even the world at large. Echoing this, the noted editor M.V. Kamath once said: "A newspaper's sense of purpose and integrity, rather than its circulation, would determine its influence." And it is the reporter who is a builder of a newspaper's sense of purpose and integrity.

It is essential for a news reporter to be alertminded and curious. In addition, one should be in excellent health and should have inexhaustible stamina to chase difficult assignments. Most of all, a reporter should be a sociable person. It is true that one must posses the right attitude toward the vocation. This would include intelligence, initiative, industry, general competence, objectivity and accuracy. There are several other features' of one's personality and character which can contribute befittingly to one's profession as a journalist. In this section, we shall elaborate the salient qualities.

The reporter is the most important functionary of a newspaper, as far as news operations are congruence. So one must know what constitutes news in order to be able to gather news. A reporter's job of discovering the news has been simplified in one way and rendered difficult in another sense, in this age of information. While there are the usual press notes on which news reports can be based, there are other sources of information on a variety of news event. The range of sources stretches from official spokespersons and press conferences to unidentified members of the public and the regular sources which one meets on the beat.

But quite often, most of the material before a news reporter may just be publicity matter or advertisements in disguise. Therefore, as a reporter, you must check the material and squeeze the news that would interest your reader. When you are overwhelmed by an ocean of facts, you can always rely on the readers' interest for guidance. Here is where Your ability to select the right information and present it to the reader comes to your help. Besides, most of the time you will cover routine matters such as press conferences and press notes that are hardly exciting At least you may have to begin at quite a low level like covering local matter. Later you may be given the opportunity to cover major national issues. For the most part you may find yourself reporting the speeches, declarations and announcements by V.I.P.s, persons in authority, politicians and political parties. Occasionally, you may get an exciting newsbreak. But your routine reporting should not prevent you from looking for something unusual that may lurk under the ordinary occurrence. You have to be a keen observer so as to discover unusual and exciting material even in routine stuff. A sharp sense, of observation may also help exciting material even in routine stuff. A sharp sense of observation may also help you to gather amusing sidelights' of interest to your readers. Your alertness will help you to discover contradictions and problems while you are on your daily beat. This can be the basis for an exciting news story even where apparently there was none.

Professional journalists are never armchair writers. Introverts normally make poor reporters. Reporters have to move about meeting people, making their acquaintance and winning their confidence. This would help them to establish contacts, which in turn helps in writing well-investigated reports. This is the era of investigative reporting and readers are keenly interested to know what is going on behind the scenes. To get that kind of stories, you have no alternative but to be outgoing. You have to develop and affable temperament and an easy-going nature.

An outgoing nature is, the basic quality to establish contact and develop sources. During the course of your duty, you may meet several people who may help you in gathering information. You must have the ability to win the confidence and respect of those who may be potential sources of news. During the course of your regular duties, people may voluntarily offer you information. Alternately, this might not be the case when you are working on an investigative story. People may hesitate to talk on sensitive matters. They may like to reveal yet are afraid to in case it were to affect them adversely. Such people may be government officials whom you may meet while investigating matters ranging from inefficiency to corruption. They could be informers of the underworld, if you are doing an in depth crime investigation. What may be at stake for them could be their jobs or their lives. It may be quite difficult to win their trust. In such situations, you must be able to assure your sources that they will remain protected and their identities kept secret if they so desire. While you are establishing contact, there may be some among them who may want to plant information on you to sever their vested interests. Such information may consist of half-truths and even lies. So, you must have other independent contacts through whom you can verify the information.

Remember, even the most ordinary source at times can become very valuable, providing important leads and a wealth of information. A couple of years ago a newspaper carried a story about a footpath hawker who once was a wrestler of international repute, thus throwing light on the neglect of the sportsmen in the country. You must make it a point, therefore, to pay attention to your sources howsoever 'ordinary' they may seem by appearance. Remember, the classic case of the Watergate scandal. The scandal that shook the United States and the Nixon presidency was not exposed by any ace newsperson, but by ordinary local reporters acting on a tip from an ordinary source. What matters is the alertness and ability to pursue your sources to get the right lead. Take the case of the securities scam. The entire expose began with a source contacting Ms. Sucheta Dalal of the Times of India, Bombay, with an unconfirmed report about some activities in the State bank of India. Ms Dalal, Assistant Business Editor of the paper, followed the lead provided by the source and got the story confirmed from reliable contacts bringing to light the stock scam concerning stock broker Harshad Mehta and others involving a staggering Rs. 6,000 crores.

The reporter must be an unprejudiced observer of events, one who presents the facts to the reader in a balanced, objective manner. Now, objectivity is a much debated topic. It has been said that reporters mix comment with fact and so their reports are quite subjective. While reporters may have their own views on the subject of coverage, they should not allow personal opinions at any place in the copy. One must be able to throw light on unclear aspects if any, of the news event. At the same time, the news reporter must endeavour to write a report which is only a statement of facts. An observation or viewpoint, might occasionally creep in and one must be alert to such strips in straight news items. How do you maintain balance and objectivity in your coverage? The first and foremost thing to do is to source your copy properly to assure the reader that what you are passing on as news, is not your opinion or some publicity matter in disguise. The sources must be quoted except when they want to remain anonymous. Even when you are not able to quote the sources, you must ensure that the story is balanced, by giving adequate coverage to all the sides of the subject. You should always ensure that the information you are presenting is true. You can do this by counter checking. Remember, what may appear fair to one group will amount to bias for another. So, always ensure that you give both sides of the picture. But, remaining an unprejudiced observer does not mean adopting what is known in American journalistic parlance as "man from the mars" stance, i.e., seeing each event afresh, unconnected to any previous expectations or future possibilities and passing them on untouched by interpretation. In an increasingly complex world, this would not amount to objectivity or fairness. In many cases, it would simply mean an irresponsible attitude, a refusal to make the reader understand the event in its proper context and realise its significance.

In many cases, you not only report the events but interpret them for the reader. But, remember, interpretation does not mean backdoor editorialising. It is not an excuse for colouring the story with your personal opinions.'

As a reporter, you may cover several complex and specialised subjects, such as science and technology, law and economics. Your command over the language must be such that you can explain even the most complicated issues in single terms to any general reader. In addition to specialised subjects such as science and technology, even government press notes are written in complicated language, burying the news point. You must be able to simplify it and bring out the news point. Except for routine coverages which can be handled by one person, many investigative stories have to be handled by a team. The Bofors Investigative stories in the Indian Express and other papers were based on reports from Geneva and Stockholm, besides New Delhi. The securities scam investigations by the Times of India involved, besides Sucheta Dalal, one more correspondent, R. Srinivasan, who posed as an investor and went to the State Bank officers in Bombay to get confirmation about the going on in the bank.

With investigative journalism seeking to bring out scandals and exposures, there is bound to be pressure on journalists to keep someone's wrong doings hidden from public view. This 'someone' is usually a person with considerable clout. The 'pressure' on journalists is exerted in the hope of preventing exposure. The concerned journalist may also be bribed with attractive favours in return for silence on the matter. As a newsperson you may provide helpful or harmful exposure to persons holding important positions in your beat. Since may of them need publicity to perform their functions, they seek you out to provide them with the required exposure. They are on the lookout for a minimum of harmful and the maximum of helpful publicity. If they consider it necessary, they may use their power and influence to pressurise you for this.

The pressure could be used to make you change the news or "kill" a story. This constitutes censorship. Pressure could also be applied with the hope of inducing journalists to volunteer the change or omission which is then equal to self-censorship. While groups like the government and the advertisers could indirectly pressurise you through your news organisation, direct pressure could also come from the government and political parties. In case you are doing stories on something which could lead to harmful exposure for someone, they could take recourse to a range of legal and illegal options, including legal action, threats and violence to pressurise you.

There are three ways of coping with pressure: fighting it, giving in, and anticipating the pressure and taking preventive measures. The first one is the most noble of the three options and history is full of shining example of this category. During the British rule in India, many papers decided to close down, rather than submit to censorship and government pressure. The father of the nation, Mahatma Gandhi, exemplified this spirit when he wrote during the Quit India Movement: "It is better not to issue newspaper than to issue them under a feeling of suppression." Even during the 1975-77 internal emergency, journals like Mainstream closed down rather than submit to government censorship. But the heroic option is not always feasible. Remember, running a newspaper is a business, apart from being a service. Thousands depend on it for a living. You are in it as a professional, seeking to earn your daily bread. So few expect you to be a hero or a missionary. If you give in to pressure which you cannot fight on your own and if your news organisation does not back you, the consequences could be disastrous for you as' a professional journalist. The reporters who generally brave powerful pressures are those who have the full support of their organisations or their professional colleagues backing them unitedly. But, still, you must have the strength of character to fight pressures that come in the form of inducements like lavish gifts, favours, etc. to influence your reporting.

Preventive measures to fight pressure could be legal steps, like seeking a court stay on any law or ordinance that could affect the freedom of the press. In case you feel threatened by some physical violence, you can always seek security from law and order authorities. The journalists of the "Punjab Kesari" group of newspapers, who have taken a courageous antiterrorist stand in Punjab, work under extremely tight security. The group has lost tow of its owners to terrorist bullets, but has not given in to pressures.

The reporting profession is unlike any other profession. At times, some slight carelessness is doing one's duty, can cause incalculable harmful repercussions, both for the news organisation and society. A slight laziness in checking or cross checking certain facts could endanger the credibility of the news organization, proving to be a major block in the way of advancement of the reporters career. A reporter has been likened to a solder on the field. Even as the quality of the soldiers on field determines to a large extent the quality of an army, so also your abilities and the way you discharge your duties as a reporter go a long way in determining the quality,and reputation of your news organisation. As a reporter, you have to follow the character, style and policy of your newspaper or magazine or news agency. There are conservative papers which may prefer to stick to routine coverage, not bothering about investigation of scandals. In such papers, you have to stick to their policy even if it cramps your style. But in a news organization with a more dynamic approach to news, you must develop the skills of an investigator. Whatever you do as a reporter will affect the newspaper and its reputation. So, you must take pains to ensure accuracy and objectivity in your stories.

Remember, your sources are sacred. Your credibility in their eyes could be a major factor in your performance as a newsperson. There are sources with whom you will have to take great pains to establish your credibility to make them open up towards you. You will have to assure them that no harm will come to them, and if they so desire, you must keep their identity a secret. There have been instances in the United States of America and some other countries where reporters have defied court orders and gone to jail rather than reveal the sources. In 1960, an American magazine reporter alerted his editors that the ruler of a Middle East country was receiving large amounts of money from several governments for his personal use. But the reporter held back the story till 1977 as he felt that its publication would compromise his source. The matter became news only when the American Intelligence Agency (CIA) files, made available to the press in 1977, contained the same information.

You may well ask whether the responsibility of protecting the sources is absolute. A situation could arise when the information given by a contact who wanted to remain unidentified could lead to a major inquiry of a court case. You may be ordered by the court to reveal who your contact is, for giving witness before the court. What would you do in such a case? Should you commit contempt of court or violate your commitment to the confidentiality of your source? If you reveal the source who wanted to remain anonymous, you could lose your credibility among your contacts who may hesitate to volunteer information in future. Such extreme cases have to be dealt with, on their individual merits. It is sufficient to say that under normal conditions, you have a commitment to protect your sources. As a news reporter, you have a duty to provide accurate, unbiased and objective information to the reader. Every effort must be made to ensure that the news is accurate, free from prejudices and that all sides of the news event are presented fairly.

To maintain your credibility with the reader you have a duty not to accept things or favours or pursue any activity that might compromise your integrity.

However, in these days, publicity seekers including those in private business, organise press conferences and conduct tours with attractive gifts and other incentives. While private firms depend mainly on advertising for publicity, they sometimes want their activities to be carried as news items since news carries greater credibility than advertisements. News reports are written by newspersons who are supposed to be independent and objective. While in these days of corporate and business journalism.

Business and corporate journalism is a field where you have to exercise a tremendous sense of responsibility. With the proliferation of big companies including multi nationals and their role in the liberalisation of the Indian economy, their activities form a major subject of public interest. But, it is a subject that must be handled with utmost care. On the one hand, you risk becoming a publicity agent for corporate houses and on the other, you may be risking people's investments and reputations. Remember, anything you write for a news organization could have its impact in terms of money and reputation.

Opinions about the newspaper industry have ranged from it being a mere business to an instrument of social change. Even if it is to be considered a mere business, it is deeply involved in matters of public interest. Every thing you write could have its repercussions in the society. Even under normal circumstances, you have to exercise great care about what you write.

You have to be particularly careful when reporting in a communally sensitive country like India. This is because there are a host of religious and social diversities and several linguistic groups. It would be unbecoming to be partisan to a particular faith, linguistic or social group. As a reporter you will have to wield your pen with due respect for everyone.

What may be considered correct by one group may be held wrong by another. Take the example of the Ramjanambhoomi,

Babri Masjid dispute at Ayodhya. Two concerned communities have a conflicting stand about the disputed structure. If you have been following the controversy in the papers, you would have found that the disputed structure is referred to neither as Ramjanambhoomi nor as Babri Masjid. It is referred either as the "disputed site" or as the "controversial structure", of simply as the. "Ramjanambhoomi-Babri Masjid site".

Apart from the Ayodhya dispute, the communal tension in the country has been aggravated by the Punjab and Kashmir problems. News organisations are extremely careful about reporting events of a communal nature.

A similar procedure is followed when reporting communal riots. The step is taken to prevent any further tension from developing between the communities if they are to be identified in the news reports. For this reason, places of worship affected in riots are not referred to, by name.

Art of Subbing

The editor and the publisher of a newspaper are responsible for whatever is printed in it. It many Indian newspaper the editor and publisher is the same Person. In such papers editors is also proprietor and manager.

But where the editor and the publisher are different people, the editor looks after the editorial Content that is anything except advertising. An a dvertising manager looks after the advertising. The publisher, general manager or managing editor or executive director look after the management of the paper.

A number of assistant editors assist the editor in looking after editorial and feature pages. The news content of the paper is looked after by the news editor under whose guidance a number of sub-editors and reporters work.

In India the entry into the profession of journalism is normally as a trainee journalist who is later absorbed as a reporter or a sub-editor.

The job of a reporter is to gather news and write it for his organisation. Sub-editor makes it fit to print. Reporters go out in the field while sub-editors work at the news desk where all the news that comes, is selected, edited, each news story is given a suitable headline and its place in the newspaper is decided.

Reporters can become senior reporters, correspondents, senior correspondents, chief reporter, special correspondent and foreign correspondent. Sub-editors are promoted to the positions of senior sub-editor, chief sub-editor, deputy news editor and news editor but the basic job of a reporter remains news gathering and filing the report or "copy" to' the news desk. Similarly, the basic job of the sub-editor also remains the same; to "sub" copy to make it fit to print which includes collecting, selecting, arranging, reducing, farming, translating and adapting for publication according to the importance of the copy, Sub-editor is also called copy editor as what he edits is called copy. Whatever is field by reporters special correspondents etc., is copy for him whatever comes to the news desk from wire services is also copy.

But reporting and editing sides are not water-tight compartments. Reporters can exchange places with sub-editors. In many newspapers it is a routine. A sub-editor is sent on a reporting assignment many a time. He is also asked to write news items from the handouts that land up in the newspaper office when reporters away.

To be a good reporter or a good sub-editor what one needs is common sense and command over language. These two requirement in fact summarise the qualities newsmen should have as other qualities flow from these two and the basic human values.

It is customary to describe desired qualities of a reporter and sub-editor separately, but as both of them deal with the same commodity, news, and their basic job is to communicate effectively many of these qualities have to be common.

News Sense: it is the basic quality of newsmen. Every reporter has to have news sense or nose for news to distinguish news from non-news. He should be able to compare various news values and decide where to begin his story and should not miss important details. News sense is essential for a sub-editor also, he is the first reader of a reporter's copy, and if the reporter has made a mistake he has to correct it. A bad copy may have the most important element of the story buried in the fourth paragraph. It will be left to the sub-editors nose for news to bring that to the first paragraph.

Clarity: A reporter should have clarity of mind and expression. A person who is confused himself cannot tell a story to others. Only clarity of mind is not enough unless it is accompanied by clarity of expression. Without clarity of expression clarity of mind has no meaning.

Sub-editor is the judge of clarity of the copy. A good sub-editor will never allow a copy escape him unless the meaning is crystal clear. He has every right to make life miserable for a reporter who is not clear and does not write is simple language.

Objectivity: reporter and sub-editor should not allow their personal bias or ideas to creep into a story. They should not take sides but try to cover all the different viewpoints to achieve balance in the story.

Accuracy: A reporter should strive for accuracy, he should check and re-check his facts till he is satisfied that he has them accurate. In this respect he should not take any chance as accuracy is directly proportional to the credibility of a reporter and his newspaper.

The role of a sub-editor is to check for accuracy, it is particularly important when background is involved. In the case of dates and names the reporter may rely on his memory but the sub-editor must check them from reference material available in the newspaper office. When there is a doubt he should leave it out this is the golden rule of journalism. It is better not to say a thing than to say it wrong.

Alertness: A reporter should always be alert while dealing with his subjects. Many major news breaks in the past were possible because of alertness of reporters. Scoops don't walk into newspaper offices-alert reporters catch them in air and pursue. A sub-editor has to be alert while working on news-desk. Lack of alertness of a sub-editor can be seen by readers in the morning for he will be leaving or introducing mistakes for everybody to see.

Speed: In today's world speed matters everywhere. A person who cannot work fast cannot be good reporter. While maintaining all other desirable qualities a reporter should strive to work faster. He should think fast, decide fast and write or type fast for he has to meet deadlines or may have to go to another assignment.

A sub-editor also has to work with speed. He cannot sit with a copy for long. He has to do swiftly whatever is required of him for a lot more copy is waiting for him. A slow sub-editor is a curse at the news desk and is treated with contempt. Such people are misfits in the profession.

Calmness: Reporters and sub-editors often work in trying circumstances. They have to remain clam and composed in most exciting and tragic circumstances. In many situations they have to be calm-devoid of hysterical actions or utterances and apply appropriate mental and physical effort to write or edit the story.

They have emotions but they have to stifle them in the face of disturbing influences-they have to develop resistances to excitability. Being in the field reporters face many such occasions when they have to control their emotions. Sub-editors should develop a temperament to work under pressure of deadlines. They should not lose their cool if they are behind the clock for calm mind can work faster.

Curiosity: Reporters and sub-editors should have an unsatiable curiosity. For reporters it is useful in developing just for facts that may lead to better stories. This characteristic will keep on improving a sub-editor for with every passing day a curious subeditor will have a better back ground to do his job the next day. Reporters and sub-editors should read as much as possible to constantly improve their awareness level.

Scepticism: It is another necessary quality which a reporter and a sub-editor should cultivate. They should not take anything for granted. They should have an unwavering posture of doubt until faced with undeniable proof. Reporters should be more vigilant for many forces constantly try to use them and through them their paper. Many people try to plant on reporters a wrong story for their own ends. Many a time reporters fall into such traps in good faith. They should have enough scepticism to avoid such plots.

Sub-editors should also be careful for some clever politicians, public relations men and product advertisers keep on trying to take them for a ride. They should not allow anything to go in news columns that should actually go as advertisement. They should not fail to check even reporters' copy for such foul play.

Punctually: It is a goods habit. For reporters it is a must for if they are not punctual they may miss something for which they may have to depend on secondary sources, it is always better to be punctual and then wait than reach late and ask others a rival may misinform, you or hide some important information.

At the desk too punctuality pays, if a sub-editor is punctual he will be treated with respect by his co-workers, if he is late he will irritate them and spoil the working atmosphere. Besides, he may have to face the problem of backlog of copy which he will have to clear under the pressure of deadline.

Patience: It is quality which helps a reporter in a big way for many a time almost daily he has to test his patience, the voluntary self-control or restraint that helps one to endure waiting, provocation, injustice, suffering or any of the unpleasant vicissitudes of time and life. Most of the time a reporter waits for someone or something and patience gives him the willingness to wait without becoming disgruntled or anxious. Many a time he has to tolerate other people's shortcomings and has to remain unperturbed by someone else's slowness or other quirks. Patience also helps sub-editors as they work long hours in trying conditions. They have to put up with many annoying situations everyday vis-a-vis reporters, proofreaders or printers.

Imagination: this basic mental faculty helps reporters in writing better stories that retain the reader's interest. For a sub-editor this creative faculty is very useful as he can add sparkle to somebody else's copy and make it lively, besides, imaginative headlines attract the reader and improve the quality of a newspaper farsightedness: An intelligent envisioning of the future helps newsmen in general. The quality helps them in identifying processes and people who will be important in future. Reporters can watch such processes and cultivate people who may become important news sources in the future.

It helps reporters and sub-editors in determining the importance of an event. A reporter with foresight can think ahead and prepare for eventualities. With a little forethought sub-editors can plan their work so as to avoid tension and it results in better functioning of the desk.

Self-discipline: One can achieve a degree of proficiency in sub-editing or reporting by systematic effort and self-control. In this sense self-discipline suggests dedication and firm commitment. It helps in Journalism as in any other field.

Integrity: It is a virtue in itself and implies undeviatihg honesty and strict adherence to a stern code of ethics. This human quality is important for journalists. It is more important for reporters for they are more exposed to temptations compared to sub-editors.

Fearlessness and Frankness: These qualities help reporters in asking unpleasant questions and taking risks,to find out truth. Nobody gives a story on a platter. The reporter will have to probe, question, authenticate and exercise his power of deduction to get a good story.

Tactfulness: A reporter should be tactful, he should have the ability to handle sensitive people and situations gracefully without causing hurt or angry feelings. He should considerate of others and should be careful not to embarrass. Upset or offend them. A reporter should have flexible and sociable personality and should have a nature that relishes variety of experiences. He should have an understanding of human behavior and emotions. This will help him in developing contacts that are so essential for news gathering.

Initiative: A reporter works in the field should have an outgoing nature with initiative and drive. These qualities will help him get acquainted with news sources and get stories from them. A meek, retiring or shy person is not fit for reporting, he may be good at his desk. Reporter need a fair mount of assertiveness and aggressiveness to be successful in their career.

Mobility: A reporter should be mobile. He should enjoy moving ground and should not hesitate travelling distances to get stories when required, he should go to his news sources as often as possible for such constant contacts help him get news. A mobile reporter is seldom caught napping when a major story breaks.

Reporters and sub-editors should be diligent. There jobs require painstaking exertion of intense care and effort, alertness and dedication to the task and wary watchfulness. They have to make extremely fine distinctions while writing or editing copy. A sub-editor should insist on perfection and should love his job for he can make or mar the newspaper.

These qualities are basically qualities of good and efficient human beings. Good and efficient human beings make good and efficient sub-editors and reporters. All other things being equal reporters need additional qualities to deal effectively with all sorts of people they meet in the field. Sub-editors should have better command over language as they improve what reporters write.

A very authentic way of gathering facts, figures and opinions on various issues is to interview the persons concerned. In this unit, we shall discuss the importance of the interview in reporting, besides the skills required to master the art of conducting an interview. Having done this, we shall proceed to the next block where our main theme will be "specialised reporting".

There are carious way of gathering information and knowledge for the media. One can do so from books, magazines and journals, or incidents, and by meeting people who hold important positions.

Meeting or interviewing them is one of the most significant and important ways of gathering information, facts and knowledge. The interview is a very useful input for all media-print and electronic. It depends on how one would like to use an interview. It may be used and a programme to make the audience/reader get information/facts from the source directly. The interview can form the basis of an article, a feature or a commentary. Or, segments of an interview can be used to substantiate an argument or a point in an article or a radio/television feature.

One may like to presume that you have written something in your life; a letter, an application, an article or a poem. One can also assume that you might not have been satisfied with the first draft. Therefore, you may have re-written it changing sentences, paragraphs, words, etc. It is also possible-that after changing the draft twice, thrice or more times, you were satisfied with your written material. Let us call this the preparatory stage. To do and interview is also something like doing an original work in which you create something. Thus, to do a meaningful interview-both for yourself and for the person whom you plan to talk to-it is necessary that you do your home work right. It is only then, that an interview conducted after proper preparation, would make a certain impact.

It is said that to speak for five minutes over-radio, a person must prepare himself/herself at least for five hours. Therefore, preparation is very important. Interviews can be on the record or off the record. On the record interviews are those whose contents call be attributed to the person interviewed.

In this lease, unless there is a prior agreement to use the whole of the interview verbatim, portions of the interview, that have some use for the reporter can be utilised and the rest discarded or canned for future use.

Off the record interviews are those in which the information is given, but the source is not to be identified by the interviewer. In such cases, the source identified is "a source in the Defence Ministry" or "a General Commanding a division" etc. In such cases it is normal to cross-check the facts from another source, since the man giving the information is not willing to stand up and be counted. There can be interviews which are partly on the record and partly off the record. That is, some information given can be attributed to the person who gives it and some can be attributed to "a source" or "a Defence Ministry Official" or "a General", etc.

The most important part of the interview is to know your subject as completely as possible. It could be a VIP, an important member from the bureaucracy, the art world or the corporate sector or just an ordinary citizen. Accordingly; you should prepare yourself by reading about the person. It is imperative for you to not only fully research the information you want from your subject, but also the person behind it. You should also have all the essential background information of the interviewee, e.g. his/her family, hobbies, interests. This will help you to build an instant rapport with the interviewee. It will enable you to get on with the job most comfortably. A reluctant interviewee only acts as an obstacle and foils the very purpose of the interviewer. It is most important to research your subject matter. It could be a subject in which you neither have any interest nor adequate knowledge. But once you are fully armed with the basic and important information acquired through books, newspapers, journals or magazine, articles, you will be much more comfortable and should be successful in your venture.

For example, if you are required to interview a criminal lawyer, a policeman or an accused, you should have enough knowledge of criminal law-congnisable and non-cognisable offences, various Acts Sections which govern the offences, and other legal provisions. This will help you extract the required information. You must know your subject matter as well as the person whom you intend to talk to about the subject matter.

All journalists must remember two fundamental factors: First, all interviews are subject to editing. So there is no harm in culling more information than you can use. The information that you need to buttress an argument or to refute another or to make a point, can be used at the appropriate place. The rest can be stored for use in future.

Second, no statement made in the interview is allowed to be used out of context. If, for instance, a Government authority vehemently denies that any human rights violations were made during a particular clash in Kashmir, one cannot quote him to create the impression that no human rights violations are made by security forces during any clashes. If the authority interviewed does not generalise it, the reporter or subeditor is debarred from generalising it.

It is important to establish contact with the interviewee much in advance of the interview. How do you do this? It could be a direct contact-physical or through telephone. More often than not, where important interviews are concerned, there is a channel yaw will have to go through. It could be the private secretary or the members of the family-referred to as the "protector of the interviewee." So, the first thing to do is to establish a rapport with the protector. To get to your subject matter or the person, you must be able to play to the gallery to defeat all the obstacles imposed by the "protectors". If the first thing is to establish contact and to build up a rapport, the most important part of the preparation is to decide what you want to get out of the interview. May be you want substantiation of a fact you have discussed; or the refutation of something; or may be you want the interviewer's views on some proposition you or someone else is making.

It is important and essential, to make a deep study of the individual you plan to interview. Let us say that he person is particularly fond of dogs. When you go to interview her/him, it will be fatal to talk about how you abhor dogs or how they are dangerous. As interviewer, you cannot afford to convey your general wariness about the capine species-not verbally, not even through body language.

The information you seek to extract from the person may have nothing whatsoever to do with dogs. Yet, the person may react by remaining uncomrhunicative through the rest of the interview if you start off on the wrong note. Paying attention to such minute, apparently insignificant matters really helps in conducting the interview smoothly. You must build a personal rapport to begin with, so you may start the interview comfortably.

In the electronic media, there are two ways of interviewing: with the Prime Minister or the President, the setting would be as designed by the Public Relation Officer or the Principal Information Officer. If it is a television interview, then you need the following: (a) cameraman; (b) sound recordist; (c) lighting technician; and (d) the sound technician.

The other way could be that the interview is to be held in a studio. In that case, you should adequately arrange the setting in the studio. For the radio studio interview, you would need a very good recording machIne. You use a lip microphone which prevents extraneous sound from getting injected into the microphone. If the interview is only a part of what you are actually going to air, then it should be transcribed. Mark the important segments, and tailor the interview to the actual slot requirements with a suitable link to give necessary continuity. To do this, you would require an editor to do a proper cut and paste work of the tape.

Getting an interview can often be difficult because the interviewer is generally viewed with suspicion. To overcome this handicap, the interviewer has to be imaginative. The interviewer labours between two competing factors. One, the public has the right to know and you are the tool employed to gather the information. Two, from the legal point of view nobody can be forced into talking and hence, the job can be tiresome and at times, very frustrating.

Be operational for the interview. This is-very important. It shows the importance of the interviewee and that he has not been taken for granted. In a nut shell, you must be ready right on time to start the interview. Arriving on time may be good in most cases, for one has to do things like setting up the camera, or recording devices before the interview. One should arrive 10-15 minutes before time in order to be operational on time. Outline your reasons for being there, unless you are working on something very sensitive. If you do not specify your reasons, it may create problems, start the interview with a broad question. This helps your to size up the person and also collect your thoughts. It also helps to receive information your may not have anticipated and to chart out your course of action-a correct direction that the interview should take. Do not interrupt until the interviewee has relaxed. Avoid making the interviewee uncomfortable at the outset. It would be of little value. An interviewee kept at complete ease can be most helpful. The interviewer must not only be conversant with the subject matter of the interview but must also be a good conversationalist. All the important features of interpersonal communication come into play in an interview. In a face to face meeting, the stress is on both the language used in speech and the no-verbal body language. But, in a telephonic interview, the stress would be on the tone and inflection given to the words. In this type of interview, it can be rather difficult to assess the intended meaning since the other person's actual expression is hidden from sight. We shall now discuss the salient points to be kept in mind when conducting an interview in person.

On occasion, an interview may not be planned or rehearsed before it actually takes place. But then there are a few thumb rules that are fundamental to any interview. Preparing oneself to interview a personality, a celebrity or eve the person-on-the-street is actually an on-going long-term process. This is because one must be well-rounded interviewer, skilled in the art of handling a variety of topics and areas as also a range of idiosyncrasies that are inherent in people in general. One must be prepared for any turn of events and still be able to take it all in one's stride, that is to say, with equanimity. One cannot acquire these skills overnight but must nurture them over a period of time. A great deal of deep study of persons and happenings is called for. The would-be interviewer must yearn to learn.

Some interviews are simply old wine in new bottles. Other seek to convey an innovation or idea that the interviewee has recently come up with. Yet other interviews are made out of the interviewer's idea(s): giving a new twist to an even, throwing new light on a discovery that had been accepted at face value, and such like. One must develop a keen sense of identifying material for use in an interview. One must also have the knack to rad more into matters that is at first apparent: something like reading between the lines. That way, a much-interviewed person may reveal a fresh side of the matter being discussed and perhaps also of his/her own personality hitherto hidden from public view.

Having a finely-turned news-sense helps to generate ideas for interviews. It enables one to capture a glimpse of the extra-ordinary in the most ordinary things and persons. It depends on the situation whether one come upon a fresh insight during the interview by asking hard-hitting questions or by putting queries in a gentle manner. These are tactics that ought to be learnt by assessing and recognising the opportune time and place when it come your way. Alternatively, you could create the right atmosphere to make your interviewee reveal material which would from the basis for a good interview. In effect, the interviewer gives shape and direction to the interview, always allowing enough leeway for the unexpected utterance. One could then build carefully on what is sometimes said in such an offhand manner. The interviewer must, therefore, remain alert and latch on to every word that is said during the conversation. One can become adept in this technique only with practice.

Advance preparation for the interview by way of well-thought out questions and a thorough consideration of approach is very helpful. One need not fear that the final outcome will sound stilted with not natural spontaneity. Usually the reverse is true. One will be able to pose the most appropriate questions when one is well-versed with the subject. But how should one conduct oneself when conducting an interview. At the outset, arrive on time for the interview. This will help keep the interviewee in good humour. Taking notes is an essential part of interviewing: the two cannot be separated. Some take down everything, even irrelevant and redundant remarks. Take down only what is important.

However, that may not always be possible. People sometimes stop taking when you start writing. Your do not always know what is to have a flawless recall. A wrong quote can be most embarrassing professionally. It costs you your credibility. Now-a-days, there is the help of a recorder. Take permission of the interviewee before using it.

Crime Reporting : Crime stories, judging from the newspapers in the country, are more the staple, of evening papers than of morningers. And since evening papers are published mostly from the major cities it is hard not to draw the inference that crime is largely urban in nature and is only of interest to urbanites.

This, of course, is not true; there is probably as much, if not more, crime committed in rural India as in urban India but a murder in a distant village does not interest the urban dweller and small town papers have still to come into existence in numbers sufficient to draw journalism students to them.

Even in the cities it is the political story that largely makes the front page and very rarely the crime story though an occasional murder such as that of Prem Bhagwandas Ahuja (in what came to be known as the Nanavati Case) in Bombay can hit the headlines.

Though writing a crime story can be as complicated as writing a political story, it is mostly the novice reporter who is assigned to the police beat. Fortunately, the police beat is the best training ground for future diplomatic correspondents. As Richard Critchfield writes in *The Indian Reporter's Guide,* "while speech reporting,rains the ear and sports reporting the eye, crime coverage gives the new reporter a broad range of events on which to exercise his talents, usually providing action stories with a narrative as well as human drama."

What constitutes crime? The dictionary meaning says crime is "a wrong act that is against the law" or "a violation of law" and it is also defined as an act or omission punishable by law.

An offence means any *act* or *omission* made punishable by *any law* for the time being in force. Offences can be *bailable* or *non bailable; bail* is security offered by the accused for his appearance before the officer or court granting him bail. Any person is eligible for bail if he is accused of a *bailable* offence and arrested or detained without warrant by an officer in charge of a police station.

Some of the more common crimes may be classified as follows:

(1) Abetment, that is, aiding and assisting, instigating or facilitating, a crime (usually the punishment is the same as for the offence).

(2) Criminal conspiracy is an agreement between two or more persons to commit an offence where some act besides the agreement is done in pursuance thereof by one or more panies to the agreement.

(3) Offences against the state. These include sedition, assaulting officers of the state and others.

(4) Offences relating to the army and navy, such as mutiny, desertion, harbouring a deserter, impersonating a member of the military and insubordination.

(5) Offences against the public tranquillity, such as rioting, being a member of an unlawful assembly, hiring persons to take part in an unlawful assembly, assaulting public servants, promoting enmity between classes or committing affray.

(6) Offences by or relating to public servants. These include illegal financial gratification, corruption, impersonating a public servant or offences by a public servant such as disobeying a law with intent to cause injury, framing an incorrect document, unlawfully buying property or unlawfully engaging in trade.

(7) Offences related to elections such as bribery, false statements, failure to keep election accounts.

(8) Contempt of the lawful authority of public servants such as-absconding to prevent service of a summons, giving

(*g*) Rape, by a man with his own wife under 12 years of age and in any other case and unnatural offences.

(15) Offences against property:

(*a*) Theft.

(*b*) Extortion: blackmail, obtaining illegal compensation.

(*c*) Robbery and dacoity such as simple robbery, or robbery on the highway between sunset and sunrise, or belonging to a gang of persons for the purpose of habitually committing theft (dacoity).

(*d*) Criminal misappropriation of property.

(*e*) Criminal breach of trust, as by a clerk or servant, banker, merchant or agent.

(*f*) Receiving stolen property, or assisting in its concealment or disposal.

(*g*) Cheating, by impersonation or by dishonestly inducing delivery of property or by altering or destroying a valuable security.

(*h*) Fraudulent removal or concealment of property or false deed execution.

(*i*) Mischief, causing damage to the amount of fifty rupees or upwards, or by rendering useless, killing or maiming any animal of value, or by obstructing ora public drainage, causing dimunition of agricultural water supply, damaging public road or bridge, removing landmarks, mischief by fire or explosives.

(*j*) Criminal trespass such as lurking, house trespass by night or dishonestly breaking open any closed receptacle containing property.

(16) Offences related to documents and to,trade or property marks such as forgery, counterfeiting seals or plates with intent to commit a forgery, defacing or destroying a will, falsification of accounts, using false trademarks, counterfeiting of bank notes.

is likely to cause death, with or without intention of doing so.

(iii) Causing death by rash or negligent act.

(iv) Abetment of suicide committed by child, insane, idiot, delirious or intoxicated person.

(v) Abetting suicide.

(vi) Attempt to murder.

(vii) Attempt to commit suicide.

(viii) Being a thug.

(b) Causing miscarriages, injuring unborn children, exposure of infant with intent of abandoning it and concealment of birth by secret disposal of dead body.

(c) Voluntary causing hurt by dangerous weapons or drugs, to export properly, information, to deter a public servant from his duty or on grave and sudden provocation.

(d) Wrongful restraint or confinement.

(e) Criminal force and assault such as to deter a public servant from his duties, to commit theft, on a woman *to* outrage her modesty, to dishonour a person or to wrongfully confine.

(f) Kidnapping, abduction, slavery and forced labour:

(i) Kidnapping.

(ii) Abduction in order to murder.

(iii) Kidnapping a woman to compel her marriage or cause her defilement.

(iv) Procuration of a minor girl, or importation of girl from foreign country of buying and obtaining possession of a minor for purposes of prostitution.

(v) Kidnapping to subject a person to slavery, grievous hurt or abducting of child with intent to take its property.

(vi) Unlawful compulsory labour.

false information, threatening or obstructing public servants.

(9) Paise evidence and offences against public justice as giving false evidence, destroying documents, harbouring capital off enders, escape or resistance to lawful apprehension, insult to public servant during judicial proceeding.

(10) Offences relating to coin and government stamps. These include counterfeiting, possession of counterfeit money if it is known to be so, fictitious stamps.

(11) Offences relating to weights and measures such as fraudulent use of false instruments for weighing or measuring or constructing such instruments for false use.

(12) Offences affecting the public health, safety, convenience, decency and morals. These include deliberately spreading disease, adulterating food and drink, adulterating medicine, defiling publie water supplies, driving or riding on a public way so negligently as to endanger human life, dealing with poisons, fire, explosives or machinery as to endanger human life, omitting to guard against probable danger by fall of any building over which a person has right to tear down or repair, committing a public nuisance, sale of obscene books, obscene songs or keeping a lottery office.

(13) Offences relating to religion such as defiling or damaging a place of worship, maliciously insulting.the religious beliefs of any class, causing a disturbance to an assembly engaged in religious worship, trespassing in place of worship or disturbing a funeral with intention to insult, or uttering any word or making any gesture with intention to wound religious feeling.

(14) Offences relating to the human body:

(a) Offences affecting life:

(i) Murder.

(ii) Culpable-homicide: act done with lmowledge that

(17) Criminal breach of contracts of service.

(18) Marriage offences such as a man by deceit causing a woman not legally married to him to think she is and cohabit with him on that belief, or enticing with criminal intend a married woman, or adultery.

(19) Defamation or printing matter known to be defamatory or selling defamatory matter.

(20) Criminal intimidation, insult and annoyance such as starting a false rumour circulated with intent of offending the public peace, or intimidation by anonymous communication, or by inducing a person to believe that he will be rendered an object of divine displeasure, or uttering any word and making any gesture to insult the modesty of a woman, or appearing in a public place in a state of intoxication and causing annoyance to any person.

This is a pretty exhaustive list of criminal acts and a reporter covering crime must familiarize himself with it. It is equally important that he is familiar with the processes of dispensation of justice.

In India there are following classes of criminal courts. To begin from the lowest:

Magistrates of the Third Class: He may pass a sentence of imprisonment not exceeding one month and a fine not exceeding Rs 50.

Magistrates of the Second Class: He may pass a sentence of imprisonment not exceeding 6 months, including solitary confinement and a fine not exceeding Rs. 200.

Presidency Magistrates and Magistrates of the First Class: He may pass a sentence of imprisonment not exceeding two years, including solitary confinement and a fine not exceeding Rs. 1,000.

Courts of Session (Sessions Judge or Additional Sessions Judge):

He may pass any sentence, but a sentence of death is subject to confirmation by the High Court.

High Courts: They may pass any sentence, authorized by law.

Above them all, of course, is the Supreme Court of India. When a person is arrested and charged with crime, he is first taken to the police station where he is held until he is produced before a magistrate. Arrests may be made with or without a warrant, depending on the crime. (As an example, if someone is accused of buying or selling of any person as a slave, IPC 370 lays down that he may not be arrested without a warrant but if the crime is habitually dealing in slavery, IPC 371 permits arrest without a warrant).

A *warrant* is a written out authorization from a magistrate to the police giving them the right to carry out an arrest.

An offence can be either *cognisable* or *non-cognisable.* In the case of the former no warrant is necessary. In the latter case, a warrant will be necessary.

There is a further classification of cases into *warrant cases* (for offences punishable with death or imprisonment for a term exceeding a year) and *summons cases* (for offences punishable with imprisonment for a term not exceeding one year and fine.)

Arrest: If a person complains against another demanding the latter's arrest he must affirm under oath that he has reasonable grounds for belief in the guilt of the accused. A *search warrant* permits the search of a premise where there is reason to believe evidence of a crime may be found. But in certain specific circumstances, the police have the power to search without a warrant.

A person has a constitutional right to be brought into court promptly to be confronted with the charges against him. He cannot be held in custody for longer than 24 hours without a special order from a Magistrate (who can authorise the detention of the accused for not more than 15 days at a time).

Information relating to commission of a cognisable offence if made by a witness or informant is reduced in writing, read over to the informant, signed by him and entered into a book. This is called *first information.* Anyone acquainted with the circumstances of a case and whose statements are recorded by the police are called *witness for the prosecution.* (Remember the famous Agatha Christie play by that name?)

An *investigation* is carried out by the police starting with their first knowledge of an offence committed; this can go on until the police officer is satisfied that he has all the information necessary to form an opinion as to whether the offence has been committed or not.

An *inquiry* is begun after the police officer has sent up the case to a Magistrate. If no *prima facie* (on the face of it) case is made out the Magistrate dismisses the complaint and discharges the accused. If on the contrary, the Magistrate is satisfied that a *prima facie* case has been made out, he frames a *charge.* He may then *try* the case himself or *commit it for trial* to the Court 01 Session.

In his *charge sheet* or *completion report* that a police officer submits to the Magistrate he must state *(a)* the names of the parties *(b)* the nature of the crime *(c)* the names of persons who are acquainted with the criminal case and (d) whether the accused has been forwarded in custody or released on his bond with or without sureties. This is the final report of the police officer after completion of his investigation.

A police officer making an investigation has the following duties to perform on a day-to-day basis:

(1) He must set forth the time when the information reached him.

(2) He must put down the time when he began and closed his investigation.

(3) He must name the places he has visited and

(4) He must record the circumstances ascertained.

Trial of Summons Cases: In regard to a summons case, the accused appears before a Magistrate. He is told the particulars of the offence charged against him. He is asked to *show cause* why :he should not be convicted. But no charge is framed. If the accused *admits the offence,* his admission is recorded in his own words; he may be convicted, if he fails to show sufficient cause.

If the Magistrate does not convict the accused or the accused, *does not admit* the offence, the Magistrate *shall hear* thee complaint (if any) except where the complaint has been brought by the Court itself. The Magistrate will then *take evidence* produced by the parties or *examine* the accused and if he finds the accused not guilty, he shall *acquit* him. If he finds the accused guilty, he shall pass sentence on him providing he does not ask a higher court for an enhanced sentence, or release the prisoner on probation with an admonition. The Magistrate's finding *is not limited* by the offence specified in the complaint or summons.

If the complainant *fails to appear,* the Magistrate shall acquit the accused unless he adjourns the hearing of the case to another day. However, the complainant may, before the finel order is passed, *withdraw* the complaint with the *permission* of the Magistrate in which case the Magistrate then acquits the accused.

In a case not instituted upon a complaint, any Magistrate with the sanction of a District Magistrate may *stop proceedings* at any stage without pronouncing a judgement and *release* the accused.

Trials of Warrant Cases: In these cases the Magistrate hears the accused and any evidence produced for the prosecution. If the Magistrate finds *no case* has been made out against the accused, he *discharges* him. If he decides there is ground for presuming the accused has committed an offence, he will frame in writing a charge against the accused. This shall be read to the accused who is asked to plead guilty or not guilty and whether he has any defence to make.

If the accused pleads guilty, he may be convicted by the Magistrate. If he refuses to plead or does not plead or *claims to he tried,* he is asked to state whether he wishes to cross-examine any of the witnesses for the prosecution already examined. Thus the accused is called upon to *enter on his defence* and produce evidence. If the accused is found not guilty, he is acquitted. If found guilty, the Magistrate passes a sentence on him if he does not submit the case for enhanced sentence or release the prisoner on,probation with admonition.

Trials before High Court and Court of Sessions: In the High Court all trials are by jury, though in the Court of Sessions the jury may be substituted by assessors. The accused is brought before the court, the charge is read and explained to him and he is asked whether he pleads guilty or claims to be tried.

If he pleads guilty, the plea is recorded and the accused can be convicted. If he refuses to plead or does not plead guilty or-claims to be tried, the Court shall *choose jurors.* These are chosen by lot and their number is nine. They then appoint one of their number as *foreman* and are *sworn.* A juror may be objected to by either the prosecutor or the accused, though the Judge's decision is final. In the High Court the judge is bound by the unanimous verdict of the jury. In the Court of Sessions, the Judge, if he disagrees with the unanimous verdict, can submit matter to High Court, giving the grounds of his disagreement.

It may be remembered that in the Nanavati Case, in which the Jury acquitted the accused 8 to 1, the Judge, Mr. R.B. Mehta,-declared that the decision was "perverse" and announced that he would refer the issue to the High Court. The Jury's verdict was reversed by the High Court and subsequently the Supreme Court confirmed the sentence of life imprisonment for Commander K.M. Nanavati, for the murder of Prem Bhagwandas Ahuja.

How does one report crime cases? Here below is a partial list of questions to be asked by a reporter:

Casualties: Was anyone killed? If so, how? Similarly, was any one injured? How? What were the weapons used? What happened to the dead? Was any of the killed well-known?

Property Loss: What was the value of the property lost or damaged? What exactly was stolen, defaced or destroyed?

Method of Crime: How was the crime committed? What weapons, if any, were used?

How were the victims treated by the criminals? Was this a repetition of any similar crime? (Remember the similarity of crimes committed by the murderer Raman Raghavan in Bombay and its suburbs).

Motive: What moved the criminal to commit the crime? What did the victims report? What did the police or other witnesses have to say?

Arrest: State the names of the arrested people, along with their age and occupation. What formal charge was preferred? How did the police apprehend the criminals? Where were they taken to?

Clues: Did the criminal leave behind him any clues? What clues did the witnesses provide? What clues are the police investigating? Is there a description of the criminals available?

In the following leads, note how these different elements are emphasised:

Sample News : The city police have arrested two persons for allegedly defrauding the Jammu and Kashmir Bank Ltd., to the tune of Rs. 10,41,120. K.K. Dhar, Bombay Manager of the bank and Roopa, alias Roopmala Sain Khosla, a small-time film actress, were nabbed Thursday as they alighted from a cab at Pali Hill Bandra.

Two other accused in the case, Sudhir Sain Khosla, husband of Roopmala and S.R. Sheth, are absconding.

Sunday Standard, 1 July 1979

Casualties : Patna, June 25: At least 21 persons were killed and nearly a hundred injured in a pitched battle between Army and Central Industrial Security Force (CISF) personnel at Bokaro in theearly hours of this morning. The condition of 17 of the injured is stated to be serious.

Indian Express, 26 June 1979

Clues : The city police are on the hunt for a foreigner who has reportedly cheated several people on the pretext of providing them jobs as chauffeurs in a chain of hotels in Canada which, he said, belonged to his father.

Operating under the name of Capt. Sheisya, he extracted from each a sum of Rs. 4,000, the police said. The wanted man appears to be of Malayasian or Korean origin, is tall and slim and has an accomplice in Bombay whom the police are tracking.

Indian Express, 26 June 1979

A ticket stub to the Liberty Cinema for the 6.30, Aug 8 evening performance of "Hercules" may hold the solution of the mystery of who killed Hislop College professor Chandralal Rao and why.

The Hitavada, 29 Aug 1961

Property Loss : A hunt is on to trace a con-man who is alleged to have conned the father of Davis Cup per Sashi Menon into parting with an electronic wrist-watch presented to the tennis star. The watch had the inscription "Seiko Super Tennis" and was one of the prized possessions of Menon.

The police said the con-man goes by the name of A.B. Murthy and claims to be the Sales Executive of HMT (Watch Division), Bangalore. His *modus operandi* is that he gains the confidence of people by his glib talk and friendly ways and lures them into parting with their valuables under some pretext or other.

He was described by his victims as of medium height, wheat complexioned, long-haired and adept at speaking and writing English, his age was stated to be around 30.

Indian Express, 28 June 1979

Judgment : Found guilty of culpable homicide not amounting to murder and of causing hurt, Shamsuddin Rahim Babaji, a 32-year old fisherman residing in a hut at Ghas Bunder, Sewree, was sentenced to rigourous imprisonment for 7 years by Judge B.P. Talathi, at the Sessions Court for Greater Bombay.

The prosecution said that on November 8, 1977, at 9.15 p.m. Farida Abdul Rashid and her mother Khatija Kassam were sitting near their hut at Ghas Bunder when they heard a commotion near Kadar's garage. When they rushed to see what had happened, they saw the accused, who was in a drunken state, assaulting Ayeta, sister of Farida, with a kitchen knife. They intervened and they were also assaulted by the accused. As the accused was running toward the seaside, he was chased and caught, but he managed to throw the knife into the sea. The injured women were removed to the J.J. Hospital where Khatija died on November 10, 1977. The knife was subsequently recovered from the seashore. The accused denied the charges. Mr. G.M. Coehlo appeared for the prosecution. Mr. P.K. Nair defended the accused.

Indian Express, 27 June 1979

Suicide : The compound of the Air Force station at Madh Island was the scene of a tragedy in which a 21-year old aircraft maintenance man was found with a bullet in his head in the early hours yesterday, According to the Malavani Sub Police Station which received the information of the death from the Station Security Officer, they rushed to the spot to find Nilkantha Bhikari Raut, lying on the ground with injuries near his right ear and the left side of his head. Inquiries revealed that the tragedy could have occurred any time between 11.30 p.m. on Wednesday and 3 a.m. on Thursday. An empty shell was found in the rifle chamber and the weapon itself was entangled in his legs. The body was taken charge of by Inspector Gaikwad under a *panch name.*

A poignant note was struck when, on a search of his personal effects, the police turned up six letters written by the deceased and all addressed to relatives. On the envelope of one of them was the plea: "Please post this as soon as possible". Raut had no relatives in Bombay and was a resident of Orissa. His relatives are being informed.

No information was forthcoming as so the possible motive of the apparent suicide. Neither is any foul play suspected.

Mid-Day, 29 June 1979

It is the duty; of the reporter to check in every day with police sources,,whether at Police Headquarters or closest police station depending on where the reporter is situated, for information some information is given orally; on other occasion the reporter is given a written report, which is factual, but has to be extensively rewritten to make sense to a newspaper reader. In his book *The Indian Reporter's Guide,* Richard Critchfield quotes this sample actually issued by the Nagpur Police Press Liaison Inspector:

1. PLOT TO DUPE MERCHANTS FOILED BY NAGPUR POLICE
2. THE COMPLAINANT IN A ROBBERY CASE BECOMES. AN ACCUSED IN A CHEATING CASE

On 11-8-61 one Natulal Shrawan, a Grain dealer in Dana Bazar, Itwara Nagpur had lodged a complaint with Lakadganj Police that the same afternoon while he was preparing himself in his shop situated in the upper story to go to the bank to deposit a huge amount of Rs. 23,500, some two persons (with a dagger had appeared in the shop all of a sudden and·had decamped with the entire amount after causing him injuries at two places. On this a case of robbery was registered by the Police and immediate steps were taken up to deal with the matter. It was a problem for the Police especially when the incident was reported from thickly populated area of the City where lot of sensation was obvious among the business class. The Police adopted: the best methods of elimination off acts and on the basis of certain clues and traces, it had come to a reasonable conclusion suspecting the bonafides of Natulal himself regarding the reality of this crime. They had a definite data that the incident was false and this Natulal was out with such an alarming report with, all obvious cause to maintain his credit in the market, which in fact was at stake. The Police had no other alternative except the legal means and as such they had to register case *u/s* 420 IPC against this Natulal who had very obviously planned the show to dupe the payments of other merchants to whom he owed. He was arrested and thus had an awkward position, when confronted with a data of contradictory facts ascertained through Police investigation. When firmly and cautiously interrogated by Police Inspectors Mushtaque Ahmad and Khandagale, under the direct supervision of Shri N.S. Khedkar, S.D.P.O. Kotwali Dn., he had to' divulge his secrets and ill designs and had to recover the huge amount which he had reported to be looted from his own Possession only in the dead of night.

The Police Sources have given to understand very interesting details regarding this crime, especially when the complaint of a robbery case himself is traced to be the accused of a cheating acse.

A Police report is not expected to be like a news report. It purports to give all the facts sequentially, but it is left to the reporter to make a coherent story. This is how it appeared in one daily:

An Itwara grain dealer was arrested and charged with cheating today when police discovered he had falsely reported a Rs. 23,500 robbery in his shop on August 11 to maintain his credit in the market.

Contempt of Court: It is extremely difficult to define the term "contempt of court." It is an aspect of reporting that the crime and-court reporter has to be constantly aware of and guard against. By and large contempt of court can be defined as any conduct or action that tends to' bring the authority and administration of the law into disrespect or disregard or will interfere with or prejudice the parties litigating or their witnesses during litigation contempt is of two kinds: (1) contempt committed in the face of the court and (2) Indirect contempt or contempt out of court.

Some instances of contempt are obvious: A reporter surreptitiously retorning to' the court room after having once been excluded from it violates the order of the court. A reporter who photographs an accused person in spite of the order of the court not to do so is again in violation of the court and can be cited for contempt. Similarly publication of proceedings of a case being heard *in camera* is a disobedience of the court's orders.

The out of court contempt may be divided generally into *(a)* false and grossly inaccurate report of court proceedings *(b)* such publications that may have a reasonable tendency to interfere with the orderly administration of justice and *(c)* publication that scandalize the court, judges, counsel, parties or witnesses.

Pending Cases: The courts win resent any comments or mis-reporting in pending cases where such comments or mis-reporting could, in the least, be taken to have the effect of prejudicing the fair trial of an accused person. In the circumstances a wise reporter and his editor will make no comment on a case that is *subjudice.* The reporter is well advised not to assume the role of investigator, counselor tribunal and in any event no extra-judicial opinion regarding a pending trial should be made. The point is not whether the publication in fact interferes as much as whether it *tends* to interfere with the due course of justice. If a paper reports prosecution evidence it should also report defence evidence. The paper must not appear to take sides. And reports must not be partial or garbled.

In the case of a criticism of a judge, the criticism must take the form of reasonable argument or expostulation. It must be made in good faith and must be free from the imputation of improper motive. Criticism of a judicial officer which takes the form of representation to the Government, expressed in terms which do not overstep the limits, is not contempt. It is contempt to criticise a judicial act so as to interfere with the administration of justice but it is not contempt to criticise adversely the purely ministerial act of the court.

Newspapers must be particularly careful in attributing to judge the corruption, incompetency and dishonesty, irrespective of the facts whether the offending remarks are made in a case before trial, in a pending case or a case that has been decided. Contempt may have been committed again and this is why it has been said that contempt of court is hard to define-a person may be guilty of contempt even though there was no intention of the publication of contempt. The question is not what was the intention of the publication but what was the effect of the publication. The intention is to be inferred from the consideration of the natural meaning of the words used and the impression which they convey to an ordinary reader. All that may be in favour of the publication is that want of intention may be considered as an extenuating circumstance.

When reporting proceedings of a court, a reporter must remember that there are four stages of proceedings: *(a)* before trial *(b)* pending trial *(c)* after the decision and *(d)* when appeal is pending.

Once a trial is over, newspapers enjoy the privilege of fair comment, fairness implying that criticism is based on actual fact. Newspapers may review the facts of the law and express their opinion even if their opinion may be contrary to the decisions of the court. But personal attacks on the judges attributing incompetency, and partiality, judicial dishonesty, political bias and improper motives or "other consideration" are in contempt of court.

The Contempt of Court Act XXXII of 1952 says: "Save as otherwise expressly provided by any law for the time being in force the contempt of court may be punished with simple imprisonment for a term which may extend to six months or with fine which may extend to Rs. 2000 or with both."

Provided that the accused may be discharged or the punishment awarded may be remitted on apology being made to the satisfaction of the court.

A full and qualified apology takes out the sting of the contempt. Courts shall take a very strict view where the apology is not tendered and refusal to apologise is considered an aggravation of the offence carrying deterrent punishment.

Editors, news editors, chief sub editors and reporters therefore have to be extra careful about what is written and when it is written. The majesty of the court shall not be trifled with in any way or form.

Contempt of Parliament and State Legislatures: The Parliament expects "a newspaper writer should be more cautious than a private citizen as his criticisms are widely published." Such comments in respect of Parliamentary proceedings or the performance of any member on the floor of the House, if they contain any personal attacks on individual members or if the language of the comments is vulgar or abusive, are not protected and cannot be deemed to come within the bounds of fair comment or justifiable criticism.

Such writing constitute a breach of privilege and contempt of the House on the principle that such acts tend to destroy the House and its members in the performance of their functions and duties by diminishing the respect due to them and by bringing them into odium, contempt or ridicule. (See *Searchlight* case, AIR 1959 S. C 395 and *Blitz* case-Lok Sabha debates on 20 April 1961 and 18 August 1961).

It is one thing to criticise the performance of a member of Parliament and quite another to report Parliamentary proceedings. The Parliamentary Proceedings (Protection of Publications) Act of 1956, popularly known as Feroz Gandhi Act, provides that no person should be liable to any proceedings-civil or criminal in respect of a publication in a newspaper of a substantially true report of any proceedings of either House of Parliament. This Act was repealed during the Emergency but has now been re-enacted.

The Act permits the press to report defamatory statements in parliament without committing a breach of privilege of Parliament and by implication no legal action for the publication of any such statement referring to any outsider would lië. This Act, how ever, applies only to the proceedings of Parliament and not of State Legislatures which are left free to enact their own legislation in that respect.

The Official Secrets Act, 1923: This Act consolidates the law relating to official secrets and deals with two kinds of offences: *(a)* Spying and *(b)* Wrongful communication etc. of secret information.

Under Section 3 of the Act, it is an offence if any person for.any purpose prejudicial to the safety or interests of the State *(a)* approaches, inspects, passes over or is in the vicinity of, or enters any prohibited place; or *(b)* makes any sketch, plan, model, or note which is calculated to be or might be or is intended to be directly-or indirectly, useful to an enemy; or *(c)* obtains, collects, records or publishes or communicates to any other person any sketch, plan, model, article or note or other document or information which is calculated to be or might be or is intended to be directly or indirectly useful to an enemy. Under this Act it would be hard for any Indian reporter to publish the Indian equivalent of The Pentagon Papers.

Fashion Reporting : Fashion in the modern age has become a craze everywhere. There was a time in the past, when it was thought that only the females have a monopoly over the fashion. It was then a popular belief that since women are concerned for their appearances and looks, therefore, they spend a lot of time on their make-up and dressing. But now-a-days it is not so, because both the boys and the girls are crazy after fashion. There are special magazines which are wholly devoted to different styles of fashion. Fashion is an expression of some permanent attractions of humanity, viz., sex, snobbery, beauty and money.

High fashion is very expensive and it attracts those who have enough and want to show it off. It also attracts those who do not have money but would like to adapt fashion if they ever had. Fashion now-a-days has become a big business in which huge investment is made. With the change of fashion a lot of money is lost and earned. The mini skirt, midi, and hot pants all have made news in their own times. It is a fashion to print photographs of pretty girls to make the magazines saleable.

Paris, London, Rome, Hollywood etc. are the centres of fashion in the world. Fashion shows are organized in big cities all over the world to popularise the new dresses and other fashionable wears. The moment a fashion makes appearance in these big centres, it is publicised by the fashion magazines which are eagerly awaited by the fashion conscious people all over the world. It is generally said that fashion in Paris—the home of fashion—changes very fast. At times, it changes even before it had been introduced in other centres of the world.

Fashion can be used for anything, for dress, hair style, shoes, manners, etiquettes, in all spheres of life. Some persons may be crazy to wear fashionable clothes, others to keep fashionable hair style, or to keep an expensive library, while still others may adopt fashion in their speech and manner. In fashion nothing is stable and eternal. Here everything changes fast like the law of Heraclitus, in which everything is in a flux.

Fashion moves in a circle and goes on changing like the round globe. Sometimes, past fashions are also repeated again after a long time with minor or no changes. Sometimes, the lengthy dresses are invoked and at other times mini dresses become fashionable. Sometimes, gaudy and colourful dresses enter the world of fashion, while at other times, simple and sober dresses are considered to be fashionable. Still at other times, wearing uncouth hippie dresses are invoked and sometimes wearing an indifferent dress becomes the craze.

A few years back, keeping closely cut hair and wearing tight dresses like drain pipe trousers was the fashion, whereas the latest fashion is to keep long flowing hair and wear bellbottom type loose trousers with high heel shoes. Of course, now again tight pants are making appearance.

Sometimes, what the famous actors and actresses wear becomes the fashion. Pop music, pop art and hippie-cut clothes have also been fashions for a long time. Now-a-days, youngmen and women especially students have become highly fashion-conscious. All this has increased the importance of the fashion writer.

A fashion reporter should be always on the look out for spontaneous fashion. Such fashions are self-generating and spread like wild fire. A fashion writer, of course, should be in touch with the fashion designers. He should visit the fashionable shops and attend the fashion shows. He should also visit the college and university campuses, coffee houses and restaurants for collecting new ideas about the prevalent and future fashions. Now-a-days, the masses, especially the young boys and girls, create their own fashion. It is the job of the fashion writer to observe them and write about their ideas of fashion.

Certain stores also use the media for advertising their fashionable wears. In this way, sometimes, fashion advertising and fashion articles are linked up for the promotion of certain fashions. Of course, a fashion reporter is not to be influenced by businessmen in his comments, but he has to keep contact with the stores selling the latest fashionable dresses and other goods.

Writing for Women : Many newspapers and magazines devote one page to the women's problems and their likings. This page is called women's page. It may be published once or twice a week. This page generally gives information to the women regarding the home and other domestic things. It might include features on decoration of the house, cleaning of the house, recipes for the preparation of festival foods etc. It may include articles on women's diseases and health. It might also tell the women how to reduce weight and remain slim.

In some women's pages, questions by women are also answered. Women readers may ask questions on diverse matters like health problems, domestic problems, recipes for dishes, fashion etc. In this page, features can be written about the latest fashion, dresses, decoration styles, tips on shopping etc. In this page the women can also be informed about the latest cooking gadgets available in the market. Sometimes, articles regarding women's lib and other problems faced by them can also be discussed.

Some of these women's pages give very useful information to the women regarding women's diseases as well as child care. Some magazines invite the medical problems of the women and also give solutions to cure the same. In this manner, these women's pages are becoming very popular and the reporter who writes these pages also gains much popularity and importance.

Sports Reporting : The importance of sports reporting has increased greatly all over the world. The sports fans eagerly await the news and comments concerning their favourite sport or game and the performance of their favourite players. For this reason every newspaper and magazine gives a lot of importance to its sports page or columns. Some newspapers and magazines employ the reputed sports commentators to write their sports comments. In fact, there are many magazines which are wholly devoted to the field of sports.

Sports reporting should capture the complete atmosphere of a particular game while giving the facts concerning the game or the match. There is no doubt that first of all a sports lover wants to know the facts of the match of his favourite game. Sports reporting should be done in such a way that even those readers who have no knowledge or little interest in the sports should be tempted to read it. Like other international events, sports reporting is also done now-a-days on an international scale. People all over the world are interested to know the results of the famous World Cup matches of football, lawn tennis, hockey etc.

Sports reporting has become an art. The reporter must learn properly the rules of the game about which he is asked to give his comments. He should try to know the famous players and their past performances. He should equip himself with as many facts as possible before the game starts. In sports reporting the time factor is very vital, because the report regarding today's play must reach the newspaper's office in time, so that it can be published in the next day's newspaper. It is better if you can identify the players at the very start of the game, so that you can report back the achievements of the individual player accurately.

A reporter working for an evening newspaper may have to write his report as the game progresses in the afternoon, so that his report is published in the evening newspaper. A reporter working for a morning newspaper or weekly magazine, has a bit easier time, since he may not be required to send his report by telephone in separate 'takes'.

You should try to remember the following points as far as sports reporting is concerned:

(i) You should try to know the name of the Manager and other officials of the team.

(ii) By knowing the Referee and the Manager well, you can sometimes get a good sports story from them.

(iii) Try to know something about the personal lives of sportsmen, because now-a-days readers are quite interested to know about their earnings, expenses and even the eccentricities and their love affairs.

(iv) There is a difference between a sports writer and a general reporter. The general reporter simply makes a report regarding what happens, whereas the sports writer is at the same time a reporter and a critic.

(v) The sports reporter judges the quality and the skill of the players at the same time, when he is writing his reports. But his opinion must be authoritative and effective.

(vi) The sports reporter must know the correct names of the goal scorers with their proper spellings, so that he should not misquote them at any time.

(vii) In your report you must give the essentials of the game like the names of the teams, the ground at which the game takes place and the correct score of the team.

(viii) Never try to unnecessarily exaggerate the quality and importance of a particular sporting team or a match.

(ix) You should watch out for any news-worthy event at the match site which may prove to be more important than the game itself, just like a fight among the supporters of different teams or breakdown of a spectator stand etc.

(x) Generally, every sport has its own jargon and technical terms. When you use these technical terms, you must explain them properly for the benefit of those who are not very much familiar with the game.

(xi) The successful sports reporter also justifiably accentuates the dramatic event in the game, so that those who could not see the game should feel the dramatic effect.

Reporting Abroad : Some big newspapers can afford to have their own special correspondents stationed in the big cities of the world. These foreign reporters regularly send reports to their newspapers. Sometimes, special correspondents are also sent to cover special events like a royal coronation, general election in a foreign country, death of the head of a state or some international trade fair or exhibition. Due to the faster air travel now-a-days many newspapers instead of keeping resident correspondents, send their reporters from time to time to cover important events.

Certain newspapers also keep local 'stringers' who can be relied upon to give the news whenever any event takes place. Such local stringers sometimes give information to various newspapers and news agencies. The foreign reporter is faced with the problem of the time factor. Generally, there is a time difference between his home country and the country where he is stationed. When it may be dawn in his home country, it may still be midnight in the country where he is stationed. There is a Standard Time system throughout the world dividing it into time zones. Since 1833, this has been based on the meantime of the Greenwich meridian which runs approximately through London. The International Date Line, across which the date changes, is approximately down the 180th meridian.

A foreign reporter must try to know the time difference between his country and the country where he is stationed. For example, the Indian time is 5-1/2 hours ahead of the London time. It is better if a foreign correspondent keeps two clocks, one set to the local time of the country where he is stationed and the other to his home country's time. Sometimes, a foreign correspondent has a big problem, how to send back his story, especially when he covers an important crisis in a small town of a foreign country, because he may have the problem of long delays in contacting his country by telephone or sending a cable.

A foreign correspondent should be a good observer of things, especially when he is covering some crisis, war or insurgency. Sometimes, press reporters who do not have any rivalry, join hands together to exchange whatever information they can get. A foreign correspondent should also be a good judge of things and men. People might tell him very dramatic stories, but he should assess all the information with his common sense, so that he is neither taken in by the official propaganda nor by the exaggerated unofficial reports.

Knowledge of foreign languages will be very helpful for a foreign correspondent. Of course, it may not be possible for him to learn all the languages of the world. On the other hand, if he acquires the basic knowledge of three or four major languages like English, French, German, Russian etc. it will be possible for him to travel in most of the countries of the world.

A foreign correspondent, should also remember the following points :

(i) He must have a valid passport with him.

(ii) Some countries require a visitor to obtain a visa before entry.

(iii) He must get himself properly vaccinated before leaving his country.

(iv) Generally, countries require a valid vaccination certificate for typhoid and small pox. For tropical countries yellow fever and cholera vaccinations are also necessary.

(v) You should carry your money in traveller's cheques which is always quite safe. You must also know the rules governing the export of currencies.

(vi) Before going abroad, you should also take out a personal insurance policy against sickness or death.

(vii) If you know driving, then you should try to get an international driving licence from the transport authority in your country.

(viii) You must be careful about the customs, regulations governing the import and export of goods from one country to another, so that you do not get into unnecessary problems.

(ix) If you carry a camera and a watch, then you must have their receipts with you, so that while coming back you are not charged any customs duty.

(x) You should be careful while using your camera in a foreign country. You should not photograph military installations and aerodromes, because in many countries photography of these places is strictly prohibited.

(xi) For a foreign correspondent it is a good principle to travel light. He should carry only a few clothes and a light weight portable typewriter, so as to keep the weight of his luggage quite low.

(xii) You should carry with you some woollen clothes also, if you are going to a very cold country, but on the whole there is no need of carrying unnecessary luggage.

(xiii) If you are going abroad for a short stay, then it will be beneficial to pack all your goods in a small suitcase, so that you do not have to carry a heavy hand bag.

(xiv) Do not forget to carry your shaving box, your first-aid kit, towel etc.

(xv) Also do not forget to carry a few writing pens and ball points in your hand bag.

(xvi) You must keep in touch with your home office by whatever method it is possible, like telephone, cable etc.

(xvii) You should not use the long distance telephone too often. Whenever you are going to contact your home office by telephone, it will be a good thing if you can have your reports written out before making the call, so that you can pass on the exact message properly.

(xviii) It is a good thing if you call on your national embassy in the country of your visit, because who knows you might need their help in case of any difficulty or if you are thrown into the jail.

(xix) In certain countries you enjoy a facility that telephone calls to your home office may be paid by your office, by reversing the charges. If you like you can avail of this facility.

(xx) Generally, the foreign correspondents make use of the cable to communicate with their office. For this, foreign correspondents carry a cable card which entitles them to send cables at press rates.

The main value of a foreign correspondent to his paper is the prestige that he is in a foreign country, whereas some of his paper's rivals may not be able to send their correspondents abroad. There is no doubt that a foreign correspondent can give only a single man's view, as he has only one pair of eyes and one pair of ears. There does exist a very good professional friendship among the foreign journalists stationed abroad, but in reporting the stories every foreign correspondent has to rely upon his own judgement. He must always be cautious and careful; because all that glitters is not gold, and he should try to go behind the facade of the news. Things are not always the same as they seem to be.

There is no doubt that the life of a foreign reporter is full of problems and difficulties. But it is also fall of adventure, excitement and has its own rewards. Foreign travel is a great experience in itself. It has a great educational and enlightening value.

5

Team at Work

The Hierarchy

Chief Reporter : The chief reporter has a team of reporters working with him. He holds discussions with the news editor regarding the coverage of news. He plans the special coverage of the expected news. On the basis of his planning he allocates duties to the reporters. Many of the reporters are specialists of different fields like politics, sports, business, crime etc. It is the duty of the chief reporter to see that all the activities are covered properly and nothing important is missed by the reporters.

The chief reporter decides regarding the relative importance of the happenings in the city which should be covered and reported. He receives many invitations for press conferences, public meetings, demonstrations, agitations, strikes etc. He deputes his reporters to cover these events after assessing their relative importance. Many social and voluntary organisations also invite him to cover their annual functions and other activities.

The chief reporter also receives a lot of Government handouts, press releases and other publicity material for publication. He selects the important items for printing after assessing their newsworthiness. Sometimes, he also goes out to cover some very important news or function especially when there is a heavy rush of work. Sometimes he also looks after the administration side of the reporter's holidays and other routine matters.

He has also to keep contacts with the various sources of news. He tries to cultivate new contacts of likely information. He keeps in touch with all the important happenings. He tries to be fully aware of the activities of the rival newspapers. He also plans new investigative and interpretative reports by deputing his men.

The Correspondents : There are different kinds of correspondents who work for a newspaper. Some of these are discussed below :

The Liner : The liner is not a full time journalist. He may be living in a small town. From time to time he may send news stories to the newspaper. He is paid on the basis of the lines of the news stories published in the newspaper. He is only a part time journalist whereas he regularly pursues some other profession.

The Stringer : The stringer is also not a full time journalist. His whole time profession is quite different which he is doing in addition to writing for some papers. But he is in a little better position than the liner. Because he is attached to a newspaper through a string on payment of a small amount to cover his expenses. He is generally paid some fixed amount to retain him for the newspaper.

The Correspondent : There are various categories of correspondents. The most important of them are special correspondents. They generally cover some specified fields in the capital of a country. Some of these attend the Parliament sessions. They keep in touch with the government agencies and other news sources. Sometimes, they are also assigned to cover other special areas. Then there are the foreign correspondents. Some people consider the foreign assignment as the most glamorous part of the job. They are stationed in the capitals of important countries of the world.

A newspaper may also have its correspondents at important district headquarters. Generally, they are full-fledged journalists. The correspondents of a newspaper at the stale capitals are called 'staffers'. They do full time reporting work and are the regular employees of a newspaper or an agency. The correspondents in the different state capitals are in direct contact with the newspaper office. Generally, messages and reports from them are received on the teleprinter. Similarly, instructions are also sent to them on the teleprinter.

Newspaper's News Service : Sometimes, important national newspapers also have their own special news service. This news service is run by a chief of news service in consultation with the editor. The chief of the news service keeps in touch which its correspondents stationed in the country and in other parts of the world. These correspondents, spread all over the world, send their reports to the chief and the sub-editors working under him to shape them into news stories. Sometimes they also revise or even rewrite them. These sub-editors are experts in rewriting the reports sent by the correspondents. The chief of the news service keeps himself in touch with all the important happenings in the world through his correspondents. As a head of his department he also looks after the administration side of the staff under his control.

The Ground Worker

The staff of a big newspaper consists of many persons, those who work on the front desks, like the employees in the advertising and circulation departments, and those who work behind the scenes, like the editor, leader writer, sub-editor, manager etc. But the most interesting and the most familiar person for the public is the reporter. For the public the reporter is the press itself. At all important meetings, demonstrations, national or international gatherings, and trouble spots the presence of the reporter represents the mysterious and invisible power of the press.

There is no doubt that no other single member of the staff has a greater influence upon the life of the newspaper than the reporter. The reporter is in touch with life every day under all sorts of conditions. It is his duty to go out to see, find, hear, and know about the latest events and happenings and then write about the same in his newspaper. The newspaper today is a reflex of the day to day life and this reflex is made possible through the stories of the reporter.

Prime Duty : It should be the duty of every reporter to make his copy pulsate with life and full of interest for the readers. His stories should be bright and sparkling, something that should make people think and talk and look forward to the next issue. To do this a reporter has to put his heart and soul into his work. Of course, the reporter of today has to work at a greater speed and under more stressful conditions than his predecessors in the past. But he also gets more remuneration today as compared with the past. It goes without saying that a reporter has also to sacrifice many of the pleasures of home life to answer the call of duty, at all odd hours.

A reporter must appreciate the importance of having a good reputation for absolute reliability. For this purpose he must be systematic in his habits and punctual in keeping his appointments. He should be quite careful while making inquiries to know the facts and should be fair in his comments. The most important thing is that he should be efficient and prompt in turning out his copies. By observing these principles, every reporter can make his path smooth and trouble free.

A reporter should have the ability to write good English or the language of his paper. He should possess the quality to write in a condensed manner according to the availability of space. This goes without saying that whenever a reporter writes his copy in his own hand, it must be readable. In fact, he should write his reports in such a way which obviates any possible chance of mistake and subsequent query regarding spellings of words and meanings.

The reporter should type or write his reports clearly only on one side of the paper in double space so as to allow enough space for sub-editorial corrections. Every good reporter should develop the habit of turning out a neat and clean copy. Sometimes a reporter may give headlines to the report, but generally the headlines are given by the sub-editor. Now-a-days the reporters usually type out their stories but whenever a hand written copy is to be filed, it must be written in ink.

Unique Position : The reporter of a local newspaper occupies a unique position and he becomes quite popular with the people of his town. He reports the local events, functions, fairs, socials etc. and comes closer to the social life of the town. A reporter should follow some professional ethics in his work. Sometimes, while engaged in his profession, he may come closer to some persons and develop confidential relations with them. Some persons may also tell him their personal, private and business affairs. But a reporter should never betray their confidence under any circumstances by divulging their secrets which they have told him in good faith. This quality of trustworthiness increases the popularity of the reporter and he is welcomed wherever he goes. This will also enhance his reputation in all sections of the society.

Sometimes, a reporter may be asked to write short length paragraphs regarding the local intelligence or about the city news. For this he should keep his eyes and ears open and develop a nose for local news. He should develop a system to ensure that none of the interesting news is missed by him. He should try to know the secretaries of social, religious, political, musical, dramatic, legal, official and other organisations and should call upon them regularly to get some interesting stories. He should make inquiries from the police regarding news of accidents and crime. He should also contact the fire station for the particulars of local fires. Similarly, he can contact hospitals for collecting information regarding accidents and deaths. In the same fashion, he can get a lot of good news from the sports clubs and other organizations.

Systemised Working : Every reporter should keep an engagement diary. In this way he can systematise his working and attend to all his appointments properly and punctually. By keeping an engagement diary he can know about the important engagements and other events in the future and cover them without fail. Now-a-days, it is very necessary for a reporter to possess a good knowledge of shorthand and typing. This helps a reporter greatly in writing down verbatim reports of political meetings and speeches made at some political functions.

Generally, the reporter types the copy in the office or telephones it to a copy taker. Whenever the reporter types the copy in his office, he should prepare it in such a way that it should not need much sub-editing. It should be so neat and clean that it could be photographed and put in the paper as it is.

The reporter should not forget to give a catchline to this copy. Every copy which goes to the printer to be set is given a catchline. The catchline is a key-word, because during the production it identifies all the sheets of the copy. The catchline is given on each sheet so that the printer can collate the whole story. The catchline should be chosen very carefully. It is better to choose an uncommon word, which may not resemble with another catchline. If you choose a very common word as a catchline like 'accident', it might be confused because there may have been half a dozen accident stories in that edition of the paper.

The word chosen as a catchline may not have a very close identification with the story. But there should be some mental link with it. You should put the catchline and the page number at the top. Before starting the story you should leave half page of the first sheet. At least two inches margin should be left on the left side of every page. The space which you have left at the top of the first sheet can be used by the sub-editor for writing the headlines or any other instructions for the printer. On the left side margin, the editor might write corrections if any. As already mentioned you should always type the copy in double space to leave some space in between the lines for corrections which might be made by the sub-editor.

Good Rules : It is a good rule to end the page at the end of a paragraph. Similarly, you should not continue a sentence on to the next page. At the end of each sheet you should type the word 'more', or the letters 'm.f.' or "more follows". Whenever you finish your story you should write at the end of the last page the word 'end'. All these things are very necessary, otherwise, sometimes a page or a paragraph of your copy might be lost on the printer's desk. You should also try to follow the house style adopted by your newspaper thoroughly. Every newspaper has its own style, which must be adhered to.

Besides the above a reporter should also remember the following points :

(i) As already discussed above, a reporter should never repeat a story which has been told to him confidentially or in good faith, unless he takes the prior permission of the person concerned to make it public.

(ii) While collecting the local news, a reporter should keep in mind the great value of giving the names of persons in his stories. However, the names should be spelled correctly.

(iii) Every reporter should try to develop the qualities of a descriptive writer.

(iv) A reporter must remember that practice makes a man perfect. Therfore, he should always try to improve his method of reporting and his style.

(v) Every reporter should use plain English. He should avoid difficult words. He should enable his reader to visualise the scene described by him as clearly as if he had seen it with his own eyes.

(vi) A good reporter should avoid the use of stereotyped phraseology.

(vii) A reporter should try to be accurate in his reporting. Whenever his accuracy is called in question, he should be able to produce his original note-book.

(viii) One main cause of the complaint against misrepresentation in newspapers is that certain persons in the heat of excitement say things, which they do not mean. And when reported accurately in the press, they deny having said such things.

(ix) Whenever a reporter has to report on the court proceedings, he should be very careful in his report. For example, use of a wrong name or adverse comment might land him into legal problems.

(x) While reporting ordinary public meetings, a reporter has to produce only a summary, which he should try to write up as the meeting progresses.

(xi) The reporter must master the art of condensing while reporting the speeches made in the public meetings. This will greatly help him in writing his summaries.

(xii) A reporter must know what is news-worthy and what is not. Recognition of news values implies the need of "news nose". Without it a reporter cannot hope to achieve success in his career.

Special Correspondents : There was a time when Indian newspapers had two kinds of correspondents at New Delhi: the Special Representative and the Special Correspondent. The former species seems, for a variety of reasons, to be dying. But the Special Correspondent remains, the aristocrat of the profession, often better known to readers than the editor himself since it is the former's by-line that often features on the lead story on the front page.

Special Representatives : The Special Representative, however, ruled the roost for a long time, in fact from around the turn of the century when leading newspapers used to keep high-powered; influential special representatives at Simla whenever the government shifted its headquarters there from Calcutta (the then capital) during the summer. The era of the Special Representative, then, may be said to have started in 1899 during the Vice regality of Lord Curzon. The reason for sending a special representative to Simla grew out of the fact that there was no powerful daily in the Delhi area at that time, the nearest one being the *Civil and Military Gazette* at Lahore. Leading newspapers wanted one of their men to be where power was, not only to get news, which an ordinary reporter may have obtained without great difficulty, but to negotiate favours and facilities with the high and the mighty. Since those in power were Britishers, with their own sense of racial swperiority, it was inevitable that those appointed to hobnob with them were also Britishers, naturally of some eminence, so that they could easily socialize with their fellow compatriots and wrangle favours from them. Such a one was Howard Hansman of the *Pioneer* of Allahabad who quickly earned the reputation for getting exclusive interviews. The *Pioneer,* it may be remembered, was very much a British-owned paper; so was *The Statesman* which had its own Special Representative in Everard Coates. *The Englishman,* another paper, had Sir Edward J. Buck and the *Indian Daily News* a man called Dallas. Viceroys, Governors, Commanders-in-chief and their minions patronized these men, who wore the right sort of ties and came from the right sort of schools. It was the world of the whiteman into which the brown man had no entry. It was many years later that K.C. Roy and Ushanath Sen joined that strange band of lobbyists and preened themselves as a special breed of newspaperman, with more interest in newsprint than in news.

All Powerful **:** Today, however, it is the Special Correspondent who is accredited to New Delhi and his fare is special news. He is expected to rub shoulders as did his professional forebears again with the high and the mighty, and while 'it is no more necessary to know how to tie your knot or to wear formal dinner dress, it certainly helps to have the right kind of contacts in ministerial circles. Indian ministers these days have no use for formal dinner wear and at least one minister decided he could even dispense with a tie when he was appointed Minister-in-waiting to President Carter when the latter visited India in 1977.

Nevertheless the glitter is there. As Sir Philip Glbbs, no mean. Special Correspondent himself, once said: "The noblest and most amusing career in journalism is that of the special correspondent, because the special correspondent sees a great deal of life at other people's expense and it is very much worthwhile."

That is looking at it somewhat cynically and while it is true that a special correspondent enjoys a great number of privileges, dines and wines (when that is permitted) with the powerful in the land travels abroad at some one else's (usually his government's or newspaper's) expense and comes to see a great deal more than other ordinary mortals, it is not roses, roses all the way.

Often, it is necessary to remember, the special correspondent does not reach his eminence overnight. He has probably come up the hard way, via reporting the police courts and the municipal corporations of his home town, though it is not unusual for some leading newspapers to pick up a bright young man with a foreign degree to do the job, probably on the theory that if the young man had an opportunity to study abroad, he comes from a sufficiently high social stratum that ensures self-confidence in dealing with the world of officialdom.

For certainly the Special Correspondent has not only to meet the dhoti-clad minister who would probably be only too glad to talk to him, but he will also have to deal with the Chief Secretary to a Department and some of his minions who may think they are a cut above the elected representatives. In this, as in other spheres, self-confidence and the air of a man who knows he represents a major paper and can afford to swank about, helps. If word goes round that his salary, not to speak expense account, is measurably higher than that of his less fortunate brethren, he would find that he has entry into normally reticent circles.

In Delhi, a Special Correspondent, once he is accredited, gets certain facilities that go with the job: reserved seats at public functions, entry into the Secretariat, housing facilities and of course, the right to ask questions from the Prime Minister and other ministers and get answers. This puts him in the category of a man who has access to news at the highest level. If he is familiar with ministers he would call them at their homes or be invited as their guest. All too often, if he represents a national daily, he may find that instead of his calling up ministers, the ministers, or their men may be wanting his ear. If the Special Correspondent wants news, the minister, on occasions, may be only too willing to provide it. One feeds on the other.

This, of course, puts a terrific burden on the Special Correspondent. He has to be familiar to-and not necessarily with-the minister, but he must know how to keep aloof from his source as well. He has to be especially aware of the planted story, the deliberate leak intended to damage some one else's reputation or power base. News is not always what a minister tells the Special Correspondent. It is the latter's job to find why a minister is confiding him and what axe the latter has to grind. In the circumstances, a Special Correspondent is the sifter and the interpreter, the guide and the diplomat. James Gordon Bennett once described a Special Correspondent as "half diplomat and half detective" which is a pretty good description of the job.

It is his dexterity to interpret news, as much as to get it, that marks the Special Correspondent from the run-of-the-mill reporter. A good Special Correspondent will not only get news-that, after all, is his major responsibility-but will make it meaningful to his reader. Facts, admittedly, stand by themselves and are self-explanatory. But only partly. What do the facts mean in terms of a possibly emerging pattern? What does it mean to say that the rate of industrial growth was three per cent in a given year? Is it low or reasonably high against a background of economic stagnation? What was the rate of growth a year ago? How does it compare with the rate of growth in the neighbouring countries? It is the Special Correspondent's special responsibility to inform the reader of the *meaning* of facts. This is where his talents are most called for. He has to express an opinion. But the opinion must be so interwoven with information that together they provide the reader with the full story. Facts without opinion are barren; opinion without facts is arrogance. What the Special Correspondent has always to beware of is the tendency to offer opinion without supporting data. It is difficult enough to give an opinion with available data; it is unjournalistic, if not unethical to spout opinion with no hard information to base it upon. A columnist may get away with it but a Special Correspondent cannot.

Sometimes what passes for special correspondence is a caricature of what it should be. A Special Correspondent may be called upon to provide an "intro" to long parliamentary proceedings or to. "open" stories such as are meat to the news agencies, but that is not really what a Special Correspondent is paid for. It is poor journalism to stay put in one's own office or home and then, when the evening is over, pore over the news agency reports and condescend to write an "intra." It will be more professional if the Special Correspondent attends parliament and sits through the often tedious proceedings to make his own assessment at first hand. Then his effort at providing an "intra" becomes relevant and sound.

A good news editor will ask the Special Correspondent not only to provide an "intro" but to give a running story as well, telling the reader what the parliament was discussing, with adequate background as to the importance and significance of the debate. If the newspaper has plenty of space to allot to parliamentary proceedings, it may be left to the agencies to report who said what. In any event, that is the function of the agency. But it is the Special Correspondent's particular responsibility to place debates in their proper perspective. This calls for in depth study not just of past parliamentary proceedings, but of political science, history, economics and allied subjects. Special Correspondence does not come easy. It is earned by dint of hard work and home studies. To believe, as some do, that all that a Special Correspondent does is to attend cocktail parties and drop names, is not to appreciate his avocation.

Home study includes poring over voluminous government reports and publications of all sorts relevant to a Correspondent's job. One never can tell where one can get a good lead. The Correspondent may pick one in the day's newspaper by sheer chance because he notes that a report reveals a missing link that is worth chasing. Or he may get it in a report that is hard to read but should, perhaps for that very reason, be read with greater attention. Even usual government handouts under trained eyes could yield profitable leads to be developed by further research and interviews.

So a Special Correspondent will perforce have to do a large amount of reading, not only of reports and documents available in India, but similar ones from abroad. His reading has to be very catholic and embrace a wide range of interests such as foreign affairs, defence, agriculture, industry and commerce, trade, imports and exports, taxation policy. Well might he say with Terence:

Homo sum; humani nil a me alienum puto. (I am a man, I count nothing human indifferent to me).

Friends and Foes : A high powered Special Correspondent attracts equally high powered friends and not a few enemies. He has to learn to live with them. Friends may-and often willprovide him with valuable information. He should know how to use such information. Some of it may be spurious; it will have to be checked for accuracy. Some will be confidential and then the Special Correspondent will have to use his judgment. A confidence betrayed is a friend lost for ever. But sometimes an important source will deliberately provide information in the hope that it will be used, even though he may swear you to secrecy. To assess such situations requires experience and confidence. The best thing in such circumstances is to refuse to be party to confidential secrets and information dubbed "off the record." This calls for courage. It is some what flattering to be taken into confidence by ministers or high officials. But ministers may want to take you into confidence precisely because they do not want the Special Correspondent to delve deeper into certain kinds of news.

Besides, the Special Correspondent may be aware already of what the high official seems eager to tell on an "off the record" basis. Even if he is not, the chances are that he would soon learn of it from other, independent sources and so why tie oneself to observing secrecy? It is certainly not prudent for a Special Correspondent to receive conditional information when for all he knows, his rivals may be getting it from other sources unconditionally, thereby scoring a scoop. A Special Correspondent's loyalty is not to his ministerial or official friends but to his newspaper and to his readers.

A Special Correspondent cannot afford to live in an ivory tower, nor can he disdain social life. It is at putties that he makes important contacts under relaxed conditions. But it is a woeful mistake to believe that he can get information while swapping drinks.

Some notable Special Correspondents do not touch a drop of liquor. One does not have to be a drunk to get news. Senior officials-who, after all, are the real source of meaningful news-do not pass information to Special Correspondents over a gin-and-tonic. And not even two Patiala pegs may loosen their tongues. If that happens they may find that they are transferred. A cocktail party is not a place to gather news; it is a place to make friends in congenial surroundings. It will not hurt to have a drink or two; but it will certainly be no handicap to be a teetotaller. Drinking does not make a journalist, though a journalist may drink. If that was all to journalism, pubs in every city would provide the best correspondents.

Writing in the mid-fifties, Krishnalal Shridharani, himself a distinguished journalist summed up the qualities that a Special Correspondent should possess. These are :

(1) Vast and varied contacts with official sources, with opposition sources, with embassy sources, with fellow reporters, with private secretaries and with one or two high and mighty.

(2) Ability to keep a confidence.

(3) Courage, occasionally to refuse confidences with strings attached. Ability to avoid hearing things that bind one to secrecy.

(4) A bent for research based upon previous training in social sciences and the humanities. A craving for facts.

(5) A bit of brass (especially in foreign countries and in a war zone), the knack of bluffing one's way through forbidden areas.

(6) The art of conversation which primarily consists of encouraging others to talk, without yourself being a wet blanket.

(7) The ability to get along with people and in difficult situations. A friendly smile. This will invoke "human interest" confidings.

(8) Physical stamina and moral courage. The ability to do with out sleep on occasions.

(9) Ability to be freshly impressed by action, colour, life.

(10) Imagination, and a simple, sparkling style.

Shridharani then went on to outline the pitfalls in the path of a Special Correspondent which he said are more numerous than in the case of the routine reporter. And what were the pitfalls?

They are deeper, too and their openings more obscure. He may begin to take himself too seriously because of the stir he creates and that is the beginning of the end. Then again, he might begin to accept the wishful thinkings of his 'important sources', and thus lose the power to judge and predict. And exclusively top-level contacts might make his stories hollow: they supply leads, but meat is to be found with men who work out the details. Exclusively top-level connections may turn him into a party-going butterfly, progressively more and more incapable or applying the seat of his pants to his working chair. Just when things become esay, he stands in the need of doing things the hard way.

Much of what is said about Special Correspondents holds good' for Foreign Correspondents as well. A Foreign Correspondent comes to his job with a good deal of experience behind him. He would probably have spent some years in New Delhi as a Special Correspondent, learning the nuances of being a diplomatic correspondent at home. That ought to stand him in good stead when he leaves for foreign capitals.

Indian correspondents abroad at one time were mostly concentrated in London which used to the most important capital for India in pre-independence days. After all there was a need to know the pulse of the British public and what Parliament did or said about India and its nationalist movement. Indian newspapers regularly sent correspondents to cover the Round Table Conferences come of them like Dr. Shelvankar stayed on. London increasingly became the home of Indian Foreign Correspondents.

But as the centre of political gravity shifted to the United States, so did to some extent the interest of Indian newspapers which first began to send correspondents to the United Nations and then, as the United Nations' glamour and relevance began to' fade, to Washington. Indian correspondents sent to Washington were simultaneously accredited to the United Nations as a matter of course.

Accreditation rules to Washington are simple enough. The news paper informs the State Department through a letter from the editor of its intention to appoint the correspondent-named, for guidance-to his post in the capital. The letter is processed and the correspondent thereafter is duly informed that his appointment is accepted. He is then given a press card that permits him to enter the State Department and to attend news briefings and other press conferences. He could then join the State Department Correspondents' Association which also issues him a card acknowledging his membership of the Association. He will meanwhile have to be processed by the security offices and be fingerprinted after which he will get a White House press card that will enable him to attend White House press briefings and also presidential press conferences. Armed with these he could apply for membership of the Senate and Congressional Press Association; membership would qualify him to observe Congressional sessions from the press gallery, and also to attend hearings. He will also be entitled to receive the *Congressional Record* gratis.

Foreign Correspondents : Time was when a Foreign Correspondent would have had to take his copy to the nearest telegraph office where he would have been asked-unless, by then, he was sufficiently well-known-for his press card, his telegraphic or cable authority and identity card. But time marches on and so does technology. These days it is easy to apply for and quickly get international telex machines that link one with one's own office and the world at large. The correspondent therefore does not have to go to the cable office to hand over his copy. He can have a telex machine installed in his own office or home and send his message directly to his office and have the satisfaction of knowing that it has been received without any distortions. The telex is a major boon to Foreign Correspondents. The author had the mortification to find out, while covering the non-aligned conference that met in Algiers that his copy did not land in Bombay for four days. By then naturally, the story was dead.

As long as the Foreign Correspondent remains in his chosen capital, his problems are easily handled. It is when he is sent to another capital or country that he has to be familiar with a number of items of professional interest, such as the place where the international conference is held, the facilities available for cabling, the availability of hotel accommodation, costs, distances to be covered in commuting from hotel to conference site or to cable,office, the nature and cost of transportation, the kind of medical and dental service available at short notice etc. Sometimes the government of the host country will provide the information; at other times it will be necessary to call on the local residence of the Indian Ambassador or at the Chancery to regiester one's presence. Certainly it is a wise Foreign Correspondent who will stay in touch with the Embassy of India, not only as a source of information but for safety reasons also.

It is presumed, of course, that a Foreign Correspondent will know the language of the country to which he is assigned, Russian if he is in the Soviet Union, German if in Bonn, French in Paris and Spanish in many Latin American countries.

The Foreign Correspondent will be under pressure to say kind things about the host country. He should have the courage to resist such pressures. It is also unwise to run down the host country, no matter how much its society and administration differs from one's own. It is not the task of a Foreign Correspondent to sit in judgements on alien governments and institutions but rather to explain them in the context in which they chanced to be set up. Different countries have different historical backgrounds and they are what they are because of their special and unique pasts. Wisdom lies in understanding the process of history and to interpret each nation in the context of its own history and immutable past. Wisdom also lies in knowing that several international conflicts and controversies have no simple, immediate solution, that the conflict generally is between right and right and not between right and wrong and that one's patriotic bias, although justified, is not always just. And that takes some time to learn, especially at the United Nations where the urge to take sides, to pontificate and to prejudge can be very pressing indeed.

The Foreign Correspondent, under all circumstances, will keep to the law of the host country and never break it wittingly or even unwittingly. The Foreign Correspondent is an Ambassador of the press of his own country and has to be on the best of his behaviour. A Foreign Correspondent who cheats, who indulges in questionable practices where foreign exchange is concerned and who gets a notoriety for being unscrupulous not only brings disgrace on himself, which is his private business and should be of no concern to anyone but his own office, but will make it difficult for fellow correspondents from his country to follow him. Foreign Correspondents are usually under constant and quiet observation, a fact that they must be aware of, especially in communist or authoritarian countries. Getting into trouble of any kind just would not do.

In this regard the Foreign Correspondent cannot do better than take guidance from his Embassy which could give him some simple obvious do's and dont's. Embassies are generally helpful to correspondents if only because they themselves do not want adverse publicity. Also, they would like to be briefed on what the Foreign Correspondents have learnt in the course of their work. In most instances, there is a fair exchange of information between Foreign Correspondents and their Embassies but the correspondent must remember and realize that he works for his newspaper and not his country's government and should, at all times, learn to keep his distance from officials, if for nothing else, to respect his professional ethics of independence. Over dependence on Embassies will result in Foreign Correpondents relying on what for all practical purposes become government or embassy handouts. A Foreign Correspondent is sent abroad to give his personal assessment of the situation prevailing in the host country or countries, not to peddle Embassy views on the same. To retain one's independence in foreign lands is not always easy and embassies sometimes come under pressure from host governments to keep the writings of the correspondents in check, but this is part of the game and must be faced with courage, good humour and firmness.

Of all types of correspondents, the War Correspondent is in a very special class by himself. Think of the names: Winston Churchill, William Howard Russell, Edwin Lawrence Godkin, Richard Harding Davis, James Creelman, Luigi Barzini, Irvin S. Cobb, John Reed, Ernest Hemingway, Evelyn Waugh, Herbert Matthews, Wilfred Burchett, David Halberstam.

There are very few Indian war correspondents and such wars as India was compelled, after independence, to participate in have happily been of short.duration. Frank Moraes, D.R. Mankekar and D.F. Karaka, among others covered the second world war. But they are in a different class form Ernie Pyle or Edward R. Murrow.

Actually, the war correspondent is comparatively new to history. In years gone by Generals preferred to report their own victories and resented a civilian snooping around the battlefield as William

Howard Russell of *The Times* of London quickly discovered in the Crimea. During 1914-1918 the war correspondent was very much part of the military machine and kept quiet about the extent of the slaughter till the war was over. Not until Vietnam did the war correspondent begin to emerge as a partisan for truth and compassion. The British press failed miserably during the Russian Revolution. Looking back on its own coverage of the Revolution 35 years later, *The Times* in fact, admitted its shortcomings: "The idea of a *campaign ad maiorem proletariatis gloriam* was so foreign to Wilton (the correspondent) that he never understood it..More unfortunately still, the idea was equally foreign to Steed (the Foreign Editor), Dawson (the Editor), Northcliffe (the proprietor), to Lloyd George (Prime Minister) and to Milner (soon to be Minister of War). No one had heard of the forces of the Left except in terms that indicated them to be madmen.

Not all War Correspondents were so dumb, though some were more Jingoistic than stupid. James Creelman, along with J.A Mac Gahan' and the Italian Luigi Barzini, was one of the few correspondents to protest the conduct of war and write with truth and-compassion. His report of the Japanese massacre at Port Arthur in 1894 caused the Japanese to offer him a bribe to tone down his report, but he refused. American opinion was changed overnight. Barzini was a misfit among war correspondents of his time for he saw no glory or heroics but only senseless slaughter in war. Yet newsdealers had only to shout "Article by Barzini!" for his paper, *Corriere della Sera* to sell out. American journalist and poet John Reed, auther of *Ten Days' That Shook the World* and correspondent for the radical publication *The Masses* achieved journalistic greatness with his unparalleled description of the November 1917 events in Petrograd. Ernest Hemingway, reporting from Spain for the North American Newspaper Alliance (NANA) became the most influential figurehead in the fight against fascism.

The Spanish Civil War remains a watershed in the annals of journalism. No other war has left such a profound and lasting impression on those who reported it. "Today wherever in this world I meet a man or woman who fought for Spanish liberty, I meet a kindred soul" wrote Herbert Mathews.' "In those years we lived our best and what has come after and what there is to come can never carry us to their heights again."

The second World War had its crop of outstanding war correspondents like Ernie Pyle, Drew Middleton and Edward R. Murrow. It must have taken Murrow some courage to depart from the propaganda line that the fall of Dunkirk was Britain's "finest hour" and to assert, if somewhat, mildly, that "there will be disagreement an that point" Ernie Pyle won renown by speaking up far the infantry soldier. "I lave the infantry because they are the underdags. They are the mud-rain-frost-and-wind,bays. They have no comforts and they even learn to live without the necessities. And in the end they are the guys that wars can't be won washout" was his credo.

The wars since 1914-18 have made many war correspondents heroes in their awn right. Same have 'been killed. This is the price that wars exert even an jaurnalists. A revalution, Mao Tse-tung once said, is not a teaparty. Nor is war. Those who have reported one do not glamourize it, Vietnam was probably the mast danger ous afwars-far corespondents. Forty five of them have been killed there and eighteen listed as missing.

Fortunately wars are not as regular as internatianal conferences; true, they provide all the drama far a correspondent to work an. "If you have not seen a battle" Herbert Matthews once wrote, "your education has been same what neglected-far after all, war has never been one of the primary functions of mankind, and unless you see men fight you miss something fundamental" Other jaurnalists may fervently pray they may be spared such fundamental education but the fact remains, as another War Correspondent, Charles Mohr said, wars, "in an add way provide good staries." The hell they do.

The trouble is that many corespondents fight shy of telling the truth about war far a variety of reasons: ignorance of what really is going an, a false sense of patriotism, fear of being sent back far reporting reality. In his fascinating book *The First Casualty,* Phillip Knightley, himself a special correspondent, recalls instance after instance of War Corespondents failing to tell it all, of Ernest Hemingway suppressing the unpalatable facts about Republican Spain, Evelyn Waugh making a mess of covering the Abyssinian-War but gathering material far his navel *Scoop* and the Russians crushing Quentin Reynolds because they believed that Western corespondents were spies. Perhaps they were. War is a distressing affair in many ways and the first casualty turns aut to be truth.

The Vietnam war was better reported than any other war since the Crimean was a casualty to truth. As journalist Murray Kemptan has remarked, with a millian-dollar corps of correspondents in Vietnam, the war in Cambodia was kept hidden for a year.

That takes something. The best comment on war coverage is perhaps given by Gavin Young, a British newspaperman who covered Vietnam. "Correspondents" he wrote, "are bound to be haunted by the feeling that there is probably only one way to work the various elusive aspects of the war into one wholly satisfactory picture. Apart from the aid programmes, the military operations, the political ups and downs, how can one depict the human facets of such a complete tragedy? What of the thoughts and feeling of the Vietnamese? How has the war affected their lives and art, their outlook on foreigners, and different cultures? How if at all, have the Americans been changed by contact with the Vietnamese?.. The Vietnamese war awaits its novelist."

Knightley asserted that on the whole, writers-be did *not* call them War Correspondents-for non-daily publications like *Tom* Buckley in the *New York Times Magazine*, Jonathan Schell of *The New Yorker* and Sol Sanders of *U. S. News & World Report* came out better than most of their news colleagues because, he said, they were "free from the tyranny of pressing deadlines" and could look at the war in greater depth. Are regular war correspondents, then, a useless tribe? One suspects that even at the risk of not being able to tell the whole story every day, the War Correspondent will be necessary though wars may not. Only, the War Correspondent must know his limitations and be honest enough to admit to them' It is the most important service he could do to his reader who otherwise depends upon him to tell the truth as he sees it.

The Accreditation : Every capital has its own rules of accreditation. Given below are rules for accreditation of news media representatives to New Delhi.

(1) These rules apply to the accreditation at the headquarters of the Government of India of news media representatives.

(2) An application on the prescribed form should be submitted by the editor in the news media organization concerned to the Principal Information Officer, Government of India, New Delhi. Full details about the professional experience of the representative seeking accreditation should be furnished with the application. The Principal Information Officer will refer the application to the Central Press Accreditation Committee for their advice and approval.

(3) The applicant should fulfil the following condititions for accreditation:

(a) His residence should be the headquarters of the Government of India during the period of accreditation.

(b) He should be working journalist as defined by the Working Journalists (Conditions of Service and Miscellaneous Provisions) Act, 1955 and should be whole time engaged as a correspondent or cameraman or correspondent-cameraman or a cartoonist.

(c) At the time of application he should have spent five years in the profession of journalism.

(4) The professional norms applicable to Indian newsmen will also govern the grant of accreditation to applicants on behalf of foreign media.

(5) Editors of news media may in exceptional case be granted accreditation if CPAC is satisfied that the applicant is genuinely engaged in covering current affairs and needs accreditation for this purpose. Such applications will only be considered by the CPAC. No temporary accreditation will be granted by the PIO in such cases.

(6) The Central Press Accreditation Committee may grant accreditation, as an exceptional measure, to journalists of long and distinguished service of at least 25 years who may be contributing special articles to a number of newspaper regularly but not attached to any newspaper which qualifies for accreditation.

(7) Accreditation will be granted only on behalf of a news media-organization having a minimum circulation or coverage as presciboed by the Central Press Accreditation Commitee. The Central Press Accreditation Committee will lay down, from time to time, the number of accreditations for various classes of news media organizations, taking into account the coverage required by the organizations and the service limitations of the Press Information Bureau.

(8) In the case of news, features, photo and TV news and feature agencies, following factors will be taken into consideration for determining the entitlement for and the number of accreditations:

(a) The news, features, photo or TV news and features should be based on the news emanating from the capital.

(b) The agency should provide regular service to media network on commercial basis. For the purpose of classification of the agency, only the revenue, as certified by a Chartered Accountant by way of subscriptions from news media for supply of news material will betaken into consideration.

(c) An agency whose service operations extend to at least half of the State of the Indian Union or to electronic media network shall be deemed to be an all-India agency.

(d) In case of agencies of all classes and types, accreditation will be given to the whole-time employees only.

(9) In case of daily newspapers and weeklies, the following factors will be taken into consideration for determining the entitlement for and the number of accreditations.

(a) The paper concerned should be published regularly.

(b) Its circulation should not be less then 5,000 copies as certified by the RNI.

(c) The contents of the concerned weekly should be mainly related to current affairs.

(d) For newspapers and weeklies with circulation above 50,000 copies, only full-time employees of such organization will be granted accreditions.

(e) In the case of smaller newspapers combined circulation may be taken into consideration if they ask for accreditation for a common representative or a journalist himself seeks accreditation jointly on their behalf.

(10) Periodicals of longer than a week's periodicity will not be granted accreditation. However, fortnightlies and monthlies published abroad for the benfit of Indian communities or for dissemination of Indian news would be granted accreditation on the merits of each case.

(11) A press card will be issued to each accredited representative. Admission to special functions including press conferences however, will be governed by invitation.

(12) Accreditation is personal and not transferable.

(13) Accreditation does not confer any official or special status on the news media representative. It merely recognizes and identifies him as a representative of the media organization which employ him. It must be used only for journalistic purposes. The words "Accredited to the Government of India" should not be used on visiting cards, letter-heads or any other literature.

(14) When the representative ceases to represent the media organization for which he is accredited, the fact should be brought to the notice of the principal Information Officer in writing within 15 days by both the representative and his editor. Failure to comply with this may result in withdrawal of facilities.

(15) The list of accredited news media representatives will be subject to review every year by the Principal Information Officer in consultation with the Central Press Accreditation Committee.

For the purpose of review, the PIO may call for (a) information about the revenue of the Indian agencies (b) dipping of published dispatches or photographs of dope sheets from the concerned news media organization or representative. To ensure that only genuine news media representatives remain accredited on behalf of foreign media organizations, the PIO may, from time to time, go through their published dispatches or enquire through the Indian missions abroad about the representative's work.

(16) The Principal Information Officer may:

(a) accord accreditation by issuing a temporary card in case both the applicant representative and the media organization qualify

(b) accept substitution of an accredited representative for a temporary period

(c) grant temporary accreditation to visiting pressmen

(17) A representative will be liable to dis-accreditation if:

(a) He engaged himself in work other than journalistic, such as soliciting business or advertisement.

(b) He uses for non-journalistic purposes information and facilities provided to him as an accredited representative.

(c) He publishes official secret the inviolability of which is accepted by general understanding and the Central Press Accreditation Committee concurs with this view after giving opportunity of a personal hearing to the concerned representative.

(d) In the course of his duties, he behaves in an undignified or unprofessional manner.

(e) He ignores or violates the conditions on which information and facilities are provided by government.

(f) News media organizations will also be liable to dis-accreditation if they are responsible for wilful publication of mala fide reports or abuse confidence.

(18) In all cases relating to dis-accreditation, the Principal Information Officer will take action warranted by the circumstances in each case in consultation with a locally-based sub-committee of the Central Press Accreditation Committee. All such cases will be referred to the Central Press Accreditation Committee within a period of not more than three months.

(19) These rules come into effect from 17 February 1978 and supercede the earlier rules.

6

Reporting on Subjects

Reporting on Projects

Development reporting is somewhat different from routine reporting from court, legislatures, crime, science and technology or sports. However, it may involve writing our programmes and policies resulting in economic change, social programmes and community feelings and reactions to programme and change.

Ever since India adopted a process of planned development through the five year plans in 1951, rapid transformation have taken place in all walks of life in the country. Some of these changes have been welcomed by people, but many have been opposed also. Also, as development takes place, numerous new issues are thrown up. As a development reporter, you will be required to help in creating awareness about these developmental issues. You will also be required to create an atmosphere of understanding the objectives of these schemes and ultimately mobilizing people in seeking their willing participation in development programmes. Development Reporting needs some special skills, preparations and qualities to be imbibed by reporters of print or electronic media. To be able to do this job successfully, a reporter has to collect information on different development programmes.

The Perception

Styles of Development Reporting : Development has led to some disastrous results such as widespread pollution of air, water and soil, besides deforestation. This resulted in a rethinking on what constitutes development. It has also increased the responsibility of the development journalists. Therefore, a journalist reporting on developmental issues should organize and arrange his report logically.

— He has to collect data on the area which is being developed.

— In writing development stories, you have to be equipped with factual information which is generally not easily available.

— You will have to develop your own outlook which is more important than styles and techniques.

— Your language must be as simple as possible. While mentioning the figures of development, round up these instead of using fractions.

The Development Process : The process of development is generally slow, because people are slow in adopting novel idea. The process of development also requires people's participation and acceptance. It is here that the development reporter explains to the people the rationale behind building roads, schools and hospitals, use of high yielding resistant varieties, and other such matters. But the process of development has become very complex and in many parts of the world; the people are opposing large development programmes, almost to the extent of attaining an anti-development attitude. Billions of rupees have been spent on different development programmes but not much has been achieved in terms of returns. All these issues need to be presented to the people and the authorities. Development reporter in all mass media can help a great deal in this direction.

The Development Story : There are areas of development news and ideas which are only casually or rarely covered in the media. There are thousands of development stories lying buried under realms of paper but never come out for the general public.

To be a successful development reporter one has to be mobile and meet people who are involved in researches, attend seminars and conferences, ask questions, try to keep up with the latest trends in the world of science and human endeavour.

Also, keen habit of reading will sharpen your knowledge and technique. You will never be short of ideas.

Tasks of Development Reporting : Roughly, a development reporter has three tasks to perform—inform, interpret and promote. If properly executed, a development reporter's job is more exacting than that of mere news reporters. A development report must be included with a noble motive of supporting, crusading or promoting a cause. A sincere development writer's role in the overall progress of the country is as vital as that of a person working with his own hands. As a development journalist you will have to develop a sixth sense to smell the rot before it envelops you. Avoid *'mouthpiece writing'* at any cost. Also, the reporter must be honest to highlight the achievements and laurels won by the people executing the schemes.

To be a successful development reporter, one must inculcate certain characteristics :

(a) Fostering a wide range of contacts.

(b) Contacts with International Organizations.

(c) Keep a desk diary.

(d) Maintain your own reference material.

Specialised Skills Required : Development Reporting encompasses a number of areas and every field needs and demands special skills to report on that particular area fully and competently.

As a communicator, you have a very formidable task of

collecting information, transforming it into a right format and passing it on to the users. Avoid technical jargon and approach directly in a simple language. Tap every source of information.

As a development reporter, you have a prodigious task before you. You can choose any programme and monitor its progress in a regular column in your medium. You can help in mobilising people's participation in these programmes.

Development Reporting for Press : As a development reporter, you will be required to process and present facts in an intelligible form to the reader/viewer/listener. There are more than 1500 daily newspapers published in all the 18 national and other languages. Several newspaper devote full pages to development news. Development stories are best done in the form of a feature article.

Photo features on development projects can also be presented effectively. Interviews with the recipients of the benefits of the projects already completed can also help evaluate their impact on the masses.

An imaginative development writer can do freelancing for the press, radio and television. A development reporter has a challenging job and requires hard work, commitment and dedication.

Development Reporting for Radio : In India, radio has proved its utility as a potent audio medium for creating awareness among people. It helps in promoting an instinctive urge for development, by broadcasting programmes designed to help people diagnose their problems and clarify their objectives so that they may be able to make their decisions more wisely.

From 6 radio stations in 1947, All India Radio has grown to nearly 200 radio stations. Rural Radio Forums were started in 149 stations. Each forum consisted of 10 to 20 villages. Increase in knowledge in the forum villages was spectacular, whereas in the non-forum villages it was negligible.

As a development reporter for radio, there is plenty of scope to write scripts, to devise special programmes and also the work in the capacity as a free lancer to do development field stories.

While reporting development for radio, you must remember that you are talking to the people. You shouldn't appear as if you are reading. For this purpose, you must write your script in simple language. When you want to reach people who can not read or write, or the people who live in remote villages, and when you want to teach people speedily, the radio is the answer. The 'development' is actually meant for these people. You use the radio to inform, alert, suggest, direct, interest, stimulate and motivate people.

Development Reporting for Television : Television was first started in India in a small way in 1959. As a development reporter, you can use television to spread know-how, to as many people as within the reach of television centre. However, to be effective, your development programme must be field-based. Television is a visual medium and if visuals are missing or if you fail to focus on the relevant visuals, then the television's impact will be completely lost. For making a good television programme with a view to motivate people for development require a lot of effort, research and commitment. For writing a good television script, fewer words and more visuals are needed. Much more is communicated through visuals. Never make only studio based development programme for television. Go to the spots. Visit the remote areas. A well made television programme can help you expose the loopholes in our planning and implementation of the developmental plans.

Reporting on Sustainable Development : The term 'sustainable development' was popularized by the report of the World Commission Environment and Development (WCED). To some, sustainable development is a long awaited call for political recognition of global environmental decay, economic injustice and limits to material growth. The decline in environmental quality has however underlined the need for harmonizing the logic of economics with that of ecology.

The sustainable development, represents an opportunity for humanity to correct a historical error and develop a gentle, more balanced, and stable relationship with the natural world.

A total reorientation is required in development reporting in India. When writing about any development project, you must ask questions like how it wili improve the quality of life of the people without damaging the quality of air, water and soil and also without eroding the moral and social values.

Sports Reporting : Sports writing and reporting is as specialized an area as any other. It calls for both technical know how and a good writing style. As a sports reporter, you will have to be conversant with the tactics, rules and scoring patterns of various sports and games. You will also have to be knowledgeable about the lives of top players in the sport or game.

The art of successful sports reporting and writing, and any other special work, is the art of fully knowing the various popular games and sports. You must endeavour to write a news item or feature on any game with the objectives of making it appealing to a particular class of readers interested in those games.

Even as all sports and games are competitive, so too are the areas of sports writing and reporting. In such a scenario, as a sports writer, you need to structure your story around the reader's interest. You need to be thorough with your facts and capable of churning out a report under pressure of meeting a deadline.

How to Begin : Renowned sports journalists are known to have formed the habit of jotting down every idea or scrap of information that comes their way. Thus, to be a successful sports journalist you should first of all cultivate a habit of keeping notebook and pen with you all the time to record ideas. It is also rewarding to prepare notes on the end pages of the books you read. And it is essential to preserve the material that you have collected.

Clippings Collection : While reading paper or magazines, you should mark those articles and news reports which particularly interest you. Cut them and date those marked articles and file them under the appropriate subject. You will find that from the material so collected you can obtain information about your subject and may be some views of a handful of experts. Also, you will be able to refer to these clippings for facts and figures that you may quote in your own article or report. Facts are vital to analysis and comment.

In Search of Ideas in Sports : You have to develop your own powers of observation. Keep an eye open for any interesting out of the ordinary themes that you can write an article about. It is part of training to learn to look at life with a journalist's eye. You will then not only be knowledgeable but also will broaden your outlook. A good sports journalist has not only to be conversant with important person in sports but also has to be equally proficient with the technicalities of sports.

The Ignition Point in Idea-finding : The ignition point in idea-finding is not automatic, nor does it come readily. You have to devote enough and more time and effort to become proficient in finding an idea. Be watchful, patient and gather as much experience as you can. Thereafter, you can be sure to locate and identify ideas.

Putting Ideas in Writing : Think and think clearly before you start writing down your thoughts. In case you have not formed the habit of clear, constructive thinking, your story will reflect the confusion of your thoughts. Clear thinking will help you to write a thought provoking piece in lucid style. And also generates a flow in your ideas.

There is no better way to learn than self-analysis.

Style in Sports Writing : In order to write well, you must develop an easy, conversational style and tone that enables you to gain and hold the attention of the readers. You must learn to write simple sentences and use simple words instead of resorting to high-sounding words. Learn to write in a simple style.

Importance of a New Angle : Every sports reporter is faced with the task of discovering a new angle to a sporting event. You would probably be up against this kind of difficulty in the beginning of your career as a sports journalist. If you take the right and professional approach, you will find that the readers will read your entire report through.

Keep Your Eyes and Ears Open : Howsoever good your writing abilities, your network of contacts or even the sphere of your influence as a sports reporter, you can not escape the rigours of painstaking research, so necessary for any news item. You must keep your ears and eyes on the alert. Sometimes, even an innocuous meeting or drab cocktail party may provide a clue, or a lead for a sensational exclusive story, known as a 'scoop' in the newspaper world.

The Professional Approach : You must write for the people who were not lucky enough to be present at the site of the match. When you write a sports report, you must first consider which point you would like to highlight in your lead. Your report will be natural or original only when you lend a fresh perspective on the sporting event. You must give your best to the report that you have written. If you develop this kind of attitude, you will find that you will neither let yourself down.

Writing to Length : The most important aspect of sports journalism is precis-writing. The more precise you are, the more you will impress your readers. Readers are generally very busy, they do not have the time to read lengthy and vague news items.

Your have to possess enough knowledge, have information at your finger tips in order to write sports news. Space is allotted on the basis of relative importance of the news topics. It is better for you to revise your own copy thoroughly before you submit it at the sports desk.

How to Write ? When you report sports events and issues, you must know how to find the news and write the report. The most important thing is that a reporter wanting to make a mark in the profession must inspire confidence. You should, therefore, know landmarks in the history of the game, its rules, terms etc. The background information and achievements of players should be on your finger tips.

The readers are interested in the prospects of the individual players and of the team as on the day of the match, also all possible information about the event and finally, a post-mortem of the contest.

Good sports writing is good news writing. Sports news reporting is slightly different from general reporting because a sports reporter enjoys great freedom of self-expression.

One should rely on accurate and objective writing, stressing simplicity and clarity while avoiding unfamiliar terminology. Avoid writing vague reports when writing about stars and professional players, choose your words with care. The profession is quite hazardous. Do not make indiscreet comments.

Need for Specialisation : The arena of sporting activities is indeed a vast one. As a sports reporter, you have to know something about every sport, at least the salient features, rules and regulations. Also specialise in one or two disciplines (games). Much depends upon your interest and inclination.

Specialization, however, comes much later in one's career graph. You must train yourself to write on a variety of topics. At the same time your must also specialize in style that is both refreshingly different and illuminating to the general reader. To succeed in this, all that is required is accuracy of reportage and an original style of writing.

Facts for the Advance News Story : You have to depend upon the concerned officials, coaches and managers to get details for an advance copy. In the face of a defeat, an official may yet be willing to speak to you provided the two of you enjoy a good equation. The temperament and psychology of the players are equally important, if not more important than technique and skill. Finally, a sports reporter has to exercise tact and perhaps persistence when seeking information from officials. You have to study the situation well before you ask questions.

Covering the Game : You must learn to take notes systematically. Remember all the important incidents and happenings including the major moves or strategies that had a bearing on the outcome. When you write your copy, tell the story immediately. Avoid showing off your vocabulary. Report the action of the sport or game in as much detail as the word limit permits. While there is no rigid formula for a sports reporter, there are some conventional rules about the structure of the sports story. These are listed below :

Lead : Who won where, where, why and how.

Major Details : Star players, breaks and weather, if necessary

Minor Details : Other players, other plays and the behaviour of spectators

Other Details : Statistics, line-ups and substitutions.

Tips for Sports Reporter

— Study the rules of the game in question.

— Study their history.

— Cultivate friendly relations with officials of various clubs and associations.

— To specialise in reporting a particular sport, you must first acquaint yourself with every aspect of the sport.

— Read the journals pertaining to your particular sport.

— Try not to have confrontation with players and officials.

— There is no sports reporter who does not err. Accept the lapse instead to defend the indefensible.

— Have a positive outlook and think constructive.

Science Reporting : The laws of Nature are revealed to human beings through science. Technology involves the application of science to invent, innovate and improvise newer machines, products and services.

Must for A Science Reporter

Recapitulate School and College Science Studies : Recapitulation here means going over again and again, or revising the main points. All science reporters must have a basic knowledge of the elementary principles of science. A knowledge of scientific vocabulary is necessary.

That does not mean only science graduates can report happenings in science. Science education at school is broad-based and can be built upon.

Tips on Science Communication Awareness : Communication is sharing of information. As a science reporter, one must have the curiosity to know the latest happenings in the field one is covering. The moment one has learnt about a particular happening, must write a report for publication.

The best way to develop science communication awareness is by reading good science books and journals and by watching popular science programmes.

Checking Facts through Reference : There is no scope for factual errors, half-truths, exaggeration and hoax in Science. So also in science reporting. Scientific truths and technological facts are verifiable. It is always safe to check the facts with the source of the news or from other sources. A reporter who verifies facts as a matter of habit will earn the reputation of being credible.

Verification through Interviewing : Always keep a list of scientists and technologists of merit, living in the city or town where you are functioning as a reporter, so that the scientific facts and principles can be verified. It is important for the reporter to go ahead and cultivate an acquaintance with these scientists and technologists.

Personal Glossary : A science reporter, like all reporters is hard-pressed for time. They have deadlines to keep. As a science reporter, one will often be faced with technical terms. Scientists and technologists and indeed all specialists, are used to speaking in their own technical language. While taking down notes, one may not be ablc to translate these into common language. Therefore, prepare and keep the glossary of commonly used technical terms, arranged in alphabetical order. And should always be kept updating.

Institutions of Research and Development : As a reporter covering science and technology in India, you must have a comprehensive knowledge of the institutions of research and development in the country. India has built up one of the world's largest network of R&D facilities. They will be a major source of science-technology news.

The Department of Science & Technology of the Government of India looks after the policy planning and administrative details of the largest chain of national laboratories. These come under the council of Scientific & Industrial Research (CSIR). There are about 40 major research laboratories under CSIR. Atomic Energy and Space are two of the areas where India can boast of frontier research and development. Technical departments under other control ministries too have their research programmes.

Science-Technology Induced Development : In modern times, much is said and written about the human environment, both physical and social. The print and electronic media put out almost a daily dose of news and features about the environment. A science reporter must have a deeper understanding of the environment. The deeper the understanding of the environment, the higher would be the scientific temper.

One basic principle of mass communication is that you should not clutter up your news reporting with too many, facts. Also, you must not talk or write in complex terms. That way, people with different levels of understanding will not be able to grasp your meaning.

Language in Science-Technology Reporting for Popular Appeal: Journalistic writing must be a precise form of communication.

Science reporting calls for even greater precision. Science deals with laws of nature. Ideas and images in science communication should flow in logical progression. The skill of good writing improves with usage. As a reporter you have deadlines to keep and so may not have time for re-writing. Good science technology reporting needs language that communicates clearly and here comes the matter of grammar and usage. One has to follow the grammatical practices that make the writing orderly for others to follow.

The English language is today considered as the window to the science-technology information of the world.

Words, Sentences and Readability : Words denote images. There are tested patterns of constructing newspaper stories. The opening sentence must say the most important point of the news. The first two to three sentences should give the gist of the story. The paragraphs must be small. The story must move on from sentence to sentence and paragraph to paragraph.

Report Structure : A good beginning has the more important news point at the top of the story, and the lesser ones mentioned, as you go down. All the five Ws and H need to be cluttered in the introduction. Nothing is ever printed without being edited. Science-technology news reports are almost never rewritten, because nobody wants to be accused of having tampered with its precision.

Human Interest : People are interested in reading something which concerns them directly. If your science-technology story says something which people are interested in, just make it feel. Seek to be the best source of information for your reader, the consumer. Make the readers feel that you are their monitor and reporter.

Avoid Exaggeration and Sensationalism : Science-technology facts simply can not hold exaggerations. If a discovery, invention, or improvisation has an element of sensation, you should not be inhibited in including some of the sensation in your story. Do not make an invention look like something the world has been waiting for, when it is just an improvement on something that already existed.

Sensationalism and exaggeration can only do harm to the publication and to the credibility of a reporter. Just like the scientist, a science reporter also should be a seeker of truth. Like a technologist, a technology reporter too should be one who believes in precision and in updating knowledge.

The Importance of Rewriting : A sentence, a paragraph or a piece of writing can never be perfect. Only when a reporter makes sense to the largest section of readers does he or she qualify to be a professional writer. The first draft of any writer may need a lot of tightening up, chipping and polishing. So rewrite whenever your first effort is unsatisfactory for the reader's sake.

Place the important points at the precise junctures of your story. One needs to revise the copy and make it crisp.

Legislature Reporting : Legislature Reporting, an essential part of mass media function, is a significant feature of Parliamentary democracy. Both people and the government are benefitted by legislature reporting. Parliament or state legislature, Vidhan Sabha and Vidhan Parishad, is called 'legislature' and reporting the day-to-day proceedings of these bodies is called legislature reporting.

Reporting the proceedings of a legislature is a highly responsible job, for which an experienced reporter is sent to cover the proceedings. The reporting job includes the complex process of legislature, debates on subjects of public importance, writing for the media about several other features that go to make Parliamentary proceedings.

Parliament Structure : The constitution of India provides for a bicameral Parliament consisting of the President and the two houses-Lok Sabha (House of People) and Rajya Sabha (Council of States).

The Lok Sabha is composed of representatives of the people chosen by direct election. Unless sooner dissolved, it continues for five years from the date of its first meeting. The maximum strength of Lok Sabha is 552 members. 525 are from states, 20 from Union Territory and 2 nominated by President from Anglo-Indians.

In Rajya Sabha, 12 members out of 250 are nominated by President for their special knowledge and the remaining seats are allocated to the various states and Union Territory.

Like Parliament, there are some states which have a bicameral legislature-assembly and the council-i.e., Vidhan Sabha and Vidhan Parishad. But there are also states which have only the Vidhan Sabha and no Vidhan Parishad.

Parliament and State legislatures become great sources of news when in session. The government makes all the major announcements in Parliament. There are moves and counter-moves by ruling and opposition parties which are grist to the news person's mill.

As a reporter covering parliament, you should know the rules and procedures of legislatures. By and large, these are the same for both the parliament and the state legislatures.

Essentials of Parliamentary Proceedings : The various features essential for the parliamentary proceedings (on a normal day) can be listed as :

(1) Question Hour

(2) Papers to be laid on the table of the house

(3) Zero Hour

(4) Legislative Business

Question Hour : The first hour of every legislature sitting is normally devoted to questions. Questions are of three types :

Starred Questions : A "starred question" is the one to which a member desires an oral answer in the House. Other members can ask supplementary questions which are relevant to the main question. Generally, the answer to the main question which is listed, is in written form with explanatory statement. But supplementaries will have to be answered orally by the minister concerned.

Unstarred Questions : An "unstarred question" is one to which an oral answer is not called for in the house and on which no supplementary questions can be asked. To such a question, a written answer is deemed to have been laid on the *'Table of the House'* after the question hour by the minister to whom it is addressed.

Short Notice Questions : It is related to a matter of urgent public importance and can be asked with the consent of the minister concerned, at a shorter notice than the period of the notice prescribed for an ordinary questions. While 20 questions can be listed for oral answer on a day, as many as 230 questions can be listed for written answers. And it is through questions in Parliament, that the government remains in touch with the people. Questions bring to the notice of the ministers many an abuse which otherwise would have gone unnoticed. Sometimes questions may lead to the appointment of a commission, a court of enquiry or even legislation. Therefore, seasoned parliamentary correspondents are generally entrusted with the task of covering the "question hour". The reporter should remain alert when the minister answers or tries to answer probing questions by members on matters of national importance.

Thus, Parliament questions cover all the ministries and give authentic information. They should be kept by the correspondent for future use as they may provide leads to other stories.

Papers Laid on Table : After the Question Hour is over, the House will take up papers to be laid on the table. These are official documents relating to various ministries and departments and are tabled by ministers concerned. These papers often yield good stories. As a reporter in-charge of papers laid on the table, one should carefully read the agenda paper of the House.

Zero Hour : The zero hour which follows immediately is the most challenging for a young reporter. For, this is the time when members belonging to various parties spring on their feet and try to draw the attention of the chair to the issues they think important and need the government's response. It becomes very difficult to pick up the words of the members as many speak at the same time. All your attention should be centered on what is happening and must note down as quickly as possible what the members say.

The reporter, with his notes and a fair background knowledge of the issues raised, will be able to write a good copy. It is also important for the reporter to be thorough with the morning newspapers, at least with the stories likely to figure in parliament in the day.

Legislative Business : Legislative business consists of introduction, consideration and passing of government bills. After a bill is passed in both Houses, it goes for the Presidential assent, following which it becomes an act of Parliament. The stages through which a bill, which is a legislative proposal, has to pass are :

Introduction of the Bill : The bill can be introduced in either house by a minister in-charge of the subject of the bill. Once the House, that is the majority of members, gives leave to the minister for introduction, the bill is deemed to have been introduced.

General Discussion : At the second stage, a general discussion takes place on the bill as a whole followed by a clause consideration of the bill. At this stage it is open to the House to decide to refer the bill to a select committee of the House or a joint committee of the two Houses.

Voting : When all the clauses and schedules of the bill have been considered and voted upon by the house, the minister in-charge moves that the bill is passed.

Call Attention Motion : Essentially an Indian procedural innovation enables a member to draw the attention of the government to development of public importance and to elicit government views there on.

Adjournment Motion : This is a motion by any member to demand the adjournment of all other business in the house to discuss the issue he may raise. To raise a discussion on the issue, the member must ensure that his motion is supported by the majority of members present.

No Confidence Motion : The motion is at times brought by the opposition to express its lack of confidence in the government. After the motion is allowed, a detailed discussion takes place. After the discussion, voting may take place.

Privileges of Parliament : The concept of privileges of Parliament rests on the principle that a sovereign legislature should be able to perform its legislative and deliberative functions independently and effectively. For this it should possess certain inherent or conferred powers to punish for breach of such privileges. Articles 105(3) and 194(3) of the constitution empower Parliament and State Legislatures respectively to enact laws codifying their privileges. However, neither parliament nor any of the legislatures of the states has so far done so. Breach of privilege of either House of central or state legislature is usually known as 'contempt of parliament' like the contempt of courts.

A journalist or editor can be punished with imprisonment or administered a warning, admonition or reprimand for the breach of privilege of the House. He can be asked to publish an apology. However, no fines are imposed.

Contempt has a wider sweep than breach of privilege. Contempt can be committed by an act or utterance which undermines the dignity of the House even without violating any particular privilege of the legislature.

But, it is not a breach of privilege to publish without malice a substantially true report of the proceedings of the house even if it is defamatory, seditious or obscene in nature. The legislature in India has not enacted any law codifying its privileges, mainly because any such law will be subject to a judicial review in respect of the citizens' fundamental rights. The Press has been rightly demanding that the privileges of parliament should be codified so that it knows the scope and limits of its freedom vis-a-vis the legislature.

Breach of Privilege : Article 361-A of the Constitution of India protects publication of proceedings of Parliament and state legislatures from any civil and criminal action. No person commits any civil or criminal offence, if he publishes substantially true reports of the proceedings of a House. However, if the publication has been done with malice, the protection conferred by Article 361-A does not apply. Publication of the expourgeal portion of the proceedings of a House, is a breach of its privilege. Article 361-A was inserted in the constitution in 1977.

The House is the custodian of its own privilege and is empowered to take action against a reporter, if his conduct or writing is in breach of its privileges. Since the scope of parliamentary privilege has not been codified, the reporter has to use abundant caution in reporting the proceedings.

Deliberate, distortion of speeches, aspersions cast on a members behaviour in the House, and imputation of motives to him for his speech or behaviour in the House are serious transgression of the privileges of the members. It is one of the privileges of the Parliament and State legislatures to exclude any stranger, including press reporters, from the sittings of the House and from the press gallery.

Reporting the legislature's proceedings by the media is extremely useful for the common people in a democratic set-up. Journalists have to be on the constant look out for publishing important decisions taken or not taken in these houses as it is the day-to-day reporting of the legislature's activities that electorates perceive as to what these elected representatives are doing in Parliament and other legislatures. But in doing so the journalists are sometimes likely to err on the wrong side of the law. Thus, a number of laws have been provided to ensure that media do not cast aspersions on their conduct or adversely comment on their report in a House. These laws govern the powers and privileges of legislatures in so far as these common journalist's work may interfere with the right to the freedom of the press or reporters.

The representative of the press are generally provided facilities to cover the proceedings of legislature from the press gallery by issuing an accreditation card to press persons. The reporters should however study parliamentary privileges and Article 361-A of the Constitution of India to safeguard themselves against any default that may occur in reporting proceedings of a legislature.

Court Reporting : Here we shall discuss five different areas of reporting-Court Reporting, Legislature, Science & Technology, Sports Reporting and Development Reporting.

Who are Court Reporters : There are too many courts, and newspapers have neither the time nor the space to cover everything that happens in the court. Papers cover only those stories in which their readers are interested.

There are only a few big newspapers in India who have full time correspondents exclusively for their court beat. These correspondents generally have adequate legal background. Other newspapers mostly hire stringers to cover court stories. A newspaper which does not have a full time law reporter may send its regular staff correspondent to cover an important court story.

Must for a New Law Reporter : One would expect the Law Reporter to be knowledgeable about legal matters. The range and nature of information one must have at one's finger tips are following :

Knowledge of Court Jurisdictions, Procedures and Hierarchy : A trainee journalist aiming to be a future court reporter must at first acquire some understanding of the court jurisdiction, its procedures and its hierarchy. If a reporter is acquainted with the jurisdiction of different courts, then one can easily locate the specific court for a particular matter. Similarly if one is familiar with the hierarchy in the courts, one can easily guess where the appeal would be filed.

Some Legal Terms : For a court reporter, some basic knowledge of some of the most frequently used legal terms is a must.

Professional journalistic practice requires each technical term to be briefly explained when it is used in a story for the first time. A legal term, not used in the story, confuses the reader.

The English knowledge is predominantly used in the higher courts of India. Therefore for a reporter of a non-English daily, some knowledge of English language always helps.

News Sources : Much of a reporter's success in the coverage of the courts depends on one's contacts and sources, and one's ability to gain access quickly to records. For a reporter the key person in the court is the clerk of the court. A court clerk prepares and keeps the records. Court reporting involves diligent checking of records. The judge who presides a trial is seldom one's source. A court reporter should also have good contacts with the lawyers working on a case and with the respective parties.

Trial Coverage : While taking notes in a trial coverage the reporter needs to have a sixth sense. Guided by this news sense, one could begin to take notes of important dates. When a reporter misses an important testimony, one can always regain lost ground during the recess by consulting one's colleagues in the court, or the court stenographer.

Writing with Quotes : In trial proceedings, wherever possible, the reporters must learn to quote the questions and answers or comments and remarks that arise in the course of court's sittings. A story with quotes makes fascinating reading though sometimes, due to paucity of space. Many comments may not be quoted in the news item.

Precautions in Writing Court Stories : While writing stories one must be cautious in avoiding any contempt of court.

Sometimes, a reporter files the court story without comments and sometimes with one's own or someone else's comments.

Contempt of Court : The law relating to contempt of court can be braced from the Contempt of Court Act, 1971 and from various case laws. A contempt can be civil or criminal offence.

Civil Contempt : It means wilful disobedience to any judgement, decree, direction, order to other process of a court, or wilful breach of an undertaking given by a person to a court. There will be no civil contempt where there is ignorance of the order of a court leading to unintentional breach.

Criminal Contempt : It mainly means publication of any matter, or the doing of any other act, which :

(i) Scandalises the authority of any court; or

(ii) Prejudices or interferes with the due course of judicial proceedings.

Scandalising the Court : Under the law, publication of matter which creates doubts about the ability or fairness of a judge of a court is prohibited. A newspaper should not impute of improper motives to a judge. Casting defamatory allegations against a judge or judges, with or without reference to particular case, is contempt because it creates distrust in the popular mind and shatters confidence of the people in the judiciary. However, the Contempt of Court Act 1971, is basically designed to protect the judiciary from unwarranted allegations, and not to safeguard corrupt judges.

Prejudicing Fair Trial : Court reporting prejudicing fair trial may be of various forms. It is contempt-

(a) If a newspaper report deters a person from giving witness in a court;

(b) If the report offers threats or is written in abusive language compelling a party to discontinue the court proceedings;

(c) If the report discusses the merits of a case pending in court.

The Safeguards

According to Section 5 of the Contempt of Court Act, 1971, a person shall not be guilty of Contempt of Court for publishing any 'fair comment' on the merits of any case, which has been 'heard and finally decided'.

What is Fair Comment? There is no single formula to decide the fairness of a comment. The matter depends on the facts and circumstances of each case. To comment on the correctness of a judicial decision is not contempt. Similarly, to point out inequality of sentences in two different cases of the same nature, is also not contempt.

However, while commenting on the merits of a case if improper motives are imputed to the judge, then the comment ceases to be fair. Similarly, to express that the judgement was arbitrary or the judge was incompetent is also contempt.

Heard and Finally Decided : A fair comment on the merits of a ease be made when it is heard and finally decided. A case can not be said to have finally decided until the period of limitation for filing appeal has expired. Where an appeal or revision has been filed the comments on the merits of the case should not be published until the appeal is finally decided.

Ignorance of Pendency : If a court story interferes with the course of justice, but its reports had no reasonable ground to assume that the proceedings were pending, then one will not be guilty of contempt of court. Prior to the enactment of Contempt of Court Act, 1971, ignorance of pendency was not a defence or excuse.

Fair and Accurate Report : According to Section 4 of the Contempt of Court Act, 1971, fair and accurate report of the court proceedings is lawful.

However, a report will be contemptuous if it has been prohibited by the court or is forbidden by any law.

Truth No Defence : Though truthfulness of a statement is a good defence in an action for libel, it is no defence when it comes to contempt of court.

Academic Writings : Academic writings or a report written academically on a point, of law is not a contempt of court, just on the ground that the law discussed is at issue in a court.

Punishment : The maximum punishment for contempt of court is simple imprisonment of six months, or fine of two thousand rupees or both. If the accused apologies, the person, may be discharged by the court without punishment. It is for the court to decide whether the apology is acceptable. Generally, an apology, to be acceptable by the court, should be sincere, unconditional and without delay.

7

Analytical Reporting

There are as many definitions of 'depth reporting' as there are reporters. Or almost Editors are often heard to remark that there is so little of depth reporting in their papers that they feel the news they provide is incomplete. What is depth reporting?

The Concept

Here are a few answers:

> Depth reporting is what makes readers aware of all aspects of a given subject by giving them all possible information, including, background and atmosphere.

Depth reporting treats a story with a kind of thoroughness of detail and background that a 300-word story cannot. It tells the reader not only what happened but why it happened.

Depth reporting means giving the reader the entire story, an exhaustive, balanced and well-organized way with full backgrounding.

Depth reporting is simply good reporting with an eye for accuracy and detail.

Depth reporting is the explanatory story that accompanies or follows a breaking news story.

Depth reporting means going into a news development and explaining its significance with the possible accompaniment of photos that help illustrate the story.

Depth reporting is sound planning in anticipation of news and vigorous execution while the news is fresh.

Depth reporting is not a one-man job but is the product of teamwork, allowing for maximum flexibility.

Depth reporting deals in explanatory facts and not explanatory opinion.

Depth reporting is that which leaves no occassion for more questions to be asked by the reader.

Depth reporting is not just presentation of facts as they appear at first, but which delves into the origins, the logic, the pressures and the interests involved, making the reader understand not merely who and what, but how, and more importantly, why.

Depth reporting is digging beneath the surface and coming up. With facts that aren't immediately visible, but which nevertheless contribute to an understanding of the story.

No matter how it is defined, in-depth reporting, in the final analysis should tell us the whole, unvarnished story as it is.

His a mistaken notion to think that an in-depth story should necessarily be long, though *New Yorker* reports which are magnificent examples of in-depth reporting run into several thousand: words. Length has nothing to do with depth. And, while obviously it is not always easy to cram many facts in a short piece, a perceptive reporter should be able to provide the maximum information in the fewest necessary words. Wordiness is not wisdom and padding is usually seen for what it is.

Often the best in-depth reporting is done by a team, especially if one has to consider the time factor. While the total number of man hours put in pursuing the facts and writing the story may be about the same if the piece was written by just one reporter, team writing has the additional advantage of bringing the thinking of several men to the final story and should generally be preferable.

The line dividing an in-depth from a feature article or an investigative report is pretty thin indeed and one can often be confused for the other. The presumption usually is that in an investigative report the object is to ferret out important secret information which somebody is determined to keep secret. But there is no hard and fast rule which says that a writer of a feature article should not reveal secret information or that in-depth reports should confine themselves strictly to presenting background information in detail. The *Indian Express* in late April and early May 1979 ran a series on what it is like to be in a jail by one of its reporters Ashwini Sarin. Sarin got himself arrested and provided some excellent inside information about life in Tihar Central Jail, Delhi. The four-part serial was part in-depth reportage, part feature and part investigative reporting at its best.

Investigative Reporting: Ever since Woodward and Bernstein of the *Washington Post* broke the Watergate story and followed it up to the point where President Nixon finally had to resign, investigative reporting has received a fillip out of proportion to their real contribution to journalism. For the fact is that much of what the two reporters put out was based on FBI reports that were passed on to them by sources that had their own axes to grind.

And while this is not to minimize what Woodward and Bernstein had done, it is well to remember that investigative journalism is more than rephrasing leaks. At its best, investigative reporting is master detective work. It is a *way* of reporting that makes it a tool of the in-depth writer. Also, it is *situation reporting* rather than *event reporting,* although events may be involved.

An investigative reporter starts with the hunch that there is more than meets the eye in something of which he had heard. But he can only function best if he is assured of strong editorial direction and backing. Without that the most perceptive reporter would,be wasting his time and the paper's money.

This means that the investigative reporter will have to clear his assignment with the editor and function with the knowledge and-consent of his seniors, if only because no investigation can be successful without the time to do a decent job. A City Editor of-the Detroit *Free Press* is quoted as giving the following suggestions to the prospective investigative reporter:

Don't overlook a tip from any source. Some of the best leads may come from the tips that don't look promising. Many-perhaps most-won't pan out. But don't overlook any possibilities.

Stay within the law. Don't attempt to open safes or burgla Tise offices for 'evidence'. Don't be a policeman.

Make plans from the start. Don't leap into it. Check the evidence and keep checking as you go along. Keep up your lines of communication with those working in the field.

Keep going. The investigative way is hard, but don't stop if you think you have something. If your curiosity is burning you as it should, you won't.

'The curiosity of Ashwini Sarin of the *Express News Service* got the better of him in wanting to know what conditions in Tihar Central Jail, Delhi, were. One-fifth of India's Jails were built in the 19th century. Another two-thirds were built 60 to 80 years ago. But concerned citizens eager to help improve conditions in jail were repeatedly denied access to them. Sarin volunteered to get himself arrested on a minor charge and file a first-hand report on conditions in Tihar Central Jail. Following is an extract from,part one of his four-part report, a good example of investigative reporting:

New Delhi: I still shudder to recall the experience. "Never again." I prayed as I stepped into the waiting taxi on the night of April 20 (10.30 p.m. to be precise) after my release from Delhi's Tihar Central Jail. I had been lodged there two days earlier charged with disorderly behaviour in a public place under the influence of alcohol.

"A day more here and I would have turned mad" I told' B.M. Sinha, my chief reporter who came to take me home from an assignment which turned out to be something I had not bargained for.

The idea was to know at first hand what exactly it means to be an under-trial in Tihar Jail. Our earlier efforts to penetrate the secrecy behind the high walls through official and other sources had failed.

I was to get myself arrested on a trumped up charge and then, refuse bail.

My first effort to create an unruly scene, without consuming liquor, at the Delhi Haryana border on April 17 was futile. A burly police sub-Inspector gave me a long lecture on cultivating good habits. "You seem to come from a good family" he said. "Care for their honour if not your own." He hailed a taxi and put me in with instructions to the driver to "unload" me safely at my house.

I left the taxi at Kalkaji, tipped the driver and took a bus home.

The next day, April 18. I left home after a hearty breakfast of boiled eggs and toast. "Have your fill because there will belittle to eat for the next three days," Mr. Sinha cautioned me. About 11.30 a.m. we took a taxi and headed towards Badarpur. The arrangement was that Sinha would shadow me after my arrest.

This time I choose a spot very near the Badarpur police station. I abused a shopkeeper with an empty beer bottle in one hand and using the other to stop the traffic trying to enter the old Badarpur settlement from the historic Agra Gate side. My torn faded jeans and the ageing check-shirt with the upper two buttons missing suited my role nicely.

The word soon reached the police station and within minutes I was dragged into it. The old lanky Sub-Inspector and the baton-wielding constables were not too rough. Sinha was watching from a distance.

They put me under arrest. Within half an hour the papers charging me under Section 93 and 97 of the Delhi Police Act were ready. A police pick-up took me to the Patiala House Court and I was produced before the Magistrate who remanded me to jail custody till Monday, April 23, if I failed to produce a bail bond. The court allowed my application that I be allowed to take Rs. 25 to jail.

Outside, some touts offered to get me out on bail. "This is a very minor offence. Why are you spending five days in jail? I will get you bail for 20 rupees" one said. I thanked him as the cops took me to the lock-up room in Patiala House. I was already in low spirits. This was going to be no fun.

In the succeeding three parts Sar.r. gave a vivid account of what it was like to be in a jail with professional criminals. And whether, in the end, the revelations achieved anything is beside the point. What is relevant is that the four-part series was a professsionally, competent one.

Investigative stories may be written in a variety of ways. When the subject matter is familiar and little explanation is called for, the story can be written as straight news. But if the investigation,deals with complicated issues, then a good deal of interpretative material will become necessary. The important thing to remember is that the writer must remain calm, restrained and detached if he is to make any meaningful impact on his reader. The hystorical I-am-a-detective who-dug-it-all style is unbecoming and could even be counterproductive.

Reporting in Depth

In a sense all good editors are crusaders for a cause or causes.

In the early thirties and forties, till indeed India became free, journalism in our country was largely crusading journalism where the national press was concerned. And the crusade, understand ably, was for freedom. *The Free Press Journal* in its early days ran strong stories supporting the cause of Indian shipping.

A crusade implies not merely a cause to be fought for but steadiness and constancy, a stout heart and an unflagging interest. A crusade is not fought by writting one editorial or one news story. Perseverance, often against entrenched hostility from the powers that be, is the hallmark of a crusade. Bal Gangadhar Tilak was a crusader; so was Mahatma Gandhi. At the turn of the century, Lovat Fraser, then editor of the *Times of India* ran a crusade exposing the inhuman working conditions in Bombay's textile mills where men worked 12 hours a day. Fraser ran a tearing campaign :starting with an article entitled "Bombay's Slaves" which was to result in a succession of Factory Acts that brought the Indian industrial system in line with world practice. A crusade can be for any good cause: against child marriage, in favour of prohibition, for ushering in linguistic states...several are the causes that the Indian press has fought for over the years. The obvious characteristic of a crusade is that it is concerned with the public good as seen by the editor. In conducting a crusade, the editor may bring all the ammunition he has to the battle: editorials, depth-reporting, investigative reporting, even cartoons. It was Joseph Pulitzer who first established the crusade as a way of life for American newspapers by setting up a prize for such kind of journalism. He himself ran crusades against predatory financial interests, bad housing, the white slave traffic to menion only a few causes that he strenuously espoused. Today, in the United States, the Pulitzer Prize remains a major incentive for journalists to carryon with the Pulitzer tradition.

It may be mentioned in passing, however, that neither in the United States nor in any other country, India included, is a crusade necessarily inducted in the public interest. It does happen all too often that a crusade is just one more gimmick to raise the paper's circulation. Not that this is necessarily wrong; if the public interest coincides with the paper's interest, that is no reason why eyebrows should be raised. But nevertheless it is just as well to remember that what shines for public weal may turn out to be another way to augment private profit.

In itself, a crusading newspaper is neither good nor bad. That depends, as a distinguished American publicist, Robert J. Blakely pointed out in his Don R. Mellett Memorial lecture, in large part upon its motivations. There are newspapers that 'crusade' for ulterior reasons-to build up circulation or to grind an axe rather than to sharpen the sword of justice. These are contemptible. They injure the innocent. They rarely accomplish beneficial results that endure, always stopping short when the cream of sensationalism has been skimmed and never pressing to where they touch the really powerful and dangerous elements of the community.... But to me the free press reaches its zenith in a good newspaper looking for a fight in a good causein its own avenues and alleys. Few personal satisfactions can match the knowledge that one is making one's community a better place in which to live".

The value of a true crusade is that it quickly endears itself to the reader. And the newspaper which shows that it is unafraid or the powerful is quickly recognized as a trustworthy watchdog. More, once the public realises that the local newspaper is interested in exposing scandals it will come forth with a surprising amount of information. Trust begets trust.

A crusade can be most productive when the situation is ripe for action. A little corruption does not invite much attention. Large scale corruption does. Mr. Amitabh Chowdhury won an award while assistant editor of *Jugantar* by exposing graft in Calcutta. The graft was of such a kind that it could not go unrecognized. During his years as editor of *The Times of India,* Mr. Frank Moraes ran a crusade against prohibition. It took courage to buck the Establishment of that time. Mr. Moraes had to pay for it. An editor who runs an unsuccessful crusade *pari passu* runs the risk of losing his job.

Feature Writing : The standard English dictionary defines the word 'feature' as follows: 1 part of the face. The nose, mouth, chin and forehead are features, 2 features the face. 3 distinct part or quality; thing that stands out and attracts attention. 4 a long motion picture. 5 a special article, comic strip etc. in a newspaper.

To say that a newspaper feature is a "special article" does not say much about the nature of that article. What, then, is a feature article? Too many newspapermen think vaguely of features as something of a timeless nature-a story that can be pushed in when there is not much news, or a story that reads well on a Sunday in the magazine section. In fact one thinks of features strictly in terms of magazine reading.

What is there about a feature that makes it attractive to readers? Contrary to some belief, it is its *timeliness.* A feature to be read and appreciated, must have immediate reference to what the reader knows only sketchily. A feature, in the circumstances, must fill in the reader with new information of which he has been hitherto ignorant. It must provide him with all that he wanted to know but had no time to inquire about.

A feature can be written on any subject. Think of all the features that have appeared, for example, in *The Illustrated Weekly of India.*

News Item: Dr. K. Shivarama Karanth has been awarded the Jnanpith Award for 1978.

Feature Story: Who is Dr. Karanth? Why was the Jnanpith Award given to him? What is the source of his greatness as a writer? A discussion of the quality and content of some of his books with, possibly, an interview with the award winner.

News Story: A child is born conceived in the laboratory, a miracle of modern science.

Feature Story: What is the ballyhoo about a "test-tube" baby all about? Who are the scientists who made the birth of the first testtube baby possible? What techniques did they use? What are the lessons to be learnt from them?

News Item: On September 9, 1978, the Soviet Union celebrated the 150th birth anniversary of Count Leo Tolstoy.

Feature Story: What is the relevance of Tolstoy to India? What are his links with India? What was the nature of the correspondence between him and Mahatma Gandhi?

News Item: On August 17,1978, three Americans landed their giant helium-filled balloon in France to become the first aviators to balloon across the Atlantic.

Feature Story: When was the last attempt at crossing the Atlantic by balloon made? What is the history of ballooning? How many attempts have been made at all? Where? With what success? At what cost?

News Item: The Government of India has placed a ban on foreign film units making a documentary of the Rajneesh Ashram.

Feature Story: What kind of ashram is run by Bhagwan Rajneesh? What are his antecedents? What is his philosophy? Why is he so controversial? News item: The site of the Mathura Refinery has been chosen on the basis of techno-economic studies, but without going into the problem of pollution.

News Item: A proposal has been made by Mr. George Fernandes, Minister for Industry for the nationalization of the steel, aluminium and automobile industries.

Feature Story: Are the three concerned industries really in bad shape? What motivated the Minister to call for the nationalization of manifestly profit-making units? What does the Minister have to say in defence of his proposal? What do the stalwarts of the industries themselves have to say in defence of the private sector?

It will be noticed that every feature arises out of a news item; the news does not tell the whole story; it is left to the feature writer to fill in the blanks. The feature becomes attractive in direct proportion to the element of curiosity stirred by the news item.

In fact, there is a direct co-relation between a news item and a feature and the writer who is quick to grasp it can be the first in the market to sell it.to a magazine or a journal. A feature is saleable to the extent that it strikes reader interest when the news is still "hot."

Though Some magazines have a regular feature editor, more often than not it is the free lance writer who provides the features. The topics for the features literally suggest themselves to the perceptive free-lancer or professional writer. A film actress commits suicide. That is the news. Topic for a feature: how many people commit suicide in a year? Who are more prone to commit suicide: men or women? In India which state has the highest rate of suicides?

Which country in the world has, similarly, the highest rate of suicide? Why do people commit suicide? What can be done to prevent them from killing themselves?

Or again: Mr. Zulfikar Ali Bhutto is hanged. Topic for a feature: Is Mr. Bhutto the first political leader to be hanged for alleged crimes committed while in power? Who other have met a similar fate? Is hanging desirable?

When it was reported that there had been a sudden spurt in cases of jaundice in Bombay city, *The Illustrated Weekly of India* commissioned a distinguished medical practitioner to write about why and how jaundice strikes and what remedial measures could be taken to prevent its occurrence. It was a sell-out issue.

A feature is expected to give the background to the news, which includes analysis, explanation and discussion. It should document facts, possibly anticipate developments. Perception is a great gift for a feature writer who wants to make his mark as a knowledgeable person. In fact the more of a specialist he is, the better are the feature writer's chances of selling his product.

A feature can be based on a news item. It is a news feature.

A feature can be based on sports. It is a sports feature.

A feature can be based on adventure (mountain-climbing, hunting). It is an adventure feature.

A feature can be on science. It is a science feature... and so on.

A feature becomes attractive to editors if it is *(a)*'timely *(b)* written by an authority, *(c)* illustrated suitably. Magazines, especially, prefer features that can be richly illustrated.

But there are other kinds of features as well. A cartoon strip is.a feature. A personal diary is a feature; a column is a feature. A '"middle" is a feature. So are book reviews, film criticism, art and, theatre criticisms-all features in their own right. Feature writing, in the circumstances, is an art that is best handled by an expert-or specialist in his field.

A personal diary is something intensely intimate. It records the impressions of the writer in subjective terms-the 'I' predominating. President Franklin D. Roosevelt's wife Eleanor wrote a personal column for many years and it was widely read because of the position she held as the President's wife. Mrs. Roosevelt was also, controversial as any good personal columnist should be in a healthy way and often readable as well.

Among the more distinguished personal diarists in India was Pothan Joseph whose column "Over A Cup of Tea" which he began during his days at the *Bombay Chronicle* and continued to his last years on the *Deccan Herald* was one of the most widely-read in India. He wrote in snippets. Below are examples:

> "The consequences of abolishing Guindy races would be the sacrifice of our horses" writes a Khadi-clad sportsman mournfully. Aswamedha represented supreme attainment, you ass. Become a member of the Turf Club, support "Government policy, do your betting elsewhere, vote for the liquidation of properties, see to the sale of land at high prices, take your share of the :proceeds, and go home, singing in the rain.

Pandit Nehru warns us about, the possibility of Englishmen (before they quit) of "wreaking damage on our minds and hearts and producing a dangerous ulcer." Not to mention an Ulster.

"There is no room for goondas in any religion" says Mahatma Gandhi. Scarcity of accommodation in the cities is largely responsible for their being underground.

A new member of a certain Government bureau made life miserable for his associates by pretending absolute infallibility. One, day, however, he startled his co-workers by admitting that 'once" he had been wrong. "You wrong?" exclaimed one of them, "Impossible!" "Yes," replied the infallible one, "once I thought I was wrong, when I wasn't."

General Manager T.A. Joseph says that Janata trains are not popular in South India. The South Indian is a born democrat and likes the higgledy-piggledy form of trayel, mob-style, that keeps him in athletic fitness. With bodies normally bare as Mother Nature meant it, airconditioning interferes with his perspiration,.. and with music freely rendered by mendicants, he can do without artificial luxuries offered by the coaching department.

Jawaharlal is sorry to hear of the Andhra Kesari's passing, but President Prasad has been more liberal in his eulogy. When Sikandar Hyat Khan died, Jinnah was in Delhi, rather cross about the unenthusiastic views on partition entertained by the Punjab Premier. A statement was requested of the Quaid-e-Azam by the present writer. The tribute expected for record on a long sheet of paper ran: "I am sorry to hear Sikandar is dead." There it ended, like a knife-clasp.

In a newspaper, the columnist is something of a privileged person. He can venture into fields that are forbidden territory to reporters. He can say his piece with little fear of being called on the coals by the editor. But, as with Pothan Joseph or M. Chalapathi Rao, an editor may both write an editorial and a column as well. In fact many editors have their special columns. In his time, Frank Moraes wrote a column for the Sunday *Times of India,* M. V. Kamath wrote a gossip column for the *Free Press Bulletin* and Chalapathi Rao himself wrote a column called *Off the Record:* under the pseudonym Magnus.

Although the word "column" might indicate that the contents run to the conventional 1,000 words or so of the usual newspaper column measurement, the length of a column varies. Some columnists may turn out the full 1,000 words, some would be satisfied with much less and D.F. Karaka, writing for the defunct *Bombay-Chronicle* wrote a "half-column" under the pseudonym Dim that was often less than half a column in length. And fans of the celebrated American humourist Will Rogers will attest to the fact that he wrote a famous column which averaged but one paragraph!

There are, in a manner of speaking, several popular types of columns:

(1) The signed editorial column: Here we find what resembles an editorial in form, but an editorial so palpably personal that it is a cross between an editorial and a column. When an editor writes a piece under his own name he is trying to lay his prestige on the line, Frank Moraes used to write front-page editorials for emphasis. This kind of column is resorted to but rarely by editors.

(2) The standard column: This type of column handles editorial subjects of lesser importance and deals with each in a paragraph or two. A good example is "Current Topics" in *The Times of India*. These are primarily backgrounders and not really opinion pieces. They are unsigned and are frequently the work of two or more members of the editorial staff. Outstanding columns in this category are "Topics of the Times" in the *New York Times*.

(3) The hodge-podge column: Here the columnist presents to his reader a hodge podge of stuff of little or no consequence on the principle that variety is not only the spice of life but a sure formula to catch reader interest. Pothan Joseph's *Over a Cup of Tea*-very nearly approximates to this description.

(4) The middle: The "middle" is so-called because it occupies a position on the editorial page between the main article and the standard column, Current Topics in the case of *The Times of India*.

    The middle's sole purpose is to lighten what could otherwise be serious reading which an editorial page normally is and is expected to be. It is generally humourous and in any event it should be entertaining and is usually written in a lighter vein. In length it is about 500 words and the more off-beat it is, the better.

(5) The essay column: This type of column is rare today. Students of English literature will recognize the essay columns of Joseph Addison, Charles Lamb, Oliver Goldsmith, G.K. Chesterton and A.A. Milne. As an essay, it has style. Its range is unlimited but it must stick to one rigid rule-it must never be didactic or dull.

Consider this piece on C.K. Nayudu by Chalapathi Rao (Magnus):

C.K. Nayudu was too alive for long to have become entirely a legend. It is difficult to bury him, as other great cricketers are buried, under a mound of metaphors, though the language of cricket is rich in them. He combined Spartan physical strength with an artist's grace. To think of him mainly in terms of his sixes is poor appreciation, like his Padma Bhushan which was poor recognition. His sixes were only the sparks of his scientific hitting. Nor is it adequate to recall Neville Card us with his poetic phrases borrowed from the language of music, because Cardus had only a glimpse of Nayudu's greatness.

Nayudu could be said to be the father of modern Indian cricket, the man who stamped the age with his strength of character. He is often compared to Jessop, to Trumper, to MaCartney, or to Woolley; with similar grace and freedom from care, Woolley was probably the closest to him. In Indian terms, Nayudu's place was by the side of Ranji, Duleep and Pataudi. Ranji was remote to the modern generation. Dulip with his tulip's delicacy gave of his best in England's green fields. Pataudi was not the success he had been at Oxford when transplanted. Nayudu was wholly indigenous, almost self-taught and self-schooled. Like others, he had to suffer from the imposition of princes in the privilege-ridden days of cricket. Nayudu was a commoner, but a commoner who was king.

It would be ceremonial piety to say that his death is a loss to cricket. He lived a life of achievement, more than that, of fulfilment, and his death is a loss in the sense that a magnificent personality, a magnificent presence, has been withdrawn from a greying landscape. His qualities as a cricketer have been described by many, from Hobbs to Miller, and by a variety of writers using a rich vocabulary. But for those who saw him at his best, no mere tribute to his technique is ever adequate. He was a Greek or a Roman at the wicket; every stroke spoke of power and thinking, the merest gesture was an eipression of a powerful personality. The way he used his athlete's physique enabled him to use his springy wrists and supple footwork to impart a rare strength to his strokes. It was an attitude of mind, an attitude of adventure and daring. There was security about his centuries but there was a dignity even about his ducks. Statistics tell nothing and it was ill luck that he was passing his prime when India entered Test cricket, and even then he showed without doubt what he could have done in the age of statistics.

Even Wisden speaks of his promise, not of fulfilment. He had stature and grace; if strength is added to grace, it results in grandeur. He was an all-rounder who did not cease to be a front-rank batsman. As a bowler, he could be as wily as Odysseus. To see him field was to see a panther at work. But it was as captain that he was at his best and his character was fu1ly expressed. He was a leader of men, alert, stern, encouraging, forbidding, and bringing out the best in them. It was as a captain of India and as a captain of Holkar that his personality found full play, and cricket politics, which prevented him from presenting fully his wisdom to the generations which grew under his shadow, withered in his presence. As leader, he was a maker of men, some of them princes among men, like Mushtaq Ali.

(6) The gossip column: No daily newspaper carries a gossip column and its natural habitat is the film magazine which flourishes on gossip, some malicious, some harmless but unquestionably titillating. *Stardust* sells largely on the strength of its gossip column Neeta's Natter which is about film stars and their doings. The columnist is fed

with juicy tit-bits sometimes by the actors and actresses themselves and sometimes by their PR men on the principle that the more they ate talked about, the greater the chances of their successes at the box office. Few, if any, of these show biz people are known to resent the gossip written about them though there are no reports lacking of actors punching the gossip-columnist on the nose for exceeding the bounds of decency.

Consider this sample from *Stardust:*

> It may not be the only one, but definitely the *main* reason why Rishi is marrying Neetu Singh is because his pappa (Raj Kapoor) advised him that it is the right thing to do and the right stage (image-wise) to do it. Which means that Raj is once again playing favourites with his sons. Remember how vehement he had been when Daboo had wanted to marry Babita? He had given his consent only at the twenty-third hour and that too when he realized that Daboo intended marrying Babs anyway.

Reena Roy refuses to let anyone call her by her original 'Surname-Rai! Because, according to her, "It sounds so middle class." Web, it's easy enough for a person to change a name. Isn't it a pity that one can't do the same to a face?

After the release of "Baton Baton Mein" everyone criticised Basu ("he is a fluke director") and Tina ("she can't act for nuts") and the only guy who got away with the applause was Dhruv. A very close friend of his (no, not Shabana) confided that he was playing his real life role. Now I wonder if Ms Azmi would agree to that!

Ex-Mrs. Bedi, Protima, happily played *kabab mein haddi* between Kabir and Susan and sportingly smiled away the moment') when Kabir, suddenly overcome with love for his new wife, would peck her tenderly.

(7) The Question and Answer column: The Question and Answer column comes in various colours. It could be a

medical column in which a qualified doctor answers queries on health. It could be a sobsister column in which readers ask questions about their personal problems and get appropriate answers depending on whether the questions are plain, plain silly or serious. Filmfare ran a column in which I.S. Johar, the well-known film actor replied to questions the best of which were awarded cash prizes. Filmfare still runs such a column with Johar's scintillating replies. Sample:

In our films, when somebody is about to die, the earthen lamp starts to flicker. When the flame dies, the person dies. Why not take more care of the lamp, and put more oil in it?

A.K. Das Gupta, New Delhi.

This letter won a prize of Rs. 50.

In more serious magazines, the column could be run to elicit, serious replies. Thus, *Science Today* runs a Question and Answer column. The questions apparently are from readers-it is not specifically stated-but the answers are from experts. The questions are somewhat on the following lines: Why do waves break? What is a mirage? Why is the sky blue?

(8) The Sports Column: There was a time when some leading Indian newspapers had their daily sports column, but this is getting to be rarer these days. Among the distinguished sports columnists is A.F.S. Talyarkhan, who, indeed, is the doyen of sports columnists and whose column *Take It From Ale* was once read avidly by sports fans. Presently he writes a column for *Blitz* under the title *Knock-Out!* Take this example:

Very recently, going through some old clippings of my scriblings, came across an article on the need to go back to three day Tests before boredom sets in. That was written about fifteen years ago and if this is raked up here it is because there are clear signs that too much, over too long a period, inevitably causes reflection:

> The just-concluded limited overs competition sponsored by Wills is why am stressing today that the answer to many problems afflicting the Cricket Championship (call it Ranji Trophy if you prefer) is largely due to the want of attraction where the lover of the game is concerned.

If some one was to work out the figures, am almost sure that ninety five per cent of the preliminary rounds of the Championship are decided on the result of the first innings.

So much so that reporter after reporter writes about a team gaining the VITAL LEAD, quite rightly, too, because it is only to get the lead on the first-innings of a three day (never to be completed) match that the State teams battle for. No, not battle, struggle is the better term. You never await a report or a broadcast of an outright win, it is always the vital lead on the first innings of a pure farcical three-day Ranji Trophy match that counts. On most Indian wickets, and at the time of the year we choose to play much of our big cricket, conditions are more or less static so that it is solely the first innings lead that a team, strives to achieve thus claiming "victory" and the right to progress further in the tournament.

This being established fact, the answer seems to be to change the early rounds of the Championship matches to limited over matches thus retaining the magic "vital" first innings lead, but changing the tempo of the cricket which will make for more dynamism among players and keenness among followers of cricket.

Thus the present farce of deciding a three-day first-class match on the result of the first innings will remain but since there is a limit to the: overs to be bowled, the striving for the precious "lead" and "victory" will yet be there but there will be purposeful cricket all the way.

The purist will not like this much-I do not-but what's to do when in truth the Championship has been transformed into a positive force by deciding on the result of the first innings lead.

So, since we cannot decide a so-called three-day Championship fixture in the allotted period of three days, and know fully well that all that counts is the "vital lead" on the first innings, why not stick-to this formula and make the cricket trebly exciting and competitive by switching to limited overs matches? The Board might care to give this a thought for they cannot deny that as things are, the Ranji Trophy matches-the vast majority-are decided on the first innings. So make the innings lead a specified fight.

A columnist who signs his wares may express himself with the utmost freedom so long as he steers clear of libel and obscenity. Newspaper publishers who take on columnists often give full freedom to them to air views contrary to those editorially held. This is particularly true of American newspapers which may give hospitality to columnists of various political shades of opinion. Indian newspapers haven't yet come to that stage fully, partly because Indian cities have more than one newspaper while most American cities have only one newspaper and it cannot appear to stifle contrary opinion.

The columnist is generally a specialist, like Talyarkhan whose knowledge of sports in unchallenged. But there could be generalists like Khwaja Ahmed Abbas whose *Last Page* originally a feature of the Sunday *Bombay Chronicle* (now defunct) has been transferred to *Blitz*.

Whether he is a specialist or a generalist, a columnist who is reasonably aware of his limitations and does not stray beyond what is permissible, considering his talent has no difficulty being accepted. The criticism against columnists is that, once they are established, they tend to consider themselves as specialists one very thing in the heaven above, on the earth beneath and in the waters around. Publishers sometimes are reluctant to let them off their pages and they develop inflated egos and traits of omniscience. Westbrook Pegler, no mean columnist himself, once commented on this tribe with unusual candour:

> Of all the fantastic fog shapes that have arisen off the swamp of confusion since the big war, the most futile

and at the same time, the most pretentious, is the deep-thinking, hair-trigger columnist or commentator who knows all the answers just off hand and can settle great affairs with absolute finality three days or even six days a week.

What causes us? Well, as nearly as I can figure it out, this trade began as a sort of journalistic vaudeville intended to entertain the customers and exert a little circulation pull of a slightly higher tone that that of comics.

(9) The humorous column: Morning papers in India still fight shy of having a regular daily humorous column, but an evening paper in Bombay carries a column by one of its staff men under the pseudonym Busybee. Busybee's column *Round and About* is one of the best-known columns in Bombay. Here is a sample.

According to a report in the morning papers, jawans serving at high altitude will be given coffee, tea, milk and dry fruits instead of rum, once total prohibition is introduced. Which does not concern me. But what does concern me is hostesses doing the same at cocktail parties in Bombay. I visualize the following situation:

> Wife and I arrive at a cocktail party and the hostess greets us. and says: "So glad you could make it. Now what will you have, coffee, tea or milk?"

"Coffee to start with" I say.

The wife whispers in my ear: "I thought you had promised not to touch a drop of coffee and restrict yourself to milk."

A waiter serves me coffee and dry fruits and, as I am sipping it, the host comes up and says: "Come on, drink it up. There's plenty more where that comes from."

The wife tells the host: "He has not been feeling well all this week and has decided to go easy on coffee. Just one cup should be enough for him."

A guest at the party who in the pre-prohibition days enjoyed getting everybody slightly drunk at parties, pushes another cup of coffee in my hands and says: "If you don't drink, then the party just won't start rolling."

I have two more cups of coffee and a third one when the wife is busy talking to some guest. After that I am feeling a little sick, though only very little.

The hostess says: "Here, eat some dry fruits, you will feel better." By this time the party is really swinging. Some of the men have consumed pots and pots of coffee, others have finished' equal quantities of tea. Most of the women have been drinking milk. And, as it happens at such parties, the dry fruits ran out.

Late in the night, after one last coffee for the road, we leave the party. And, on the way home, the wife says: "You have' started getting as tight on coffee as you used to on rum."

In a sense all these, in essence, are opinion pieces, as are editorials, theatre, film, art and music criticisms. It is nct every reporter who can aspire to be a humorous columnist, an art critic or a sports commentator. From each a certain amount of expertise is called for; the critic, in the first place, must have credibility. In other words, he must be knowledgeable in his chosen field of comment. But above and beyond expertise, he must have a wider knowledge of life and letters. The narrow specialist may have credibility but it is the specialist generalist who will have the audience.

To review any piece of creative work, the reviewer must not only be aware of the artist's own past work but must be able to judge it in the context of other works of the same genre either of his contemporaries or his predecessors or preferably both. In others words, the reviewer must judge against a comparable background. While a review is primarily a subjective piece of writing-the reviewer, after all, can only write in terms of his own knowledge and understanding-it would be a mistake to think that opinion, howsoever well-based, is all.

To project too much of the critic's own viewpoint or to criticise a work for the sake of criticism or even worse, to set off a controversy, is to misunderstand the nature and function of criticism. A-critic must *describe* a work as faithfully as possible, assess it as *fairly* as possible and suggest improvements as *comprehensively* as possible, taking care to see that he will not write anything that he-could not defend before a jury of experts or will be ashamed to tell the artist to his face. The critic must remember that the reader will quickly see through bias or hasty judgements and that, inasmuch as the critic judges the artist, the reader will judge the critic.

A critic must be an ornament to his profession. He must be a father figure to artists, criticising them when criticism will do good, cajoling them when cajoling will help, praising them when praise is called for and encouraging them when necessary. A critic is the watchdog of good taste. A well-informed critic is a nation builder in that he helps push the creative talent in the land to greater and greater heights. In the repertoire of a good critic, there can be no malice or ill-will.

Expertise involves study in depth. It is not enough to see plays to be a drama critic any more than it is enough to see films to be a film critic. It helps to read up on theatre and films, to be in constant touch with playwrights and dramatists, actors and actresses,-directors and cameramen, musicians and stage hands. In other words, there must be total involvement on the part of the critic to be effective as a critic. The ivory tower critic remains what he is a man far removed from reality.

Some of the best advice on how to review a play was given by Alexander Woollcott, himself a distinguished play-reviewer and essayist.

"The review of a play" he wrote, "as it appears in the morning papers, is addressed not to the actors nor to the playwrights, but to the potential playgoer. The dramatic critic's function is some what akin to that of an attendant at some Florentine court whose uneasy business it was to taste each dish before it was fed to anyone that mattered. He is an ink-stained wretch, invited to each play and expected in the little hour that is left after the fall of the curtain, to transmit something of the play's flavour, to write with whatever fond tribute, sharp invective or amiable badinage will best express it, a description of the play as performed, in terms of the impression it made upon himself.... If he be skillful at his task, the interested playgoer ought to be able to guess pretty shrewdly from his report whether or not the new play in town is of the kind he or she would enjoy.

Woollcott himself was great at giving what he called the play's "'flavour." To him the quality of *Cradle Song*, the lovely drama of a founding baby girl left on the steps of a convent was "like the-chime of bells on a clear frosty night." Woollcott could also be :sharp but perhaps not as sharp as the late A.B. Walkley of *The Times* of London who showed a mastery of succinct as well as sharp inventive when he described a play entitled *A Dreadful Evening* in just one word: "Exactly!" Below are a few examples of good criticism that are worth noticing:

Theatre: The World Turned Upside Down: Cottesloe

The Times, London

In his book *The World Turned Upside Down*, Christopher Hill gave the lie to those who define history as the propaganda of victors. A study of the long-submerged radical movements that flourished in England in the decade,after the Civil War, it is a lasting memorial to the Socialist Britain that might have been, but for the factor which Cromwell's contemporaries termed "sin."

Some of Hill's heroes have already made a theatrical return in plays like John McGrath's *Comrade Jacob* and Caryl Churchill's *A Light Shining in Buckinghamshire*, but the idea of a piece daimed as an "adaptation" of Hill's book, with its hydra-headed sectarian factions confusedly evolving political doctrines out of a world of religious magic, strikes one in advance as an impossibility.

What Keith Dewhurst has done in his play for the Cottesloe is to limit the action to a bare 18 months from the execution of the

King to the dispersal of Winstanley's Digger settlement at Cob ham and to admit only the Diggers, Levellers and Ranters as radical spokesmen. It is a sign of our times that throughout this treatment of one of the most fervently God-fearing episodes in our history, there should be no scene of radicalism from the pulpit. For Bill Bryden and Sebastian Graham-Jones production, the interior of the Cottesloe has been remodelled by William Dudley into a timber-floored traverse, bounded at one end by huge emblems of state power and at the other end by a towering liberty tree; boundaries that determine the entrances of the royalist and Cromwellian top brass and of the common people or mutineers arriving for trial and execution.

The setting has a Handelian clarity, lending itself to civic processions, marching songs (musically this is a splendid occasion), and enactments of ritual death. It also lends itself to confrontation debates and to elaborate spectacle, such as a prolonged display of musket drill by a firing squad, or an orgiastic love-feast for the Ranters who wind up skipping in the nude.

But despite its severe editorial restrictions, the play does not convey a clear account of the hopes and disillusionment of those who welcomed Charles execution as the planting of the liberty tree the production operates by means of rapid synaptic leaps into particular situations, briefly evoking the Lockyer rebellion or the dispersal of Winstanley's followers, and leaving you to develop an interest in the connecting historic threads.

On those terms, the production is dazzlingly successful. Unlike some of is forerunners, this is not a romantically left-wing occasion, and no false climaxes are introduced to drive home the message Instead there is a crack ensemble accommodating a great variety of dramatic colours and stylistic changes.

Western Music: Allegri Ensemble: Wigmore

The Times, London

Since demand for tickets for the Allegri-Robles Ensemble on Tuesday again exceeded supply, as at Christa Ludwig's recital on

Saturday, Wigmore Hall's new chamber music festival seems to be meeting a real need. With harp, flutes and clarinet at hand as well as string quartet, the programme was ideal for a summer night.

The first half went to Mozart, with the clarinet quintet as *piece de resistance.* That brought first-rate teamwork with Jack Brymer's clarinet never dominating, but beautifully intertwined with the light texture of the Allegri team. His own nuances in cantible and the liquidity of his appeggio flourishes were a delight.

The D major flute quartet, K 285, represents a less mature Wolfgang, and we know from published correspondence how severely Leopold Mozart chastised his son for not trying hard enough with this particular commission. Its brief slow movement is a minor miracle, all the same. Christopher Hyde-Smith's phrasing here was a little unyielding, but he made amends in a sparkling finale.

Whether the unremarkable set of variations included by Marisa Roblesin the first halfwere composed by Mozart remains a moot point. She played them boldly; but inevitably more the spellbinder we remember of old, in terms of magical sonority, in Bax's one-movement Elegaic Trio of flute, viola and harp (a feast of nostalgia) and Ravel's still more seductively scored *Introduction and Allegro* which united all seven artists. At first it seemed as if the attack of out-of-tuneness that had marred Schubert's *Quartettsatz* from the Allegri team might bedevil the Ravel, too. But once the introduction was passed, those players found their form. The *Allegro* was subtly balanced, coloured, and phrased, with smouldering embers bursting into flame at the climax of the development in preparation for the harp cadenza beautifully weighed and measured by Miss Robles.

INDIAN MUSIC: DUET BY SALAMAT AND NAZAKAT

The Times of India, Bombay

The vocal duets of Salamat Ali and Nazakat Ali, who gave a three hour performance under the auspices of Arun Sangeetalaya at Khar Saturday might have been the subject of much animated discussion in the musical milieu of Bombay ever since the two Pakistani artistes made their first appearance in the city four years ago. After having heard them at several concerts during their first visit to the city, this reviewer had a feeling that the controversy touched off by the music of Salamat and Nizakat was not so much a measure of the aesthetic awareness or capacity of the average connosieur to understand and appreciate the subtle refinements or traditional music. If anything it was rather indicative of this era of mass-culture values-where the box office takings come to determine the greatness of an artiste! Indeed, Salam at and Nizakat-the latter, by the way, is more or less a sleeping partner in the team-work-possess talent in ample measure. They have a winsome command of technique and an acute sense of rhythm. They are, above all, quite novel and unconventional in their singing. But that is not all. Their singing, on the contrary, does not have a refined sense of design and proportion. It is unimaginative.

Saturday night's concert only served to confirm my earlier impressions. The artistes chose for their fare the ragas *Malkouns, Darbari* and *Adana.* In between they rendered two lighter pieces in *Mishra Pahadi* and *Multani Kafi.* The concert started an hour behind schedule. The popular sarangi player, Ram Narain, who was to accompany the principal performers did not show up at all. Then there was the erratic behaviour of the microphone which posed a great problem throughout the concert.

The presentation of the opening item in *Malkauns,* which Salamat and Nazakat rendered in *vilambit, drut,* in *jhaptaal* and then in *tritaal,* to be followed again by a *tarana,* lasted well over an hour and a half. It gave the impression that while the technical virtuosity of the artistes was unquestioned, their main obsession was to display their tonal facility, vocal gymnastics and grasp of the intricacies of their melodic theme instead of to employ them for a really aesthetic presentation of their art. Added to this was the reckless fondness for ornamentation and catchy, theatrical improvisations in *sargams* that carried but momentary appeal.

Frankly, the rendering was overdone. The exposition in *Darbari* which the artistes rendered in *viambit, drut* and *tarana,* was decidedly the best item of the concert. It was marked by a better sense of purpose and clearer sense of direction. Theitem that followed, namely, *raga adana* in *jhaptaal, tritaal* followed by a chaturanga-like piece, could have been equally good if it were not beset with out-of-tune patterns every now and then. The tabla wizard Alla Rakha, and the vocalists also engaged in a race of melody and rhythm and the entire performance degenerated into unmusical acrobatics. As for the two lighter pieces, there was nothing much to say. They were sung light-heartedly.

The newer technique of musical expression sought to be popularised by Sahmat and Nazakat is something of hectic experimentation at achieving something new that is trying hard to take root in the soil. A good many people have called them,prodigies. Some call them gate-crashers and to many others the artistes seem to be a musical. enigma. It may, therefore, be hazardous to suggest that these musicians disappointed the audience. After all, most of the listener; did get what they wanted the,acrobatics and pyrotechnics of music and not necessarily the aesthetics of it!

Book Review: Reviewing a book is as much an art as putting a-chair together or doing heart surgery. To review a book calls for considerable knowledge not only of the subject covered by the book, but of the author, his previous works, his expertise as measured against his compeers and of its relevance. Nothing is more degrading in journalism than to assume that *anybody* can review a book.

A competent book review-especially of fiction-reports to the reader on the following lines:

(1) It gives an understanding of the nature, but not the surprises of the plot.

(2) It tells of its type or class-historical novel, psychological novel, mystery story etc.

(3) It indicates the locale in which the story moves.

(4) It gives a hint of the book's tang and flavour through short quotes.

(5) It introduces the chief characters.

(6) It expresses an opinion as to how the author has handled his material.

Book reviews can be short, of medium length or longish, in the style of the *New York Review of Books.* Where space is lacking,some books are dismissed in one para notices that just mention the 'name of the book, the name of the author, the name and full address of the publisher, the number of pages and the price, as well as the year of publication.

And no matter whether the review is short or long, this is the basic information that must necessarily be provided. It is the first courtesy due to the publisher who sends a book to an editor for review.

It is often customary to first outline what the book is about to acquaint the reader what to expect in it. The critic will then assess its merits, literary, stylistic, technical or otherwise. Is it a scholarly' piece of work? Does it stand up to scrutiny? Is it socially relevant? How does it compare with works of like nature? In this the critic will bring to bear on his own writing a measure of scholarship worthy of the book.

Consider this review of a Bengali novel that appeared in *The Book Review;*

Ami Anupam (I, Anupama Bengali novel) by Nabaneeta Deb. Sen; Ishan Publishers, Calcutta, 1978;pages 180; Rs. 8. Reviewed by Meenakshi Mukherjee.

This is the first novel of a writer who has so far been well known to Bengali readers as a poet. But her novel is not poetic in the usual sense of the term.

In a style that is cerebral as well as graceful, Nabaneeta Deb Sen writes of a situation uneasily familiar to most of us-the conflict between integrity and expediency. This is done not in terms of a simple statement, but is concretized in a situation that has all the unedited and unexpurgated complexity of real life. Contrary to current expectations, her protagonist is neither a common man nor anti-hero, but a brilliant academic who has succeeded in everything he has done so far. Anupam Roy at the height of his career is a national figure whose weekly broadcast and newspaper column of poetical analysis influences public opinion and sparks off controversies. He is respected not only for his intellect and fearless views, but also because he has refused many lucrative high level jobs in order to maintain his, intellectual independence.

In his personal relationships also Anupam is impeccable. Although he does not believe in extremism in politics, he loves. many of the extremists personally, and gives shelter to Naxalite young men at home. He helps the Legal Aid Committee for justice to political prisoners. To his old mother and less successful younger brother, he is tender and dutiful. If women find him, irresistible he cannot help it,,and is human enough to recognise his occasional need but he lets women enter his life only for as long as they do not threaten his freedom.

Summarised thus, the portrait of Anupam Roy seems to be a broad brush-stroke job, but actually in this novel, *Ami Anupam,* nothing is stated-the details are gradually and subtly revealed through action and conversation, specially conversation between Nabaneeta Deb Sen-excels in catching accurately the subtle nuances of speech. Only when the image of Anupam Roy is established well, the layers can be peeled off effectively to show what lies within. The gap between the public image and the private self is seen to be wide and yet the result is not the unmasking of the hypocrite. One sees the dilemma of choice, sympathises with Anupam Roy's predicament, and realises that in real life the- option between right and wrong is hardly unequivocal.

Toward the end of the novel Anupam Roy faces a moral crisis, aggravated by an almost symbolic physical infirmity, th e loss of his voice. After a period of nightmare and self-searching, he wakes up to find many of his problems recede because he can now come to terms with a different view of himself. The end comes dangerously close to sentimentality, specially in the affirmation of the values of his mother, a temptation no Bengali writer can resist (Is idealisation of the mother-figure an essentially Bengali trait or is it Indian?) yet the competent blend of circumstantial realism with evocative use of language finally steers the novel clear of mushiness.

Of the positive qualities of this rather remarkable novel I will single out only two. One: the authentic potrayal of a character in terms of his work and professional commitments. Very rarely do we see in Indian novels such a credible, convincing character seen largely in terms of his own career. Popular fiction and films have conditioned us into accepting career stereotypes too easily-the reference to a test-tube makes a scientist, khadi kurta a politician and absent-minded idealism a professor. But Anupam Roy is a three-dimensional individual, whose complex predicament is seen in terms of his changing political views, his rewriting of a particular piece for a newspaper, his guilt at the recognition of the gap between his academic stand and his personal behaviour. The first test of his integrity comes when a high official of the intelligence branch invites him to his club for lunch and in between gin-and-tonic and sizzler steak, with the accompaniment of polite pseudo-cultural talk on Kurusawa, Joan Baez and Satyajit Ray, lets him know that the police is aware of a kit bag in his house left there by a young Naxalite; and if he values his own life, he should give it up to the police.

A period of conflict follows, but the decision is not difficult Roy surrenders the bag to the police which is found to contain, among other things, a note book with names and addresses. So it is possible to bring many young men to the torture chamber for confession. One of the boys Anupam Roy knew well is found murdered soon after.

His guilt becomes difficult to live with. His facile and fearless-pen is unable to churn out the brilliant pieces he was so famous for. His own servant, the only witness to his act, accuses him silently-and a drunken artist in a bar publicly charges him of betrayal. At this point 'he becomes aware of a strange affliction he is losing his voice-possibly for ever.

Several issues converge after this. The necessary surgical operation for restoring his voice can only be done in Europe for which he urgently needs money. There is a growing guilt about the two women whom he rejected for his own convenience, and his hatred for his dead father becomes obsessive. He hates himself because he carries his father's genes. Having lost his voice and his ability to write, his self-confidence ebbs away, and his favourite metaphor of a proud charioteer holding the reins of his seven horses firmly in hand, no longer applies to his own life. A mute contrast develops between Anupam and his ordinary middle class brother Niru, who stayed with the mother while the elder brother was busy getting international recognition. Niru had the courage to marry the girl he loved while Anupam spurned emotional entanglements; Niru loved animals, collected maimed creatures around him to feed them, while Anupam hated animals and the orised about the way they exercised tyranny of the weak. Finally when there was this desperateneed of money for Anupam's surgery, Niru was ready with his meagre provident fund money and his wife's unit trust, while Anupam could not only think of accepting the editorship of a national daily which would advance him a large sum in return for his freedom of belief. "Niru does not earn much" his mother told Anupam, "but he is richer than you."

The second strength of the novel is the solidity of a specification which gives the moral and ethical issues a concreteness and credibility. Lower middle class life has been portrayed in Bengali fiction often very effectively, but is very rare to find an unbiased documentation of the life of successful people. The fact that the affluent level of society is seldom presented in Bengali novels without exaggeration or satire may have interesting sociological implications. But in this novel Nabaneeta Deb Sen portrays this life effortlessly with a very sure touch, although in very rare movements, it seems that because she can do this so easily, there is a slight tendency toward over-indulgence.

In the early chapters of the novel she establishes Anupam Roy's character by a simple device-describing a routine day in his life. The busy and varied life of this international-known man is indicated when he quickly goes through his morning mail consisting of a letter from Geneva in connection with a conference, a Sapru House circular about a seminar, the current issue of South Asian Bulletin, a request from an ex-student for a testimonial, a letter from a professor in Tokyo commenting on his recently published paper, a love letter from a woman (which he tosses away without reading) and a telegram about a selection committee meeting in Hyderabad. As we follow him through the course of one day we learn a lot about him-his ability to handle difficult situations without losing his calm, his 'calculated control over himself and others including the woman with whom he spends one measured hour each day, and the charisma that he has acquired. The collage of conversation at the tobacco executive's party, the coffee-house talk where the writers congregate, the four-lettered words of a drunken artist at the bar or the rhetoric of the lunatic at the Gariahat cross roads, all these have a ring of authenticity that vividly recreates contemporary urban reality in India. One wishes the novel could be translated into English or other Indian languages so that it becomes available to more readers, because the issues and conflicts dealt with here have relevance beyond the merely local.

Note how the reviewer subtly interweaves story-telling and apt comment, how analysis is blended with narration. The reviewer provides us with the full flavour of the work making the piece an adequate study of the times in which we live. This gives added relevance, while giving details of the book, to the mentioning of when it was published. The time frame of the novel would thereby be firmly established.

The Editorial: The editorial has been grandiloquently described as the mirror of the newspaper's opinion, its great and undying soul and its conscience. Like John Brown's body, the souls of many dead newspapers keep marching on. There is no doubt whatsoever about it.

Though a newspaper is hardly ever known as a *views* paper, it is remarkable how often a newspaper is known not for its news, but its *views*. Foreign correspondents especially are aware of how often they quote the major newspapers of the country they are assigned to. "*The Times* said today...", "The New York Times said today..." "In an editorial *Die Welt* said today..." are common enough beginnings to them. While news is sacred and opinion free and possibly profane, it is the opinion, evidently, that counts. News frequently is transient, but views have the aura of a certain permanency about them. Today's news may be tomorrow's garbage, but today's views can remain fresh for a long time to come.

Considering that not more than 15 per cent at any time read an editorial, it is still an impressive fact that editorial writers are held in such awe. The truth is that though only a few read editorials, the latter help form and nurture public opinion, especially opinion of the elite that alone frequently counts. A good editorial can incite action, inspire deeds, subvert legislation, stir revolution. Ideas, a public opinion expert once remarked, have legs and they can run.

There are editorials and editorials. Long ones and short ones, pompous ones and perceptive ones, thoughtful ones and titillating ones, editorials that are hard-hitting as well as caressing, inspiring as web as denigrating, editorials, in fact, that reflect as wide a range of human emotions as are known to man.

In the early days of journalism, news and views were published separately, the one in newsletters, the other in pamphlets. It is said that Daniel Defoe first united these two journalists streams in one publication in *The Review* which he published in London in 1704.

In the early days again, the newspapers had no separate editorial page. Opinion merely took the form of observations tacked on to the end of the news or more usually of letters to the editor signed by some pseudonym. To Noah Webster goes the credit for first placing his editorials under the masthead of his paper.

In those days editorials were written by one man-the editor and every reader was aware of the fact. Today newspapers have a battery of editorial writers-leader writers, as they are sometimes known-who write anonymously, but obviously under the guidance and direction of the editor to whom, of course, all opinion is attributed. This is only but natural and as it should be, for no single man these days can emulate Francis Bacon and "take all knowledge for his province."

The complexity of our world is such that too often no single person is competent even to write on a single topic-say, Foreign Affairs. So there are in some of the great newspapers of the world men who specialize in European, African, Soviet, American or Asian Affairs.

The men and women who write editorials have a heavy responsibility to bear. They have the obligation to read extensively to be well-informed. As Geoffrey Parsons, when chief editorial adviser' of the New York *Herald Tribune* said: "The richer the writer's background, the larger his ability to stimulate thought about anything. A good editorial writer addresses the largest classes ever 'reached by a teacher, philosopher or critic. He cannot know 100 much, if he is to hold their attention."

An artificial difference is sometimes made between an editorial and a "leader." The "leader" is defined as the principle article in a newspaper. But definitions have revealed a great deal of confused thinking. One writer insists that it is the first editorial; another derives its origin from the practice of "leading" out the article in order to draw greater attention to it; and yet a third would restrict it to editorials which give a lead to the readers. As S. Natarajan, a former editor of the *Free Press Journal* has noted, "neither position nor manner of display can lend importance to an article." The difference between an editorial and a leader, in the circumstances, can only be a matter of personal consideration.

That editorials writers both individually and collectively realize their responsibility as moulders of public opinion is evidenced by the tone of the Code of Ethics which the U.S.

National Conference of Editorial Writers compiled and adopted. The preamble to this code points out that "the editorial writer, like the scientist, must pursue Truth no matter where it leads if he is to be faithful to his craft and to his society." The basic points of the code are the following:

(1) The editorial writer should present facts honestiy and fully.

(2) He should draw objective conclusions from stated facts, basing them upon the weight of evidence and upon the considered concept of the greatest good.

(3) He should never be motivated by personal interest.

(4) He should realize that he is not infallible and should give voice to those who disagree with him in a public letters columr and by other suitable devices.

(5) He should review his own conclusions and correct them should he find them based on previous misconceptions

(6) He should have the courage of well-found conviction and never write anything that goes against his conscience. Where editorial pages are more than the product of one mind, sound collective judgement can be achieved only through sound individual judgements. Therefore thoughtful individual opinions should berespected.

(7) He should support his colleagues in their adherance to the highest standards of professional integrity.

This editorial code though compiled in the United States could well serve as a model for editorial writers everywhere. They may even remember what ortegay Gasset once wrote:

The present-day writer, when he takes his pen in his hand to treat a subject which he has studied deeply, has to bear in mind that the average reader, who has never concerned himself with this subject, if he reads does so with the view, not of learning something from the writer, but rather, of pronouncing judgement on him when he is not in agreement with the common places that the said reader carries in his head.

The ultimate purpose of the editorial, of course, is to express the editor's opinion. A distinguished editor, Arthur Brisbane, who had a vast following in his time, believed that the editorial writer's opportunity was four-fold: he could teach, attack, defend, and praise. He explained this further:

Teaching is the most important and the most difficult.

Attacking is the easiest and most unpleasant though sometimes necessary. The defending of good causes, of the weak against the strong, of the new idea against ridicule; is important and usually neglected by editorial writers.

Praise also is neglected, except in a partisan sense without meaning... First have something to say. Then say it so that people will see it, read it, understand it, and believe it.

The editorial writer must have first something worthwhile to say writing an editorial just for the sake of filling in space is both a waste of time and space. Some editors prefer not to write an editorial if there is no subject worthy of editorial attention. This should lend credibility to an editorial when it is subsequently written.

To have something to say, an editor must take as his theme an, event of significance. In other word, he must hang his editorial on a news peg. The editorial could then explain the event in its perspective, when it would be informative, comment favourably or unfavourably on it, when it would be reactional or subject it to objective and constructive scrutiny, when it would be deliberative. Frequently the caption of the editorial will reveal the motivation of the writer. Mahatma Gandhi was a past-master in the art of chosing titles, as editorials in Young India will aptly testify.

An editorial writer should not only have encyclopaedic knowledge, at least in his own particular field, but should have an easy, graceful style that endears itself to the reader. He should remember that the enemy of style is pomposity and verboseness. At its best an editorial is creative writing. When it is imbued with passion and earnestness it rises to Garrison's credo that appeared in each issue of the now defunct *The Indian Social Reformer:* "I *will* be as harsh as truth and as uncompromising as justice. I am in earnest-I will not equivocate-I will not excuse-I will not re treat a single *inch-and I will be heard."* It is this spirit that was immortalised in Lowell's poem on Garrison:

In a small chamber, friendless and unseen,
Toiled over his types one poor, unlearned young man;
The place was dark, unfurnitured, and mean;
Yet there the freedom of a race began.
Help came but slowly; surely no man yet
Put lever to the heavy world with less;
What need of help? He knew
How types were set,
He had a dauntless spirit, and a press.

Most newspapers in India carry three editorials and just as often only two. What is known as "The Third Editorial" is usually given to light treatment of subjects. There is no fixed style of editorial writing, though, obviously, an editorial has a clear beginning, a well-argued middle and a distinct ending that sums up the editor's views on a given subject. An editorial that hangs loose reflects,poorly on the writer.

But an editorial point can be made in many and diverse ways.

The space meant for an editorial could even be left blank-as-some editors ordered, during the Emergency-to make a point. 'The space could be filled by an apt quotation as one Indian paper indeed did when it published Rabindranath Tagore's Prayer during that same period. Henry L. Mencken on 10 February 1938, filled six columns of editorial space of the Baltimore *Evening Sun* 'with black dots-some 10,00,725-to dramatize the number of,Federal employees. The late Rollo Ogden, when editor of the New York *Evening Post,* commented on The odore Roosevelt's early procedure (in Panama by reprinting from Kings 1: 21, the 'story of King

Ahab's seizure of Naboth's vineyard under the caption: "Panama, 899 B.C." During his great days as editor of the *Free Press Journal* of Bombay, S. Sadanand would recount stories from the *Mahabharata*, the *Ramayana* or even Aesop's Fables, drawing a parallel with contemporary events, to great effect. Originality kowtows to no fixed formula. Communication is all.

Not least of the editorial's function is to entertain. Many editors do this with the "Third Editorial," writing done with tongue,firmly in check, often in the manner of a "Middle."

Take this from an American paper, the Richmond Va., *Times Dispatch:*

PUT THOSE PREPOSITIONS WHERE THEY BELONG TO

Columnist Robert Ruark made some strong statements Monday concerning the rule against using a preposition to end a sentence with. He said there was no logical reason why you shouldn't put one of those "lousy, skimpy little words" at the tail end of a sentence if you wanted to.

There's really nothing for Columnist Ruark to get excited about. Prepositions always are supposed to govern other words, called their 'relatives', and only the laziest writer should find it difficult to arrange the sequence of his words so that the relative is last and the preposition is before.

Sometimes, with all the belittling of the old tried and standard rules, we wonder what modern literature is coming to Instead of polishing their sentences, as did the old masters of the language, many of today's writers sit down and simply dash something off. Prepositions are left dangling naked at the end of sentences, and you can't tell where they are going to or where they came from. These unclad words, tied on to nothing, appear about to take off.

In the speaking art, too, conformity with standard rules or grammar should be striven after. Here errors are easier to fall into. A person who wishes to leave a good impression with his listeners should use the very best grammar he is capable of. With anything less, he should refuse to put up.

It is a sad commentary on the literary world today that fundamental rules of grammar are laughed at. This is the age or skepticism where there's little left to cling to. Fortunately, however, there are a few purists in the writing and speaking arts who refuse to cut corners and whose work can be depended on.

Yes, Ruark, end your sentences with prepositions if you want to. But don't try to influence other writers, who to such a flagrant violation of rules of grammar will never give into.

Note how the editorial begins. It takes a statement by a columnist to hang its theme on and has a hilarious time putting the unfortunate writer in his grammatical place. The editorial is "timeless" since it can he enjoyed any time; in fact a third editorial deals often with timeless things.

As an example of how a "timeless" theme is handled, here are two editorials on the same subject, "The Resurrection" from *The' New York Times* and *The Washington Post* that appeared on the same day (14 April 1974).

REBIRTH AND RESURRECTION

Now comes the festival of spring, of rebirth, of resurrection. The whole earth celebrates. The religious holiday we call Easter is its spiritual symbol, but even the grass in the meadow and the trees in the woodland participate, even the beasts of the field and the birds of the air. This is the time when the winter of the earth, as we know it, as well as the winter of the soul, yields to the universal urgency of life and more exalted being.

Easter is everywhere. Winter has run its course. Spring returns. Out of dark desolation and chilling doubt comes the inevitability of new life, of enduring truth beyond the words or the management of man.

The Psalmist, knowing the wonder and the glory of life resurgent on the hills, in the valleys, in the woods and fields, sang, "The little hills rejoice on every side". They shout for joy.

They also sing. And again he said, "I will lift up mine eyes unto the hills, from whence cometh my help." His symbolism was broad as well as deep: for the world of faith and the human soul was also the rich, green world that his God had made. Man's arrogance was tempered by humility in the face of spring.

The hilts still stand. The grass still grows. The still waters and the green Pastures endure. Man may search the infinite and probe the infinitesimal, but the essence remains close at hand.

All around us is the evidence, the truth of life, rebirth and resurrection, which at least approaches understanding.

The New York Times

THE RESURRECTION

In the Jewish community of Jerusalem when Pilate was the local representative of Rome, the Day of Rest was Saturday. It was on this day, after dying on the cross on Friday, that the body of Jesus was laid to rest in the tomb. Early on the following morning-the first day of the Jewish week and what is now Sunday-a woman who had overcome her past reputation came to the rock—hewn tomb to minister to the body with ointments and spices, as was the burial custom.

But the stone before the walk-in tomb was moved from place. Mary Magdalen left. St. John in his gospel does not tell us if she fled in fear or confusion but, whatever the reason, she :sought the advice of her friend Peter. Alarmed, he and John came immediately, though we are told that Peter-evidently overweight and unused to morning sprints, no matter what the occasion-was not as fast as the other disciple. On examining the tomb, the two men saw evidence that indeed it had been vacated, because the burial linens were left behind. Weare not told in St. John's narrative what Peter said-doubtless the excitable Peter had plenty to say-but are given only the information that he went back home, perhaps because it was nearing breakfast time.

Mary stayed on. Full of natural emotion, she wept. After a

time, a man-it was still dark and Mary took him for the gardener-came before her and asked why she was weeping, and who did she seek. "Sir, if you have removed him, tell me where you have laid him and I will take him away." To this the man answered one word: "Mary." She knew immediately it was the risen inaster (Rabboni) and she moved to embrace him.

Although each of the four gospels provides slightly different accounts of the details of the resurrection, the major dramatells us of Christendom's greatest moment: when a mystery of faith was joined by a triumph of life. In the masterful book "Easter" by Alan Watts, the author writes that "the story of Jesus lives on, not because he was an innocent man who died a cruel death with bravery, for others have done as much; not because he was a great teacher of spiritual principles; for there was nothing peculiarly original in his doctrine; not even because he returned from death, for that, too, has been recorded of others. The Christ story lives because it has fascinated man's mind with the thought of a God who had shared the life of his creatures, a King who has become his own subject. It is the revelation that the Lord of the universe is not a cruel puppet master who watched his playthings writhe in the toils of tragedies which he has plotted. It is that he himself has entered the play, has become the victim of the tragedy, and has turned it into triumph."

Of the two great feats of Christianity-Christmas and Easterit is usually the former that receives more celebrational attention. Yet in both the liturgical and biblical expressions of these two events, the greater by far is Easter. The liturgy of the Resurrection includes 40 days of lenten preparation; while the advent season for the Nativity is much shorter, almost by half.

In the four gospels, only two writers, Matthew and Luke-tell of the birth of Jesus, whereas the details of the Lord's death and resurrection are reported by each of the four writers.

The original agony, death and resurrection of Chirst was singular also because the entire community was involved-from the crowd outside Pilate's praetorium who called for

Barabbas to Joseph of Arimathea who took away the body from the cross.

Deep human emotions stirred, as in no other places in the gospels, from the blunt doubts of Thomas who would not believe until he had seen for himself to the denials of Peter whose faith was troubled even though he did see. About the latter, though, the wavering was only temporary; in the poem *Saint Peter* Daniel Berrigan, the poet, writes:

> No Christ at a tombstone knocked me awake. A cock mounted the tall rock where his body bled. I choose that rock to stand: man and clean of hand and blessed, whose even second choice was Christ.

The alleluias of Easter not only commemorate an event to be celebrated but express a hope to be shared. Those who keep Easter know the rites of its liturgy are embedded in the renewal of the earth's life in another spring. All mysteries are reflected in reality, but where the mystery reveals a coming of life-a resurrection-it is hard not to share in the joy.

The Washington Post

The same theme, but two different voices that tell us that no matter how routine an event-and Easter comes every year-it is a dull and unimaginative writer who cannot see the beauty and mystery In Its recurrence.

Letters to the Editor: Few features are held in greater disdain than the Letters to the Editor column. In the first place it is presumed that, as with book reviews, *anybody* can write a letter to the 'editor. Anybody, of course, can, but as Shakespeare makes one of his characters say, you can summon the spirits from the deep, but will they come? And will editors accept such letters and publish them? The main characteristic of a letter should be that it should be timely and appropriate. Writing a letter to an editor about last year's tidal wave would be irrelevant unless the writer wants to suggest that another, and deadlier wave is due and could be more devastating. Letters, in the circumstances, could be in the nature of a warning against disaster, crime, riots or whatever. The sheer variety of letters that an editor receives on any given day reveals the nature of the needs of the community and the need to communieate between man and man. Most letters are commentative; they are natura, reactions to something that the editor has said or a newspaper has reported or a magazine has featured. They could raise new issues, seek to bury old ones, be laudatory in content or querulous or argumentative. Some letters may merely be informative-the London *Times* has carried letters from readers who claimed that they were the first to see a hedghog at a particular time and place.

The New York Times once ran a lively controversy as to whether white eggs were better than brown and distinguished men and women engaged in scholarly and hilarious debate.

In fact it is not uncommon for some newspapers to start off a,controversy by "planting" a letter in the letters to the editor column that was written in the newspaper office itself. While this practice may be deplored by the purists, the fact remains that recourse is often taken to it to get the circulation going.

The letter to the editor reveals not only the nature of the paper's readership but also the nature of the problems confronting it. It-is an excellent feedback for the paper. An editor should be concerned if he does not get this feedback for then it would be clear that *(a)* either his readers do not care *(b)* or that they do not have an opinion. And if they do not have any opinion, what role can an editor possibly fulfil as an opinion-maker?

Letter-writing, like all other features is an art, but an art worth cultivating. The best letters are those that are contemporaneous, that come to the point and are courteous. The reader may be instifiably angry with the editor but that is no reason why he should be abusive and vituperative. Politeness always pays, beside which a polite rebuttal always is sure to win the approbation of others. Anger is by and large counterproductive.

It is well to remember that newspapers belong not just to proprietors and editors but to readers as well. As one journal put it, because newspapers are bought every day, a habitual choice in time becomes an emotional allegiance. And that is further strengthened when the paper creates close links with its readership. Whatever the reader may think of *his* paper's policy, he should be certain that he will always have access to its letters to the editor column to air his own views. Apart from anything else, the letters to the editor column is a safety valve.

A good editor will never be afraid of publishing letters criticising him and his views. In fact he will quickly learn that the more hepublishes such critical letters, the more his credibility is restored.. And he will also come to appreciate the further fact that in addition to getting unpaid material, he can use those very critical letters to increase his circulation.

Some useful hint to editors:

(1) See that every letter is recorded and acknowledged.

(2) The acknowledgement serves two purposes: first, it is an actor courtesy But even more importantly, if some malicious person has used a false name and address, the acknowledgement card will come back.

(3) Beware of bores (those who write regular letters or who sign under a pseudonym like *pro bono publico),* sycophants and pressure groups, also of fakes and malicious writers who could land you in trouble.

(4) Beware of begging letters, for if you give space to one charity appeal, you may find it hard to deny others.

(5) *Never* print a letter from someone whose identity you do not know. Many newspapers check on letters that could be potentially damaging by trying to identify the writers. Some papers like the *London Times* provide the full address of the writer so that it is clear to the other readers that the writer is real and could betraced.

A letter to the editor column-especially if it is just one column in length-cannot take more than 1,000 words in all; short letters therefore would get preference. If they are overly long, then it is the editor's privilege to shorten them. It is courtesy, again, to seek the writer's permission for doing the editing. The shorter and snappier the letter the better are the chances of its getting published.

Anti-features: Editors are often flooded with articles that have no compelling merit other than that the writer thinks it has. Recapturing the heroism of old battles because the anniversary has come round may be patriotism but can be done once too often. It is no good writing about a foreign country just because the public relations department in the tourist office is pushing or the editor has been given a free, all-expenses-paid trip. That is no reason to saddle the reader with a general article on the country, unless the magazine happens specifically to cater to the tourist trade. And all copy submitted by Public Relations men should be put to the sternest of scrutiny, no matter how well it is sugar-coated and made to seem relevant.

8

Reporter's Profile

A journalist must posses and uphold certain noble qualities in order to be professional. Integrity of character, commitment to the truth and a reasoning power of mind are essential to any reporter. These qualities also contribute to the credibility of the reporting organization. Besides, a journalist has to be truly responsible. This responsibility extends to different groups of people at the same time. A journalist is responsible to the audience as much as to the news organization. Again, a journalist is always responsible to the source(s) who reveal information. Should the need arise, a reporter has to submit to a source who may request anonymity. A reporter must also have a healthy respect for news values. A journalist must inculcate other positive features besides clear perception. For instance, one must have specific skills to elicit information in a question-answer session.

The Duties

It is said that a reporter is both eyes and ears of a news organization, it is not possible to strictly prescribe qualifications which a good reporter must posses. However, novice reporters must train themselves informally for the job so that they would be able to discharge their responsibilities with confidence, courage and competence. In order to quality the role of a reporter you must prepare yourself in many ways.

It helps to be well-read, and you can do full justice to your reporting beat. You must equip yourself adequately with all aspects of your beat. If you are covering the civic body proceedings, you must be fully knowledgeable about several laws and rules under which the proceedings are regulated. In addition, you must know its various functions, areas of operations and jurisdiction. You should cultivate wide contacts with all kinds of sources in your beat, some times even outside your area of activity. As a reporter, you should be able to find out information; you should have a bent of mind for research. You should be a perfect talker, you should possess inexhaustible patience and the ability to get along with any kind of people in difficult situations. To be a successful reporter and to accomplish your job competently, you must be able to perceive, calculate, predict and plan your action appropriately in anticipation of a news event. The sole aim of good news reporting should be writing with a certain amount of responsibility to oneself, to an organisation, to society and to humanity at large. You must use your pen consciously, carefully and should bear full credit (or discredit) for what you say: "Just as an unclaimed torrent of water submerges the whole countryside and devastates crops, even so, an uncontrolled pen serves but to destroy." Besides, as you must write everyday, you should write to build your own image, as well as the image of your institution. You have a responsibility towards your city, state, region, country, even the world at large. Echoing this, the noted editor M.V. Kamath once said: "A newspaper's sense of purpose and integrity, rather than its circulation, would determine its influence." And it is the reporter who is a builder of a newspaper's sense of purpose and integrity.

It is essential for a news reporter to be alertminded and curious. In addition, one should be in excellent health and should have inexhaustible stamina to chase difficult assignments. Most of all, a reporter should be a sociable person. It is true that one must posses the right attitude toward the vocation. This would include intelligence, initiative, industry, general competence, objectivity and accuracy. There are several other features of one's personality and character which can contribute befittingly to one's profession as a journalist. In this section, we shall elaborate the salient qualities.

The reporter is the most important functionary of a newspaper, as far as news operations are concerned. So one must know what constitutes news in order to be able to gather news. A reporter's job of discovering the news has been simplified in one way and rendered difficult in another sense, in this age of information. While there are the usual press notes on which news reports can be based, there are other sources of information on a variety of news event. The range of sources stretches from official spokespersons and press conferences to unidentified members of the public and the regular sources which one meets on the beat.

But quite often, most of the material before a news reporter may just be publicity matter or advertisements in disguise. Therefore, as a reporter, you must check the material and squeeze the news that would interest your reader. When you are overwhelmed by an ocean of facts, you can always rely on the readers' interest for guidance. Here is where your ability to select the right information and present it to the reader comes to your help. Besides, most of the time you will cover routine matters such as press conferences and press notes that are hardly exciting. At least you may have to begin at quite a low level like covering local matter. Later you may be given the opportunity to cover major national issues. For the most part you may find yourself reporting the speeches, declarations and announcements by V.I.P.s, persons in authority, politicians and political parties. Occasionally, you may get an exciting newsbreak. But your routine reporting should not prevent you from looking for something unusual that may lurk under the ordinary occurrence. You have to be a keen observer so as to discover unusual and exciting material even in routine stuff. A sharp sense of observation may also help exciting material even in routine stuff. A sharp sense of observation may also help you to gather amusing sidelights of interest to your readers. Your alertness will help you to discover contradictions and problems while you are on your daily beat. This can be the basis for an exciting news story even where apparently there was none.

Professional Reporters

Professional journalists are never armchair writers. Introverts normally make poor reporters. Reporters have to move about meeting people, making their acquaintance and winning their confidence. This would help them to establish contacts, which in turn helps in writing well-investigated reports. This is the era of investigative reporting and readers are keenly interested to know what is going on behind the scenes. To get that kind of stories, you have no alternative; but to be outgoing. You have to develop and affable temperament and an easy-going nature.

An outgoing nature is the basic quality to establish contact and develop sources. During the course of your duty, you may meet several people who' may help you in gathering information. You must have the ability to win the confidence and respect of those who may be potential sources of news. During the course of your regular duties, people may voluntarily offer you information. Alternately, this might not be the case when you are working on an investigative story. People may hesitate to talk on sensitive matters. They may like to reveal yet are afraid to in case it were to affect them adversely. Such people may be government officials whom you may meet while investigating matters ranging from inefficiency to corruption. They could be informers of the underworld, if you are doing an in depth crime investigation. What may be at stake for them could be their jobs or their lives. It may be quite difficult to win their trust. In such situations, you must be able to assure your sources that they will remain protected and their identities kept secret if they so desire. While you are establishing contact, there may be some among them who may want to plant information on you to sever their vested interests. Such information may consist of half-truths and even lies. So, you must have other independent contacts through whom you can verify the information.

Remember, even the most ordinary source at times can become very valuable, providing important leads and a wealth of information. A couple of years ago a newspaper carried a story about a footpath hawker who once was a wrestler of international repute, thus throwing light on the neglect of the sportsmen in the country. You must make it a point, therefore, to pay attention to your sources howsoever 'ordinary' they may seem by appearance. Remember, the classic case of the Watergate scandal. The scandal that shook the United States and the Nixon presidency was not exposed by any ace newsperson, but by ordinary local reporters acting on a tip from an ordinary source. What matters is the alertness and ability to pursue your sources to get the right lead. Take the case of the securities scam. The entire expose began with a source contacting Ms. Sucheta Dalai of the Times of India, Bombay, with an unconfirmed report about some activities in the State bank of India. Ms Dalai, Assistant Business Editor of the paper, followed the lead provided by the source and got the story confirmed from reliable contacts bringing to light the stock scam concerning stock broker Harshad Mehta and others involving a staggering Rs. 6,000 crores.

The reporter must be an unprejudiced observer of events, one who presents the facts to the reader in a balanced, objective manner. Now, objectivity is a much debated topic. It has been said that reporters mix comment with fact and so their reports are quite subjective. While reporters may have their own views on the subject of coverage, they should not allow personal opinions at any place in the copy. One must be able to throw light on unclear aspects if any, of the news event. At the same time, the news reporter must endeavour to write a report which is only a statement of facts. An observation or viewpoint, might occasionally creep in and one must be alert to such strips in straight news items. How do you maintain balance and objectivity in your coverage? The first and foremost thing to do is to source your copy properly to assure the reader that what you are passing on as news, is not your opinion or some publicity matter in disguise. The sources must be quoted except when they want to remain anonymous. Even when you are not able to quote the sources, you must ensure that the story is balanced, by giving adequate coverage to all the sides of the subject. You should always ensure that the information you are presenting is true. You can do this by counter checking. Remember, what may appear fair to one group will amount to bias for another. So, Always ensure that you give both sides of the picture. But, remaining an unprejudiced observer does not mean adopting what is known in American journalistic parlance as "man from the mars" stance, i.e., seeing each event afresh, unconnected to any previous expectations or future possibilities and passing them on untouched by interpretation. In an increasingly complex world, this would not amount to objectivity or fairness. In many cases, it would simply mean an irresponsible attitude, a refusal to make the reader understand the event in its proper context and realise its significance.

The Interpretation

In many cases, you not only report the events but interpret them for the reader. But, remember, interpretation does not mean backdoor editorialising. It is not an excuse for colouring the story with your personal opinions.

As a reporter, you may cover several complex and specialised subjects, such as science and technology, law and economics. Your command over the language must be such that you can explain even the most complicated issues in single terms to any general reader. In addition to specialised subjects such as science and technology, even government press notes are written in complicated language, burying the news point. You must be able to simplify it and bring out the news point. Except for routine coverages which can be handled by one person, many investigative stories have to be handled by a team. The Bofors investigative stories in the Indian Express and other papers were based on reports from Geneva and Stockholm, besides New Delhi. The securities scam investigations by the Times of India involved, besides Sucheta Dalai, one more correspondent, R. Srinivasan, who posed as an investor and went to the State Bank officers in Bombay to get confirmation about the going on in the bank.

With investigative journalism seeking to bring out scandals and exposures, there is bound to be pressure on journalists to keep someone's wrong doings hidden from public view. This 'someone' is usually a person with considerable clout. The 'pressure' on journalists is exerted in the hope of preventing exposure. The concerned journalist may also be bribed with attractive favours in return for silence on the matter. As a newsperson you may provide helpful or harmful exposure to persons holding important positions in your beat. Since may of them need publicity to perform their functions, they seek you out to provide them with the required exposure. They are on the lookout for a minimum of harmful and the maximum of helpful publicity. If they consider it necessary, they may use their power and influence to pressurise you for this.

The pressure could be used to make you change the news or "kill" a story. This constitutes censorship. Pressure could also be applied with the hope of inducing journalists to volunteer the change or omission which is then equal to self-censorship. While groups like the government and the advertisers could indirectly pressurise you through your news organisation, direct pressure could also come from the government and political parties. In case you are doing stories on something which could lead to harmful exposure for someone, they could take recourse to a range of legal and illegal options, including legal action, threats and violence to pressurise you.

There are three ways of coping with pressure: fighting it, giving in, and anticipating the pressure and taking preventive measures. The first one is the most noble of the three options and history is full of shining examples of this category, During the British rule in India, many papers decided to close down, rather than submit to censorship and government pressure. The father of the nation, Mahatma Gandhi, exemplified this spirit when he wrote during the Quit India Movement: "It is better not to issue newspaper than to issue them under a feeling of suppression." Even during the 1975-77 internal emergency, journals like Mainstream closed down rather than submit to government censorship. But the heroic option is not always feasible. Remember, running a newspaper is a business, apart from being a service. Thousands depend on it for a living. You are in it as a professional, seeking to earn your daily bread. So few expect you to be a hero or a missionary. If you give in to pressure which you cannot fight on your own and if your news organisation does not back you, the consequences could be disastrous for you as a professional journalist. The reporters who generally brave powerful pressures are those who have the full support of their organisations or their professional colleagues backing them unitedly. But, still, you must have the strength of character to fight pressures that come in the form of inducements like lavish gifts, favours, etc. to influence your reporting.

Preventive measures to fight pressure could be legal steps, like seeking a court stay on any law or ordinance that could affect the freedom of the press. In case you feel threatened by some physical violence, you can always seek security from law and order authorities. The journalists of the "Punjab Kesari" group of newspapers, who have taken a courageous antiterrorist stand in Punjab, work under extremely tight security. The group has lost tow of its owners to terrorist bullets, but has not given in to pressures.

The reporting profession is unlike any other profession. At times, some slight carelessness is doing one's duty, can cause incalculable harmful repercussions, both for the news organisation and society. A slight laziness in checking or cross checking certain facts could endanger the credibility of the news organization, proving to be a major block in the way of advancement of the reporters career! A reporter has been likened to a solder on the field. Even as the quality of the soldiers on field determines to a large extent the quality of an army, so also your abilities and the way you discharge your duties as a reporter go a long way in determining the quality and reputation of your news organisation. As a reporter, you have to follow the character, style and policy of your newspaper or magazine or news agency. There are conservative papers which may prefer to stick to routine coverage, not bothering about investigation of scandals. In such papers, you have to stick to their policy even if it cramps your style. But in a news organization with a more dynamic approach to news, you must develop the skills of an investigator. Whatever you do as a reporter will affect the newspaper and its reputation. So, you must take pains to ensure accuracy and objectivity in your stories.

Remember, your sources are sacred. Your credibility in their eyes could be a major factor in your performance as a newsperson. There are sources with whom you will have to take great pains to establish your credibility to make them open up towards you. You will have to assure them that no harm will come to them, and if they so desire, you must keep their identity a secret. There have been instances in the United States of America and some other countries where reporters have defied court orders and gone to jail rather than reveal the sources. In 1960, an American magazine reporter alerted his editors that the ruler of a Middle East country was receiving large amounts of money from several governments for his personal use. But the reporter held back the story till 1977 as he felt that its publication would compromise his source. The matter became news only when the American Intelligence Agency (CIA) files, made available to the press in 1977, contained the same information.

You may well ask whether the responsibility of protecting the sources is absolute. A situation could arise when the information given by a contact who wanted to remain unidentified could lead to a major inquiry of a court case. You may be ordered by the court to reveal who your contact is, for giving witness before the court. What would you do in such a case? Should you commit contempt of court or violate your commitment to the confidentiality of your source? If you reveal the source who wanted to remain anonymous, you could lose your credibility among your contacts who may hesitate to volunteer information in future. Such extreme cases have to be dealt with, on their individual merits. It is sufficient to say that under normal conditions, you have a commitment to protect your sources. As a news reporter, you have a duty to provide accurate, unbiased and objective information to the reader. Every effort must be made to ensure that the news is accurate, free from prejudices and that all sides of the news event are presented fairly.

To maintain your credibility with the reader you have a duty not to accept things or favours or pursue any activity that might compromise your integrity.

However, in these days, publicity seekers including those in private business, organise press conferences and conduct tours with attractive gifts and other incentives. While private firms depend mainly on advertising for publicity, they sometimes want their activities to be carried as news items since news carries greater credibility than advertisements. News reports are written by newspersons who are supposed to be independent and objective. While in these days of corporate and business journalism.

Corporate Journalism

Business and corporate journalism is a field where you have to exercise a tremendous sense of responsibility. With the proliferation of big companies including multinationals and their role in the liberalisation of the Indian economy, their activities form a major subject of public interest. But, it is a subject that must be handled with utmost care. On the one hand, you risk becoming a publicity agent for corporate houses and on the other, you may be risking people's investments and reputations. Remember, anything you write for a news organization could have its impact in terms of money and reputation.

Opinions about the newspaper industry have ranged from it being a mere business to an instrument of social change. Even if it is to be considered a mere business, it is deeply involved in matters of public interest. Every thing you write could have its] repercussions in the society. Even under normal circumstances, you have to exercise great care about what you write.

You have to be particularly careful when reporting in a communally sensitive country like India, This is because there are a host of religious and social diversities and several linguistic groups. It would be unbecoming to be partisan to a particular faith, linguistic or social group. As a reporter you will have to wield your pen with due respect for everyone.

What may be considered correct by one group may be held wrong by another. Take the example of the Ramjanambhoomi Babri Masjid dispute at Ayodhya. Two concerned communities have a conflicting stand about the disputed structure. If you have been following the controversy in the papers, you would have found that the disputed structure is referred to neither as Ramjanambhoomi nor as Babri Masjid. It is referred either as the "Disputed site" or as the "controversial structure", as simply as the "Ramjanambhoomi-Babri Masjid site".

Apart from the Ayodhya dispute, the communal tension in the country has been aggravated by the Punjab and Kashmir problems. News organisations are extremely careful about reporting events of a communal nature.

A similar procedure is followed when reporting communal riots. The step is taken to prevent any further tension from developing between the communities if they are to be identified in the news reports. For this reason, places of worship affected in riots are not referred to, by name.

Relation with Desk

The editor and the publisher of a newspaper are responsible for whatever is printed in it. In many Indian newspaper the editor and publisher is the same person. In such papers editor is also proprietor and manager.

But where the editor and the publisher are different people, the editor looks after the editorial content that is anything except advertising. An advertising manager looks after the advertising. The publisher, general manager or managing editor or executive director look after the management of the paper.

A number of assistant editors assist the editor in looking after editorial and feature pages. The news; content of the paper is looked after by the news editor under whose guidance a number of sub-editors and reporters work.

In India the entry into the profession of journalism is normally as a trainee journalist who is later absorbed as a reporter or a sub-editor.

The job of a reporter is to gather news and write it for his organisation. Sub-editor makes it fit to print. Reporters go out in the field while sub-editors work at the news desk where all the news that comes, is selected, edited, each news story is given a suitable headline and its place in the newspaper is decided.

Reporters can become senior reporters, correspondents, senior correspondents, chief reporter, special correspondent and foreign correspondent. Sub- editors are promoted to the positions of senior sub editor, chief sub-editor, deputy news editor and news editor, but the basic job of a reporter remains news gathering and filing the report or "copy" to the news desk. Similarly, the basic job of the sub-editor also remains the same; to "sub" copy to make it fit to print which includes collecting, selecting, arranging, reducing, farming, translating and adapting for; publication according to the importance of the copy Sub-editor is also called copy editor as what he edits is called copy. Whatever is field by reporters special correspondents etc., is copy for him whatever comes to the news desk from wire services is also copy.

But reporting and editing sides are not water-tight compartments. Reporters can exchange places with sub-editors. In many newspapers it is a routine. A sub-editor is sent on a reporting assignment many a time. He is also asked to write news items from the handouts that land up in the newspaper office when reporters away.

To be a good reporter or a good sub-editor what one needs is common sense and command over language. These two requirement in fact summarise the qualities newsmen should have as other qualities flow from these two and the basic human values.

It is customary to describe desired qualities of a reporter and sub-editor separately, but as both of them deal with the same commodity, news, and their basic job is to communicate effectively many of these qualities have to be common.

News Sense: it is the basic quality of newsmen. Every reporter has to have news sense or nose for news to distinguish news from non-news. He should be able to compare various news values and decide where to begin his story and should not miss important details. News sense is essential for a sub-editor also, he is the first reader of a reporter's copy, and if the reporter has made a mistake he has to correct it. A bad copy may have the most important element of the story buried in the fourth paragraph. It will be left to the sub-editors nose for news to bring that to the first paragraph.

Clarity: A reporter should have clarity of mind and expression. A person who is confused himself cannot tell a story to others. Only clarity of mind is not enough unless it is accompanied by clarity of expression. Without clarity of expression clarity of mind has no meaning.

Sub-editor is the judge of clarity of the copy. A good sub-editor will never allow a copy escape him unless the meaning is crystal clear. He has every right to make life miserable for a reporter who is not clear and does not write is simple language.

Objectivity: reporter and sub-editor should not allow their personal bias or ideas to creep into a story. They should not take sides but try to cover all the different viewpoints to achieve balance in the story.

Accuracy: A reporter should strive for accuracy, he should check and re-check his facts till he is satisfied that he has them accurate. In this respect he should not take any chance as accuracy is directly proportional to the credibility of a reporter and his newspaper.

The role of a sub-editor is to check for accuracy, it is particularly important when background is involved. In the case of dates and names the reporter may rely on his memory but the sub-editor must check them from reference material available in the newspaper office. When there is a doubt he should leave it out this is the golden rule of journalism. It is better not to say a thing than to say it wrong.

Alertness: A reporter should always be alert while dealing with his subjects. Many major news breaks in the past were possible because of alertness of reporters. Scoops don't walk into newspaper offices-alert reporters catch them in air and pursue. A sub-editor has to be alert while working on news-desk. Lack of alertness of a sub-editor can be seen by readers in the morning for he will be leaving or introducing mistakes for everybody to see.

Speed: In today's world speed- matters everywhere. A person who cannot work fast cannot be good reporter. While maintaining all other desirable qualities a reporter should strive to work faster. He should think fast, decide fast and write or type fast for he has to meet deadlines or may have to go to another assignment.

A sub-editor also has to work with speed. He cannot sit with a copy for long. He has to do swiftly whatever is required of him for a lot more copy is waiting for him. A slow sub-editor is a curse at the news desk and is treated with contempt. Such people are misfits in the profession.

Calmness: Reporters and sub-editors often work in trying circumstances. They have to remain clam and composed in most exciting and tragic circumstances. In many situations they have to be calm-devoid of hysterical actions or utterances and apply appropriate mental and physical effort to write or edit the story.

Reporter and sub-editors are human beings. They have emotions but they have to stifle them in the face of disturbing influences-they have to develop resistances to excitability. Being in the field reporters face many such occasions when they have to control their emotions. Sub-editors should develop a temperament to work under pressure of deadlines. They should not lose their cool if they are behind the clock for calm mind can work faster.

Curiosity: Reporters and sub-editors should have an unsatiable curiosity. For reporters it is useful in developing just for facts that may lead to better stories. This characteristic will keep on improving a sub-editor for with every passing day a curious sub-editor will have a better back ground to do his job the next day. Reporters and sub-editors should read as much as possible to constantly improve their awareness level.

Scepticism: It is another necessary quality which a reporter and a sub-editor should cultivate. They should not take anything for granted. They should have an unwavering posture of doubt until faced with undeniable proof. Reporters should be more vigilant for many forces constantly try to use them and through them their paper. Many people try to plant on reporters a wrong story for their own ends. Many a time reporters fall into such traps in good faith. They should have enough scepticism to avoid such plots.

Sub-editors should also be careful for some clever politicians, public relations men and product advertisers keep on trying to take them for a ride. They should not allow anything to go in news columns that should actually go as advertisement. They should not fail to check even reporters' copy for such foul play.

Punctually: It is a goods habit. For reporters it is a must for if they are not punctual they may miss something for which they may have to depend on secondary sources, it is always better to be punctual and then wait than reach late and ask others a rival may misinform you or hide some important information.

At the desk too punctuality pays, if a sub-editor is punctual he will be treated with respect by his co-workers, if he is late he will irritate them and spoil the working atmosphere. Besides, he may have to face the problem of backlog of copy which he will have to clear under the pressure of deadline.

Patience: It is quality which helps a reporter in a big way for many a time almost daily he has to test his patience, the voluntary self-control or restraint that helps one to endure waiting, provocation, injustice, suffering or any of the unpleasant vicissitudes of time and life. Most of the time a reporter waits for someone or something and patience gives him the willingness to wait without becoming disgruntled or anxious. Many a time he has to tolerate other people's shortcomings and has to remain unperturbed by someone else's slowness or other quirks. Patience also helps sub-editors as they work long hours in trying conditions. They have to put up with many annoying situations everyday vis-a-vis reporters, proofreaders or printers.

Imagination: this basic mental faculty helps reporters in writing better stories that retain the reader's interest. For a sub-editor this creative faculty is very useful as he can add sparkle to somebody else's copy and make it lively, besides, imaginative headlines attract the reader and improve the quality of a newspaper.

Farsightedness: An intelligent envisioning of the future helps newsmen in general. The quality helps them in identifying processes and people who will be important in future. Reporters can watch such processes and cultivate people who may become important news sources in the future.

It helps reporters and sub-editors in determining the importance of an event. A reporter with foresight can think ahead and prepare for eventualities. With a little forethought sub-editors can plan their work so as to avoid tension and it results in better functioning of the desk.

Self-discipline: One can achieve a degree of proficiency in sub-editing or reporting by systematic effort and self-control. In this sense self-discipline suggests dedication and firm commitment. It helps in journalism as in any other field. Integrity: it is a virtue in itself and implies undeviating honesty and strict adherence to a stern code of ethics. This human quality is important for journalists. It is more important for reporters for they are more exposed to temptations compared to sub-editors.

Fearlessness and Frankness: These qualities help reporters in asking unpleasant questions and taking risks to find out truth. Nobody gives a story on a platter. The reporter will have to probe, question, authenticate and exercise his power of deduction to get a good story.

Tactfulness: A reporter should be tactful, he should have the ability to handle sensitive people and situations gracefully without causing hurt or angry feelings. He should considerate of others and should be careful not to embarrass. Upset or offend them. A reporter should have flexible and sociable personality and should have a nature that relishes variety of experiences. He should have an understanding of human behaviour and emotions. This will help him in developing contacts that are so essential for news gathering.

Initiative: A reporter works in the field should have an outgoing nature with initiative and drive. These qualities will help him get acquainted with news sources and get stories from them. A meek, retiring or shy person is not fit for reporting, he may be good at his desk. Reporters need a fair mount of assertiveness and aggressiveness to be successful in their career.

Mobility: A reporter should be mobile. He should enjoy moving ground and should not hesitate travelling distances to get stories when required, he should go to his news sources as often as possible for such constant contacts help him get news. A mobile reporter is seldom caught napping when a major story breaks.

Reporters and sub-editors should be diligent. There jobs require painstaking exertion of intense care and effort, alertness and dedication to the task and wary watchfulness. They have to make extremely fine distinctions while writing or editing copy. A sub-editor should insist on perfection and should love his job for he can make or mar the newspaper.

These qualities are basically qualities of good and efficient human beings. Good and efficient human beings make good and efficient sub-editors and reporters. All other things being equal reporters need additional qualities to deal effectively with all sorts of people they meet in the field. Sun-editors should have better command over language as they improve what reporters write.

A very authentic way of gathering facts, figures and opinions on various issues is to interview the persons concerned. In this unit, we shall discuss the importance of the interview in reporting, besides the skills required to master the art of conducting an interview. Having done this, we shall proceed to the next block where our main theme will be "specialised reporting".

There are carious way of gathering information and knowledge for the media. One can do so from books, magazines and journals, or incidents, and by meeting people who hold important positions. Meeting or interviewing them is one of the most significant and important ways of gathering information, facts and knowledge. The interview is a very useful input for all media-print and electronic. It depends on how one would like to use an interview. It may be used and a programme to make the audience/reader get information/facts from the source directly. The interview can form the basis of an article, a feature or a commentary. Or, segments of an interview can be used to substantiate an argument or a point in an article or a radio/television feature.

One may like to presume that you have written something in your life; a letter, an application, an article or a poem. One can also assume that you might not have been satisfied with the first draft. Therefore, you may have re-written it changing sentences, paragraphs, words, etc. It is also possible that after changing the draft twice, thrice or more times, you were satisfied with your written material. Let us call this the preparatory stage. To do and interview is also something like doing an original work in which you create something. Thus, to do a meaningful interview—both for yourself and for the person whom you plan to talk to—it is necessary that you do your home work right. It is only then, that an interview conducted after proper preparation, would make a certain impact.

It is said that to speak for five minutes over radio, a person must prepare himself/herself at least for five hours. Therefore, preparation is very important. Interviews can be on the record or off the record. On the record interviews are those whose contents can be attributed to the person interviewed.

In this case, unless there is a prior agreement to use the whole of the interview verbatim, portions of the interview, that have some use for the reporter can be utilised and the rest discarded or canned for future use.

Off the record interviews are those in which the information is given, but the source is not to be identified by the interviewer. In such cases, the source identified is "a source in the Defence

Ministry" or "a General Commanding a division" etc. In such cases it is normal to cross-check the facts from another source, since the man giving the information is not willing to stand up and be counted. There can be interviews which are partly on the record and partly off the record. That is, some information given can be attributed to the person who gives it and some can be attributed to "a source" or "a Defence Ministry Official" or "a General", etc.

The most important part of the interview is to know your subject as completely as possible. It could be a VIP, an important member from the bureaucracy, the art world or the corporate sector or just an ordinary citizen. Accordingly you should prepare yourself by reading about the person. It is imperative for you to not only fully research the information you want from your subject, but also the person behind it. You should also have all the essential background information of the interviewee, e.g. his/her family, hobbies, interests. This will help you to build an instant rapport with the interviewee. It will enable you to get on with the job most comfortably. A reluctant interviewee only acts as an obstacle and foils the very purpose of the interviewer. It is most important to research your subject matter. It could be a subject in which you neither have any interest nor adequate knowledge. But once you are fully armed with the basic and important information acquired through books, newspapers, journals or magazine, articles, you will be much more comfortable and should be successful in your venture.

For example, if you are required to interview a criminal lawyer, a policeman or an accused, you should have enough knowledge of criminal law— congnisable and non-cognisable offences, various Acts/Sections which govern the offences, and other legal provisions. This will help you extract the required information. You must know your subject matter as well as the person whom you intend to talk to about the subject matter.

All journalists must remember two fundamental factors: First, all interviews are subject to editing. So there is no harm in culling more information than you can use. The information that you need to buttress an argument or to refute another or to make a point, can be used at the appropriate place. The rest can be stored for use in future.

Second, no statement made in the interview is allowed to be used out of context. If, for instance, a Government authority vehemently denies that any human rights violations were made during a particular clash in Kashmir, one cannot quote him to create the impression that no human rights violations are made by security forces during any clashes. If the authority interviewed does not generalise it, the reporter or sub-editor is debarred from generalising it.

It is important to establish contact with the interviewee much in advance of the interview. How do you do this? It could be a direct contact— physical or through telephone. More often than not, where important interviews are concerned, there is a channel yaw will have to go through. It could be the private secretary or the members of the family— referred to as the "protector of the interviewee." So, the first thing to do is to establish a rapport with the protector. To get to your subject matter or the person, you must be able to play to the gallery to defeat all the obstacles imposed by the "protectors".

If the first thing is to establish contact and to build up a rapport, the most important part of the, preparation is to decide what you want to get out of the interview. May be you want substantiation of a fact you have discussed; Or the refutation of something; Or may be you want the interviewer's views on some proposition you or someone else is making.

It is important and essential, to make a deep study of the individual you plan to interview. Let us say that he person is particularly fond of dogs. When you go to interview her/him, it will be fatal to talk about how you abhor dogs or how they are dangerous. As interviewer, you cannot afford to convey your general wariness about the canine species—not verbally, not even through body language.

The information you seek to extract from the person may have nothing whatsoever to do with dogs. Yet, the person may react by remaining uncommunicative through the rest of the interview if you start off on the wrong note. Paying attention to such minute, apparently insignificant matters really helps in conducting the interview smoothly. You must build a personal rapport to begin with, so you may start the interview comfortably.

In the electronic media, there are two ways of interviewing: with the Prime Minister or the President, the setting would be as designed by the Public Relation Officer or the Principal Information Officer. If it is a television interview, then you need the following:

(a) cameraman;

(b) sound recordist;

(c) lighting technician; and

(d) the sound technician.

The other way could be that the interview is to be held in a studio. In that case, you should adequately arrange the setting in the studio. For the radio studio interview, you would need a very good recording machine. You use a lip microphone which prevents extraneous sound from getting injected into the microphone. If the interview is only a part of what you are actually going to air, then it should be transcribed. Mark the important segments, and tailor the interview to the actual slot requirements with a suitable link to give necessary continuity. To do this, you would require an editor to do a proper cut and paste work of the tape.

Getting an interview can often be difficult because the interviewer is generally viewed with suspicion! To overcome this handicap, the interviewer has to be imaginative. The interviewer labours between two competing factors. One, the public has the right to know and you are the tool employed to gather the information. Two, from the legal point of view nobody can be forced into talking and hence, the job can be tiresome and at times, very frustrating.

Be operational for the interview. This is-very important. It shows the importance of the interviewee and that he has not been taken for granted. In a nut shell, you must be ready right on time to start the interview. Arriving on time may be good in most cases, for one has to do things like setting up the camera, or recording devices before the interview. One should arrive 10-15 minutes before time in order to be operational on time. Outline your reasons for being there, unless you are working on something very sensitive. If you do not specify your reasons, it may create problems. Start the interview with a broad question. This helps your to size up the person and also collect your thoughts. It also helps to receive information your may not have anticipated and to chart out your course of action—a correct direction that the interview should take. Do not interrupt until the interviewee has relaxed. Avoid making the interviewee uncomfortable at the outset. It would be of little value. An interviewee kept at complete ease can be most helpful. The interviewer must not only be conversant with the subject matter of the interview but must also be a good conversationalist. All the important features of interpersonal communication come into play in an interview. In a face to face meeting, the stress is on both the language used in speech and the no-verbal body language, but, in a telephonic interview, the stress would be on the tone and inflexion given to the words. In this type, of interview, it can be rather difficult to assess the intended meaning since the other person's actual expression is hidden from sight. We shall now discuss the salient points to be kept in mind when conducting an interview in person.

On occasion, an interview may not be planned or rehearsed before it actually takes place. But then there are a few thumb rules that are fundamental to any interview. Preparing oneself to interview a personality, a celebrity or eve the person-on-the-street is actually an on-going long-term process. This is because one must be well-rounded interviewer, skilled in the art of handling a variety of topics and areas as also a range of idiosyncrasies that are inherent in people in general. One must be prepared for any turn of events and still be able to take it all in one's stride, that is to say, with equanimity. One cannot acquire these skills overnight

but must nurture them over a period of time. A great deal of deep study of persons and happenings is called for. The would-be interviewer must yearn to learn.

Some interviews are simply old wine in new bottles. Other seek to convey an innovation or idea that the interviewee has recently come up with. Yet other interviews are made out of the interviewer's idea(s): giving a new twist to an even, throwing new light on a discovery that had been accepted at face value, and such like. One must develop a keen sense of identifying material for use in an interview. One must also have the knack to rad more into matters that is at first apparent: something like reading between the lines. That way, a much-interviewed person may reveal a fresh side of the matter being discussed and perhaps also of his/her own personality hitherto hidden from public view.

Having a finely-turned news-sense helps to generate ideas for interviews. It enables one to capture a glimpse of the extra-ordinary in the most ordinary things and persons. It depends on the situation whether one come upon a fresh insight during the interview by asking hard-hitting questions or by putting queries in a gentle manner. These are tactics that ought to be learnt by assessing and recognising the opportune time and place when it come your way. Alternatively, you could create the right atmosphere to make your interviewee reveal material which would from the basis for a good interview. In effect, the interviewer gives shape and direction to the interview, always allowing enough leeway for the unexpected utterance. One could then build carefully on what is sometimes said in such an off hand manner. The interviewer must, therefore, remain alert and latch on to every word that is said during the conversation. One can become adept in this technique only with practice.

Advance preparation for the interview by way of well-thought out questions and a thorough consideration of approach is very helpful. One need not fear that the final outcome will sound stilted with not natural spontaneity. Usually the reverse is true. One will be able to pose the most appropriate questions when one is well-

versed with the subject. But how should one conduct oneself when conducting an interview. At the outset, arrive on time for the interview. This will help keep the interviewee in good humour. Taking notes is an essential part of interviewing: the two cannot be separated. Some take down everything, even irrelevant and redundant remarks. Take down only what is important. However, that may not always be possible. People sometimes stop taking when you start writing. Your do not always know what is to have a flawless recall. A wrong quote can be most embarrassing professionally. It costs you your credibility. Now-a-days, there is the help of a recorder. Take permission of the interviewee before using it.

9

Origin of News

The Speeches

Speeches are a major source of news and every day many news items that appear in the newspapers can be traced back to some speech or the other. Sometimes several speeches from part of one report. This happens in reports of seminars, symposia and legislatures. In such situations the most important speech, normally from the most important speaker, gets prominence.

While covering political party conferences and international conferences on various subjects, one has to deal with several speeches in a row. Depending on the content and the speaker a reporter has to decide who should come first. Effort should also be made to generalise observations if possible and then mention who said what. In such cases the most important things said by different speakers should be mentioned and there should be no repetition of ideas. If there are contrary opinions expressed by different speakers they should be mentioned and then supporters of different schools of thoughts should be quoted. Here again repetition of ideas should be avoided.

The importance of speeches and speakers varies from occasion to occasion and relative importance of other speakers. A reporter must evaluate various factors and use judgement while writing the story. For example, if many ministers speak in a party their speeches are important and what they say will be important according to the content of the speech. But if the prime minister speaks and he touches upon points which have been covered by other ministers already and adds something to it, he will get the maximum space and the rest of the ministers will be mentioned in the story with very little of what they said.

If in a special debate in a house of parliament the speech of a minister of state gets prominence in case the cabinet minister of the same department does not speak. If the cabinet minister of the same department does not speak. If the cabinet minister also speaks then the state minister is normally pushed out of intro. If the prime minister intervenes during the debate and says something on the subject even the cabinet minister is pushed below in the body of the story. So while reporting multiple speeches the reporter must evaluate all these factors.

There are occasions when copies of a speech may be supplied in advance. Sometimes the story is prepared based on the advance copy and a reporter goes to the site when the speech is made-just to check whether the speech was made and if so whether it followed the advance copy. The advance story is subject to an embargo which is released automatically at the time up to which it is embargoed (should not be used before/ should be used on or after ...). A reporter or sub-editor who writes the story from such a speech has enough time to his disposal and should ' read the speech carefully and write the story on the top of which 'not to be used before ... on...' as mentioned in the embargo should be typed. Normally, this embargo time is the time of the event where the speech is to be made. News agencies sometimes creed the embargoed story in advance. It should be used only after the embargo is lifted.

Where advance copy is not made available the reporter must

reach the place where speech is to be delivered and check from the organisers if they are supplying a copy of the speech. If the copy is supplied before the speech then the reporter should start working on it immediately. He should go through it carefully and mark what he considers as important points.

He should also mark the order of their importance so that he loses no time when he has to type or dictate his story. He should carefully check the copy when the speech is made and see if there are any major deviations from the text supplied. Sometimes what is said by the speaker outside the supplied text is more newsworthy than all what is given in the text. Such departures from the prepared text should find place in the intro or body depending on their news value.

Many a time a speaker does not read the prepared speech and says that the speech be taken as read while what he says is in addition to that in that case the reporter is supposed to listen to the speaker carefully and read the text also before writing the story.

If the organisers promise that the copy of the speech will be supplied but it is not distributed when the speech begins, the reporter should start taking notes from the beginning of the speech imagining that the copy is not available. Many such promises of the organisers prove false and if the reporter does not take notes or record the speech when it is delivered, he will be in difficulty. Moreover he will miss any departures from the text.

A reporter should make use of the copy if he gets it within a few minutes after the event, otherwise he should rely on his notes and do the story. The copy can be used for quotations from the speech.

But there are occasions when the copy of the speech is not supplied. This happens in seminars and almost all the public meetings of political parties. A reporter can record them on a tape recorder. He must taken care to take down important points in his notebook. In this way he can do the story quickly, for he will not have enough time to replay the full speech and then write. A tape recorder is useful for it helps the reporter in reproducing exactly what the speaker might have said on a controversial or important issue.

A speech can sometimes yield more than one story. In certain circumstances a reporter can add colour to the story by describing the atmosphere or some sidelights. Such opportunities should not be missed.

It is interesting to see how the same speech is covered by different newspapers. Following is the address by the President of India to Parliament (February 20, 1986):

Honourable members :

1. It gives me great pleasure to welcome you to this first session of Parliament in 1986. I felicitate the new members.
2. The year has seen Parliament transact its business in a purposeful manner and in an atmosphere of cooperation. I extend to you all my best wishes for the successful completion of the budgetary and legislative business that lies ahead.
3. In July, 1985, the Government took a major initiative to resolve the complex and difficult problems in Punjab. Our prime concern was to strengthen the forces of unity and integrity. Policy was governed by the perspective of serving the highest national interest. The democratic process triumphed over terrorism. The peaceful elections in Punjab testified to the desire of the overwhelming majority of the people for peace and normalcy in the State.
4. A great responsibility rest on those who have secured the mandate of the people. The supreme task is to isolate those who are resorting to violence to, disturb communal harmony and peace. In this task they will have the support of all political forces committed to the unity and integrity of India. There cannot be and must not be, any compromise with the forces of disintegration. It is imperative that all

secular and democratic forces join hands in a mass campaign to safeguard the values enshrined in our Constitution-nationalism, secularism, democracy and socialism-the bedrock of India's unity.

5. The Assam settlement was followed by elections to the Legislative Assembly and the Lok Sabha. A new Government has taken office.

6. Government are committed to the fullest implementation of the Punjab and Assam Accords.

7. Government express their deepest sympathy with the families of all those who lost their lives, or were injured, or suffered loss of property in violent incidents in different parts of the country. Violence in public life is the very antithesis of the ethos of our civilization. The frequent resort to violence to settle what are perceived as grievances of one group or another should deeply disturb those who uphold democratic values. While governments must firmly put down violence wherever it may occur, it is essential that political parties committed to democratic values should deal with the root causes of violence through purposive and sustained work among the people. The temptation to seek short-term advantages from communal and other types of violence must be eschewed.

8. Communalism continues to pose a serious threat to national unity, it is being reinforced by religious fundamentalism and fanaticism. These trends represent a reactionary social outlook, directed against the struggle of the poor and the underprivileged against the vested interest. The reconstituted National Integration Council will have to act decisively and systematically to strengthen secularism.

9. In my Address on January 17, 1985, I had outlined the major policies and programmes of the Government. I recapitulate the main points:

   (i) Commitment of a clean public life;

(ii) Administrative reforms;

(iii) Judicial reforms;

(iv) A new national education policy;

(v) A new national programme for women;

(vi) Participation of youth in programmes for promoting national integration and achieving excellence;

(vii) Establishment of a Wasteland Development Board;

(viii) Formation of a Central Ganga Authority;

(ix) A new textile policy; and

(x) Thorough examination of safety measures for industrial establishments.

10. My Government have fulfilled in substantial measure the tasks they had set for themselves for the past year.

11. The anti-defection Act is now on the statute book. Contributions to political parties by the companies have been permitted by law. Government have endeavoured to set a new tone in public life. This has strengthened national confidence. A strong sense of involvement in public affairs among all sections of the people and a buoyant spirit have characterised the year that has gone by. We have to build on these assets to raise the standards of public life.

12. Vigorous steps have been taken to combat corruption and to improve the performance of the public services. Strong emphasis has been laid on sound personnel management and training of personnel at all levels. Machinery for redressal of public grievances is in place. Its results are being continuously evaluated. A new Ministry has been set up to monitor the implementation of various programmes. All Departments of Government have been directed to formulate detailed action plans for the coming financial year, against which their progress will be judged. Administrative reform is a continuous process. Detailed

exercises are underway to reorient the system to speedier decision-making and better implementation.

13. Government are determined to eliminate delays in dispensation of justice. The experiment of Lok Adalats has proved that an innovative approach is required to cure this malady. The establishment of Administrative Tribunals will also lighten the burden of the courts, enabling them to devote more time to the liquidation of arrears. However, these are just the first steps in tackling the basic problem of making justice inexpensive and easily accessible to the poor. Drastic changes are needed. Government have entrusted to the Law Commission the task of recommending such changes.

14. Government published in August 1985, a status paper entitled "The Challenge of Education". This was intended to stimulate wide and intensive national debate on issues and alternatives. Government note with satisfaction that the debate has involved all sections of the people and many useful ideas and approaches have emerged. A draft of the new Education Policy will be presented shortly to Parliament.

15. Government have set up a new department to look after the development of women. A comprehensive national programme for women is being worked out. It will aim at enabling women to play their full part in developing a strong and modern nation.

16. Programmes for youth development have made considerable headway but much more has to be done in this area.

17. The Wasteland Development Board has been set up and has started work on an ambitious programme of afforestation. In a recent meeting, all the State Governments endorsed an integrated approach to a National Land Use Policy as well as the strategies and policies for wasteland development.

18. The Central Ganga Authority has come into existence. With the cooperation of the concerned State Governments, work has started in full swing on stopping the population of the Ganga.

19. A new textile policy was announced in June 1985. It aims at production of cheaper cloth for the people. An equally important objective of the policy is to protect the interests of handloom weavers. It is envisaged that in the Seventh Plan the entire production of 700 million sq. metres of controlled and janta cloth will be transferred to be handloom sector. The Handlooms Act, 1985 has been passed to strengthen this vital sector which provides livelihood to millions. Steps are being taken to ensure full and efficient implementation of the policy.

20. Government have completed examination of issues relating to industrial safety and management of hazardous substances and legislation will be introduced in this session of Parliament.

21. Government will establish seven zonal cultural centres--three have already been set up-to promote a sense of cultural cohesion. These centers, cutting across territorial and linguistic boundaries, would project the rich diversity of regional cultural traditions and their underlying unity. They "Would take the best of our culture to the masses, harmonising it with their lives and struggles. Their essential thrust would be to break the artificial barriers created during the colonial era between the masses and the living tradition of India's age-old culture in all its forms. The centres will also aim at revitalising folk art which has enriched the country's culture life."

22. I would now refer to the major trends in our economy.

23. The seventh Five Year Plan was approved by the national Development Council. The basic strategy of the Plan is cast in a longer term perspective of eradication of

poverty and building a strong, self-reliant and modern economy. The plan sharpens the focus on the anti-poverty programmes which will have an expanded coverage. It also envisages adequate investments in the core sectors to strengthen the growth potential of the national economy.

24. The fulfillment of the- Plan required total commitment and determination to mobilise adequate resources for investment. To translate the vision of a strong, prosperous, self-reliant India into reality requires unremitting to and capacity to sacrifice and to bear hardship. Adequate savings have to be mobilised to pursue a non-inflationary path of development. More importantly, these savings have to be used effectively. The challenge has to be met. There are no short cuts to development, no alternatives to hard work.

25. Vigorous implementations of anti-poverty programmes yielded significant results. The Sixth Five Year Plan aimed at assisting 15 million families under the integrated Rural Development Programme; 16.6 million families were actually covered, of which 6.4 million belonged to the Scheduled Castes and Scheduled Tribes. These programmes are being strengthened and surplus foodgrains stocks will be used in 1986-87 to expand the National Rural Employment Programme and the Rural Landless Employment Guarantee Programme to cover one million additional families. An amount of Rs. 100 crores has been provided annually during the Seventh Five Year Plan for the construction of housing for the Scheduled Castes /Scheduled Tribes and freed bonded labour.

26. By the end of March, 1985, of a total of 2.31 lakh problem villages lacking safe drinking water supply, 1.92 lakh villages had been provided with at least one source of water supply. During 1985-86 the programme was further accelerated.

27. In 1985-86 agriculture continued to make steady progress. In November 1985, foodgrains stocks with Government were higher by nearly 15% over 1984. This has enabled Government to launch a scheme for distributing wheat and rice at specially subsidised rates in tribal areas and to other vulnerable sections, especially the Scheduled Castes, expectant mothers, children, etc. A comprehensive crop insurance scheme has been introduced in specified areas for the kharif crop. Government are considering further expansion of such schemes.

28. During the first seven months of 1985-86, industrial production grew at the rate of .3%. The policy initiatives of Government have created a buoyant investment climate. The infrastructural industries have performed well. Compared with the first nine months of the last year, power generation was up by 8.2%; saleable steel production by 12.9%; fertilizer production by more than 10%. Our ports handled 13.2% more cargo and the railways created an all time record in freight traffic movement.

29. In 1985-86 the Central Plan outlays were stepped up by 15% over 1984-85, especially on anti-poverty programmes human resource development and infrastructure. There was considerable increase in the outlays of State Plans. Government will have spent in 1985-86 Rs. 1,650 crores on food subsidy an and Rs. 2,050 crores on fertilizer subsidy. Public distribution system was strengthened and prudent management of supplies prevented shortages. It is gratifying that a significant increase in public investment was achieved.

30. Tax collections have been buoyant belying gloomy forebodings. The collection of direct taxes is up by about 23% compared to the corresponding period last year, indirect tax collection has increased by 22%. Total tax collections have increased by 22% which is the highest in the last decade. An effective drive was launched against

tax evaders, smugglers and black marketeers. Action has also been taken against personnel found guilty of colliding with economic offenders. Government are determined to cleanse the economic life and to fight the evil of black money.

31. For the first time, a long-term fiscal policy coterminous with the Five Year Plan has been announced. A long-term direction to economic policy has been provided. Government are confident that the policy will ensure economic growth and speedier expansion of productive investment and employment opportunities.

32. It is necessary to focus attention on the structural problems of the economy to further our basic objective of growth with social justice. India's development depends upon steadily rising levels of public investment. How are these investments to be financed? Massive investments made in the previous Plans must yield adequate returns. Coasts of production on have to be reduced. Every pair of national savings has to be put to the most productive use. Otherwise it will be difficult to find real resources for the larger and larger investments required for maintaining the tempo of self-reliant growth, for enlarging our antipoverty programmes and for preserving our economic independence. Sooner or later, sooner rather than later, we have to face the realities of the situation. No one should be under the delusion that growth, social justice, price stability and self-reliance are achievable without efficiency, discipline and sharing of burdens. Contemporary history warns us of such pitfalls.

33. We must reduce the costs of our inputs and prices of final products and services. We cannot afford the luxury of pricing ourselves out of both the domestic and the export markets. A modern industrial society cannot rise on the basis of continuing low levels of productivity and high coasts of production. New jobs cannot be created if existing enterprises incur losses year after year. Operational

inefficiency increases the cost of production and is inevitably reflected in increased prices which are a burden on the people. It raises costs all round, reducing real investment.

34. The future of the planning process depends on our capacity to face up to difficult questions and- to take hard decisions, decisions that may involve sacrifices but without which forward movement will not be possible. Growth is absolutely vital to raise the standards of living of the poor. Can we evade decisions that protect and strengthen this development process? Nations are built by generations that sacrifice for a better tomorrow.

35. The balance of payments position poses a similar challenge. Our exports have remained sluggish in 1985-86 but our imports have increased. The imports of petroleum products and edible oils are well above the limits the country can afford. The question basically is whether we want to stand on our own feet or not. If we do, there is no question that we have to curb the growth of consumption of petroleum products and we have to be self-sufficient in oilseeds. We also have to have a fresh look at our imports of capital goods. We do not want to shut out new technology because that will harm us, but we have to make sure that such technology meets the rigorous criteria of essentiality. External financial flows are needed but Government are determined that India is never at the mercy of foreign banks and institutions. Economic independence and self-reliance are central to our philosophy of development. We shall pay whatever price is required to maintain our economic independence.

36. The primary objectives of our foreign policy continue to be the promotion of non-alignment, advocacy of peace and nuclear disarmament, enlarging the area of friendship and cooperation and building of a just world order.

37. We welcome the resumption of high level dialogue between the Russian Federation and USA. It is imperative to take urgent steps to bring about a freeze in the nuclear arms race and a comprehensive nuclear weapon test ban treaty. The six-nation initiative has called for these measures. The Delhi Declaration of January, 1985 had a good impact on public opinion throughout the world. The leaders of the six countries are in touch with one another about further steps.

33. During the last one year the atmosphere in the subcontinent has distinctly improved. We have succeeded in making progress with our neighbours in many fields. But we remain concerned about the ethnic situation in Sri Lanka and Pakistan's continued pursuit of a nuclear weapon capability. We remain convinced that the situation in Sri Lanka can be settled only through political means; attempts to seek a military solution will fall and will only result in the loss of a large number of innocent lives.

39. The Government welcome the establishment of South Asian Association for Regional Cooperation launched in Dhaka in December, 1985. We expect that it will help strengthen forces of friendship and cooperation in our region.

40. The Government have made untiring efforts towards the resolution of the major areas of tension. At the Commonwealth Meeting in the Bahamas in October, in which the Prime Minister participated, our delegation played a leading role in the adoption of the Commonwealth Accord on South Africa. We continue to demand comprehensive mandatory sanctions against the racist regime in South Africa. If the authorities there, and other Governments in a position to influence South Africa, do not act in time, violence on a large scale will become unavoidable.

41. The Prime Minister also attended the 40th anniversary of

the United Nations. The Nassau Declaration on World Order adopted by Commonwealth leaders, contained a strong plea for adherence to international norms and principles and the strengthening of the United Nations. Support for the United Nations system is one of the corner-stones of our foreign policy. We are concerned at the growing threat to the multilateral institutions and the increasing tendency to resort to unilateral action. Government support international efforts to combat international terrorism, while recognising the rights to people under colonial occupation to use all means to attain their just objectives.

42. The Government deplore the fact that the Palestinian people continue to be denied their inalienable rights, including the right to an independent homeland of there own. Until this problem is tackled, West Asia will not see a basic lasting peace.

43. The Prime Minister paid official visits to the Russia, Egypt, France. Algeria, the USA, Bhutan, the UK, Cuba, the Netherlands, Vietnam, Japan, Oman and Maldives. Our traditionally close and friendly relations with the USSR have been further strengthened following the Prime Minister's discussions with Soviet leaders in Moscow. The visit to USA has significantly enlarged the content of our bilateral relations with the -USA. The Prime Minister visited Dhaka to express our solidarity with the people of Bangladesh during the cyclone disaster and participated in the meeting of Heads of State and Government for launching the South Asian Association for Regional Cooperation. The Prime Minister addressed the UNESCO during his visit to France. He addressed the annual conference of the I.L.O. in Geneva. We had the privilege to host visits by the Kings of Nepal and Bhutan, the Queen of the Netherlands, the Presidents of Mexico, Maldives, SWAPO, Sri Lanka, Tanzania, Indonesia and Pakistan, the Chairman of PLO, the Head of State of

Ethiopia, and the Prime Ministers of Poland, Yugoslavia, Mauritius, Britain, New Zealand, People's Democratic Republic of Yemen and Trinidad and Tobago. The Crown Prince and Princess of Norway and the Pope also visited India.

44. Let me now outline some priority areas for 1986-87 and beyond.

45. The need of the hour is to enable the poor to better their lives. Science and technology have to support this fundamental objective. To this end, government are mounting technology missions in the following areas,

    (i) Drinking water for all villages;

    (ii) Eradication of illiteracy;

    (iii) Vaccination and immunisation of children;

    (iv) Production of oilseeds and manufacture of edible oils;

    (v) Improved communications.

46. In the course of the year more thrust areas will be identified with the object of using technology for improving productivity in industry and agriculture. In selected areas science and technology missions will endeavour to place India in the front rank of scientific activity.

47. A comprehensive agriculture policy will be formulated to promote an optimal cropping pattern, to improve water and soil management, to increase productivity of all crops to enhance the incomes of small and marginal farmers and to enlarge our hard-won self-sufficiency in foodgrains through production of oilseeds and pulses. A time-bound action plan will be drawn up to take the green revolution to the eastern region.

48. It is gratifying that a national consensus has emerged on treating water as a national resource. Government attach high priority to the evolution of a national water policy

which would optimise the use of water for agricultural, industrial and other social needs.

49. Government have carried out an indepth analysis of our family planning programmes. Profiting from the experience of the past, an effective strategy for family planning is being worked out and will be announced shortly.

50. The focus on anti-poverty programmes will be sharpened. A new programme, which builds on the success achieved by the revised 20-Point Programme, is being formulated and will be announced soon. It will bring together all the elements, policies and programmes for a major national effort to tackle the problem of mass poverty in all its manifestations, specifically the problems of Scheduled Castes and Scheduled Tribes. Programme for the social economic educational and cultural development for the Scheduled castes, Scheduled Tribes and other weaker sections will be vigorously implemented. The implementation of the 15-Point Programme for thus development of minorities, with special emphasis on increasing economic opportunities will be closely monitored.

51. To rapidly increase employment to stimulate development in backward areas and to enhance the efficiency by Indian industry to serve the masses better, a more comprehensive framework of industrial policy is required. Many changes have already been made in our industrial policy which now reflects the new thrust for modernisaton, absorption of new technologies and promotion of indigenous technologies. High cost and inefficient industry hurts the poor, because it absorbs resources that are needed to create new jobs for them. A vast increase in the production of goods and services for the masses in rural and urban areas is central to our strategy for he removal of poverty. This necessitates a fresh look at policies governing the scale of production, capacity utilisation, the role of indigenous technology, labour productivity, the detailed

regulatory mechanism, thus future perspectives for small and medium industry and the existing administrative and management apparatus. Industry must serve the large masses.

52. To meet the challenge of maintaining a viable balance of payments position, a major thrust for promotion of exports and tourism is called for. Any slackening of progress on this front will jeopardise our overall development strategy. Government will take new initiatives in this critical area.

53. It is imperative to effect changes in our administrative system to bring it in tune with the objective of growth with social justice. Management in Government has to be imbued with a new social outlook. It is not a question of imposing something from above. The impetus to reform must come from within. The national community as a whole must debate issues affecting the working of the administrative system. A concrete agenda of action will thus emerge for implementation. Our watchwords must be improvement of efficiency and enforcement of accountability.

54. To safeguard the health and vitality of our basic political institutions, changes will be needed in our electoral and other laws. Government will hold wide ranging consultations with the leaders of political parts with a view to formulating concrete proposals to ensure cleaner public life.

55. The vision of a mighty Indian will be realised only in the actual lives of men and women who have strength of character, tenacity of purpose and commitment to excellence. Government's strategy for human resource development aims at developing these qualities in our national life. The new education policy will be an integral part of this strategy. It will aim at the physical, intellectual, cultural and moral development of society in a harmonious fashion.

56. It is not enough to state objectives. A national mobilisation is essential to ensure that the resources required to implement the education policy are forthcoming. Even more important is the involvement of the youth, students, teachers, the intelligentsia, workers and farmers in giving a new direction to the national effort in this area. Education has to be transformed from an activity in the classroom to a social process for building the India of our dreams. It has to be integrated more closely both with production and our commitment to conserve and enhance our cultural heritage to make us proud to be Indian.

57. The years ahead are years of challenge. Government have take a number of measures to accelerate growth, to modernise the economy and to give new content to our programmes for achieving social justice. It is imperative to impart a sense of urgency to the task of implementation.

58. Much has been achieved this past year; and the hopes and expectations of our people are high. As their representatives, you have the onerous duty to fulfill their aspirations. Above all, people's representatives and organisations of all political persuasions should work together to strengthen the secular and democratic foundations of our society. The forces of violence and fanaticism have to be fought. The economic capabilities we have built up since independence have brought us to a point where determined and concerted efforts to take us forward and to remove poverty are feasible. Now is the time it ensure greater political cohesion so that the battle against poverty and backwardness can be won. I wish you all success in the tasks ahead.

Jai hind

Now let us examine how this address is covered by newsmen. The copy of this speech was made available to all correspondents when the President began to read it. Given is the report of the speech published in the Times of India, New Delhi:

The Address

Isolate terrorists, says President

The times of India news service

New Delhi, February 20. The President in his traditional address to the joint session of Parliament outlining the agenda of the government today pointed to the "inevitability of hard decisions without which forward movement will to be possible."

The address promised a comprehensive agriculture plan to promote an optimal cropping pattern, a more effective strategy for family planning and sharpening of the anti-poverty programme.

Technology missions will be mounted to ensure drinking water for all villages, eradication of illiteracy, immunisation, oil-seeds production and improved communications.

New initiatives will be made for promotion of exports and tourism with a view to maintaining a viable balance of payments position.

There will be wide ranging discussions to formulate concrete proposals for changing electoral and other laws. Administrative reforms calculated to improve efficiency and enforçe accountability will be introduced.

The joint session, with its usual ceremonial, was still shorn off the excitement and rapture which featured in the function only a year ago. Most non-Congress groups stayed away as announced leaving gaps in rows.

Not since 1973 have so many groups joined in such a boycott. Even Congress members did-not find any cause to cheer during the entire reading of the address. They thumped the desks only at the end as the president resumed his seat.

There was a moment so suspense when the President paused at the beginning. It was then noticed he was looking for his reading glass.

At the same time, the President' address made it plain that "hard decisions" were inevitable in the pursuit of self-reliance, economic independence and eradication of poverty.

"Sooner or later we have to face the realities of the situation. No one should be under the delusion that growth, social justice, price stability and self-reliance, Are achievable without efficiency, discipline and sharing of burdens," Mr. Zail Singh said.

The President began his speech with a reference to the "triumph of democratic process over terrorism in Punjab" and held that the supreme task now was to isolate those resorting to violence.

He reiterated the government commitment to the fullest implementation of the Punjab and Assam accord.

Communalism: He acknowledged that communalism continued to pose a serious threat to national unity. "It is being reinforced by religious fundamentalism and fanaticism. The reconstituted National Integration Council will have to act decisively and systematically to strengthen secularism," he said.

He recalled the policies and programmes of the government outlined in his address last year and claimed "these have been fulfilled in a substantial measure". He cited the anti-defection law, enunciation of a new national education policy, establishment of a central Ganga authority, creation of a wasteland development board as cases in point.

As for trends in economy, agriculture made steady progress with grain stocks going up nearly 15 per cent. He described the investment climate as buoyant. Power generation, fertilizer production, steel output have all gone up.

Tax collection: He said tax collections have been buoyant, belying gloomy forebodings. The collection of direct taxes is up by about 23 per cent compared to the corresponding period last year indirect tax collection has increased by 22 per cent which is the highest in the last decade.

Fact and Interpretation

Interpretative reporting, as the phrase suggests, combines facts with interpretation. It delves into reasons and meanings of a development. It is the interpretative reporter's task to give the information alongwith an interpretation of its significance. In doing so he uses his knowledge and experience to give the reader an idea of the background of an event and explain the consequences it could led to. Besides his own knowledge and research in the subject, he often has to rely on the opinions of specialists to do a good job.

In the USA, thus first important inputs to interpretative reporting was provided by World War-I. Curtis D. MacDongall writes in his book Interpretation Reporting that when the First World War broke out, most Americans were taken by surprise. They were utterly unable to explain its causes. This led to changes in the style of reporting. The result was that when in 1939 the Second World War began, an overwhelming majority of the Americans expected it or at least knew it was possible.

MacDongall says that a successful journalist should be more than a thoroughly trained journeyman. With his reading of history, economics, sociology, political science and other academic subjects, an interpretative reporter is aware of the fact that a news item is not an isolated incident, but an inevitable link to a chain of important events. An interpretative reporter cannot succeed if he is hampered by prejudices and stereotyped attitudes, which would bias his perception of human affairs.

Interpretative reporting thus goes behind the news, brings out the hidden significance of an event and separates truth from falsehood.

The biennial elections to the Rajya Sabha took place in July. The interpretative reporter would give the reader the breakup of the results and acquaint him with he impact they would have on the various political parties and on the composition of the upper House. He would, for instance, inform the reader that the Congress Party lost its majority in the Rajya Sabha, following the elections and that the Bharatiya Janata Party emerged as the main opposition, pushing the Janata Dal to third place. He will then explain the effect it would have on the working of the Rajya Sabha and on political party affairs generally.

The election of the new President of India took place in July. The interpretative reporter would not only convey the bare news of the victory of Dr. Shankar Dayal Sharma but analyse the reasons behind it and reflect on the consequences of his victory for the future of the Congress and opposition parties.

10

News Coverage

Deeply rooted in American journalism is the notion of the journalistic reporter. Reporters are trained in the journalistic method which gives them the tools and wherewithal to cover almost nay situation they may confront. Essentially journalistic training means knowing how to gather the news—how to sift through documents, do background research, interview sources, and so on-and how to write it using the usual news and feature forms employed by newspapers and broadcast outlets. In the midst of this seemingly routinised task, however, come all kinds of ethical issues (tactical decisions) including "checkbook journalism," fabrication of sources, false identification, lying. Some of these issues, being topical, come and go. But many are recurrent.

Various Methods

As with news-gathering methods and writing methods, competent reporters and editors are expected to handle tactical or ethical dilemmas. But do these problems require precise and differing tactics for different situations, or responses based on consistent and universal standards? While such questions are regarded as worthy of debate and discussion, most reporters believe that they have somehow internalized professional values, and competencies that will help them resolve any problems that may occur.

We come now to discuss a very real and important everyday convert of journalists: reportorial tactics, journalistic ways and means of gathering and writing stories. Should these tactics be situational and relative; should they be, as Professor Dennis will argue later, consistent and universal? we maintain that they are situational and relative; even more, we insist that they should or ought to be situational and relative. This position, of course, gets us into the realm of ethics.

Opposing my view, however, is a considerable theoretical tradition in this country, even if it fails to manifest itself in common practice. It is safe to say that an accepted truth in American journalism is that journalists should be consistent in their methods and their actions: that they should all subscribe to universal standards, and should, if they are responsible and "Professional," have a profound respect for predictable an consistent practice. Consistency and predictability, we are led to believe, are foundation stones of professionalism.

Unpredictability is associated, on the other hand, with amateurism, with inconsistency and relativity, which are seen by many as deleterious to journalism, harmful to the journalist, and frustrating to the audience. We would maintain just the opposite: that consistency in journalism—the journalist always using the same tactics and dealing with the elements of the story in the same way—makes for a deadly dull journalism, keeps the individual journalist from full self -realization, and prevents the audience from being exposed to the multifaceted, rich, and diversified aspects of similar (but different) stories.

Perhaps it is more comfortable and satisfying for journalists to have hard-and-fast rules as to tactics of reporting. Most printed codes of ethics fail because they present absolute and consistent rules or standards (or because they are so fuzzily written that they, in essence, say nothing meaningful). But, perhaps, the fact that they fail is paradoxically a good thing—for their failure assures that tactical situationalism and relativism will thrive in the absence of absolute ethical codes.

Ethics, of course, is very closely related to the subject of journalistic tactics. One cannot really separate them. Should I lie, either to get a story or while, telling the story to my readers or listeners? Should I reveal the source of certain statements or quotes which I use in my story? Should I give my readers or listeners all of the information which I have collected and verified?

These are just a sampling of questions that are both ethical and tactical. I might rephrase them thus:

- Should I ever lie as a reporter?
- Should I always reveal my sources? Or never reveal them?
- Should I tell the whole truth (as much of it as I have verified) to my audience?

Here we have introduced the possibility of tactical consistency of absoluteness. Such consistency has a notable appeal, If I am going to reveal the source in one case, why should I not reveal all sources? If I am going to lie in one case, why not in all? If I am going to withhold part of a story in one case, what would be wrong with withholding parts from any story?

Let me give an example of each of the two tactical positions.

1. Absolute: always identify victims of all crimes.
2. Relativistic identify victims in some crimes but not in others.

The first tactic (the absolute) does, indeed, simplify the journalist's decision making. If this tactic is accepted all that must be done is to identify all victims—juveniles, the mentally ill, rape victims, and so on. The second tactic (the situational) is more difficult because it forces the reporter to discriminate, to think. The reporter must see distinctions, think about consequences; is short, the reporter must decide that it is not only all right but good journalism to make exceptions—to have double standards, if you will.

The Difference

The reporter who is situational recognises that there is a difference, and a very important one, between a rape victim, for example, and a murder victim. Naming a rape victim can bring mental and emotional harm to the victim: naming a murder victim cannot harm the victim at all. The thinking reporter understands that the naming of a nine-year-old boy for shooting his father is quite different (in psychological, if not in legal, terms) than the naming of a 39 year-old adult for shooting his father. The reporter believes that it is his duty to make certain editorial decisions impinging on what is and is not published. After all, he reasons, editorial decision is the nature of journalism: selection is made to some degree-among facts in every story that is written.

Reporter must play this tactical game rather loosely: that he must not strive for consistency in tactics: that he must consider the specific situation or circumstance. In short, the reporter (to be effective and in many cases to be ethical, too) must specifically determine not to be absolute and consistent, but rather to be situational and relative.

Case: A reporter cannot subscribe to a tactic of always revealing his source—even if he does, indeed, maintain that the people have a right to know. In some cases, to reveal sources would be counter productive as well as unethical. For example, the journalist may get information from a source who would be in great physical danger if his identity were know. The reporter not only wants to keep the source operative for another day, but also to avoid endangering his life. In other, similar cases, the reporter might want to keep his source from losing his job.

Case: A reporter is writing a rape story. He has the name of the person arrested on suspicion of committing the rape. He also has ascertained the name of the rape victim. He decides not to use the victim's name, although he does not hesitate to use the suspected rapist's name, although he does not hesitate to use the suspected rapist's name. Inconsistent? Yes. He is, in effect, withholding information from the reader. At the same time he is providing the name of another person connected with the case—

even though this person may not have committed the rape. He feels no qualms about this procedure, even though it is inconsistent, reasoning that in this particular case it is tactically prudent to do as he has done. He justifies withholding verified information from the reader on ethical grounds—on a consideration of possible consequences to the victim.

The reporter in the above case is inconsistent. And he certainly does not subscribe to a "universal" tactic. A universal tactic in reporting would be: The reporter is obligated to report all the facts that he has, all that he has verified, and all that are pertinent to the story. In this rape story, certainly the name of the rape victim is pertinent to the story, as we will be told by our absolutist reporter. After all, the reporter has found out who the woman is: therefore should not the name be given—especially since the name of the rape suspect has been used?

Let us reply to the above question with another question: Why should the reporter use the victim's name? The reporter is wise to subscribe to relativistic tactics, to play the story the way he wants to play it in that particular case—after consideration of possible consequences. Why should the reporter always name names? Why should the reporter subscribe to the same tactics in every story? Straight jacketing oneself does not ,assure better reportage by the reporter. In fact, a relativistic or situational tactical program in reporting is what is called for. Consider the importance of the story. Consider each story. Consider consequences or implications for certain persons in the story (e.g., the rape victim in the example above).

The Realisation

It may well be that when a reporter considers the importance to the public of a particular story, there will be a realisation that "usual tactics must be modified or changed." The reporter may decide that the story is important enough, for example, to steal files (or at least to make copies of papers and return the files). The reporter may even feel that in a particular case there is justification to pose as someone else. It may be that the reporter will decide to eavesdrop on conversations and report what he overhears, using or perhaps not using the names of those who said the things he is divulging. The reporter might decide to "bug" a room or wiretap a telephone in order to get some very important enough, for example, to steal files (or at least to make copies of papers and return the files). The reporter may even feel that in a particular case there is justification to pose as someone else. It may be that the reporter will decide to eavesdrop on conversations and report what he overhears, using or perhaps not using the names of those who said the things he is divulging. The reporter might decide to "bug" a room or wiretap a telephone in order to get some very important information which he believes the public should know. The reporter might decide, in order to get some much-needed information, to tell a source that he knows certain things or that he has heard certain things from someone else (which he really has not heard) in order to get a response. The reporter might decide to make up quotes and drop them into a story so as to prompt someone connected with the story-someone he wants to make a statement—to come forward to refute or to enlarge on the "speculated" or fabricated quotes.

Now, we can justify these tactics by resorting to the "ends justifies the means" argument. We can say that we are thinking of the public, and the public's right to know. How can the public know unless we break through the barriers of secrecy with our situational tactics? So, journalists must resort to these tactics from time to time in order to do their job, to live up to their responsibilities.

We can justify relativistic or situation tactics by contending that they are more ethical; we can also justify them instrumentally or pragmatically by saying that they are needed to accomplish our ends. If we need a further rationale for inconsistency in journalistic practice, we can always fall back on press freedom in its editorial self-determinism sense. In other words, it is the right of a newspaper reporter to be inconsistent; if he wants to use a victim's name—(or any name) in one story and not in another, that is his right.

If the reporter wants to reveal the source of a quote in one story and not in another, that is his right. In fact, if the reporter wants to reveal the source of a quotation in one part of a story and make all the other quotes in the same story anonymous, that is his right.

After all, why should the reporter be consistent or use universal tactics? Even though there may not be any evidential basis for the belief, the reporter can contend that journalistic consistency is the "hobgoblin of little minds." Journalism, it seems to the relativistic reporter, is riddled with instances of inconsistency, most of which are considered valid journalistic practices. Here are just a few:

Using the lead in one story, but not in another.

Using indirect quotations only in one story, and using direct quotations or a mixture of indirect and direct quotes in another.

Giving the addresses of persons in one story, and omitting addresses in another.

Going directly to persons for information in one story, while going to someone for second hand information in another or using old information form the files.

Giving certain personal data (such as age, race, occupation) about some persons in some stories but not about other persons.

A list of inconsistent tactics could be extended easily. What is the alternative to these inconsistent tactics? Consistent and universal tactics, we are told. The intelligent and dedicated reporter can only scoff at such an alternative, seeing it as a definite voluntary placement of the reporter in a straight jacket with little chance to achieve a primary goal of journalism: obtaining the story.

The preceding discussion of news-gathering tactics defends the status quo in American journalism. Reporters do use relative and situational methods when gathering the news. However, there are many agreed-upon general standards and practices. These practical tactics for getting information are undergirded by ethical judgements that are self-contained, based mainly on the immediate situation rather than considered against the backdrop of long experience with similar cases. There is more than a slight temptation in reinvent the wheel with each ethical dilemma that arises.

That, in our opinion, summarizes one of the most serious problems in journalistic practice today—a thoughtless, seat-of-the-pants approach to reporting that eschews planning and thinking. It is the journalism of intuition. "Do what intuition tells you; apply common sense to the situation are accepted axiom. On the face of it this doesn't sound so bad, but consider the following:

A reporter for NBC News is asked how he knows when he has enough information to "go" with a story. "How," he was asked, "can" you be sure that your information is complete, that you are not missing major sources that would turn a story completely around, maybe with a different interpretation altogether?" The reporter replied, "You just know. There is, "he added, "no answer, things just click into place an it seems right." An editor for a metropolitan daily newspaper is asked by a Harvard Law professor how far he would go to get a story. "Would you lie? Would you steal?" Would you disguise your identity?" The editor thought for a moment, then responded, "Yes, under some conditions, I'd probably do all of those things even though I might personally find some of them reprehensible." The professor wanted to know, "How" do you make your decision; on what theory do you base your actions?" And the editor answered, "I have no theory, I just do what I think is right."

We would not accept this kind of thinking from other professional persons (say, doctors, lawyers, or architects) whom we expect to have standards, codes and a systematic basis for their decisions. We do accept it from journalists perhaps because we have no choice or because they convince us that news is unpredictable, a matter of timing that requires on-the-spot decisions governed solely by the facts of a particular situation. "You simply can't quantify these things," goes the incantation.

There is a prevailing myth in American journalism that planning news coverage runs counter to freedom of the press.

Planning is thought to be dull and routine, not spontaneous and timely. It is further said that writers are creative persons who, if left to their own devices, will produce a better kind of journalism. And God forbid that journalists should have hypotheses. A hypothesis, which is an assumption that becomes an organizing principle, is thought to encourage bias and run counter to journalistic objectivity. There is also a prevailing view among many journalists that news really defies definition.

Operational Rule

This kind of "every day a new beginning" theme in many newsrooms, the operational rule of the status quo, needs rethinking. While it certainly is not possible to always predict with scientific certainty what will happen on a given day, journalism is really much more routinized than most of its practitioners know or will admit. They may not know it because American journalism is insulated and parochial. Many journalists have little work-experience outside of their present assignments; few belong to national organizations where they come into contact with their journalists; few subscribe to professional publications or make any effort to keep up with the literature of their systematic research that gives us data about patterns and practices across many journalistic organisations. Individual journalists may know their own organization intimately, but they often have little knowledge about the field generally. This situation is not unusual because many professionals are so busy doing their jobs that they have little time to think about them or to make comparisons with their colleagues in other places. For a field that is supposed to demand so much creative calibration, journalism is remarkably predictable, routinized, even stodgy. Send any five reporters to cover a city council story and you can predict with almost considerably certainty what they will write. Why? Because the coverage of public affairs, in particular, has been standardized. There is much agreement about the form and format of stories, about what essential facts should be included, and about what most editors will accept. Reporters know what is expected of them and generally they do it.

Of course there are stores that are more complex than routine meetings, but even with these the traditional methods of news gathering pretty much dictate what will eventually appear. And if this were not enough, we have "rewards and punishments" built into the journalistic system to guarantee conformity. At a positive level there are prizes (such as the Pulitzers) that honour imaginative work within the framework of traditional journalism. Journalism schools help out by promoting conventional approaches to news gathering through courses and books.

There is in American journalism a serious perceptual conflict. Journalist on the one hand believe that their work is unpredictable, situational, and relative. Communications researchers say this is not true, that reporting is not nearly as uncertain as practitioners think. In a sense both are right. While there may be great similarity in work patterns and output from day to day, journalist still think tat there is little formal guidance and there is considerable latitude for individual decision making. They say that with regard to ethics, they live in a conceptual thicket which requires instant decisions of convenience if not conviction. They tend to justify what they do without worrying whether their choices about revealing sources or lying are consistent with what they did before. Scholars, on the other hand, because they are trained to look for patterns of organizational and individual activity, can see a method whether haphazard or well-though-out-in journalistic work just as they do in firefighters or farmers. The way the news paper or broadcast station is organized, the selecting of personnel, their training and socialization, all have a hand in shaping the news.

Interestingly enough, it is the once-similar (and now quite different) practices of journalists and social scientist that explain some of this discrepancy. As Philip Meyer, well known for his work in precision journalism and now a professor at the University of North Carolina, has written.

> "Social scientist used to be more like journalist. They relied on observation and interpretation, collecting

> the observations from public records, from interviews, from direct participation, and then spinning out the interpretations. Like many journalist they cheerfully accepted the American folk wisdom ... that anyone with "a little common sense and a few facts can come up at once with the correct answer on any subject".

But something changed. First with the development of inferential statistics and later with the advent of computers, social scientist no longer worked like journalist. Instead they used powerful quantitative tools to deal with unwieldy and massive data. Now, says Meyer, social scientist are doing "what we journalists like to think we are best at: finding fact, inferring causes, pointing to ways to correct social problems, and evaluating the effects of such correction". In short, he charge that journalism is being left behind because it lacks a systematic approach to news gathering.

The point of course, is that with an affective strategy for gathering information which systematically considers possible sources and mines them with care brings a far richer yield than old-fashioned, impressionistic reporting. It is now possible to determine how much information from what sources will be adequate-when enough information has been assembled and when writing can begin. This statement does not mean that journalists should be exactly like social scientist. Press people have greater time pressures and are more concerned about immediacy.

It is one thing to develop a strategy for news coverage that list the tactics to be employed, another to actually do it. No situation is ever perfect and no prearranged rules ever work in all situations. For this reason some journalist throw out the rules altogether and make expedient decisions. It is threatening to ask: Is the information complete? Have I mined all possible (and reasonable) sources? Is the evidence strong enough to warrant the conclusion actual or implied? Are various interpretations and leaps in logic justified?" If such questions could have been avoided in the past, such is no longer the case.

Systematic Way

Systematic newsgathering tactics are not simply a theory for journalism schools to trumpet, but something being demanded by the rests of society. One of the most compelling calls comes in the courts. Frequently in libel suits news organizations must offer evidence that the story is not marred by "knowing falsehood" or "reckless disregard" of the truth. How is this honesty of intent determined?" By showing that reasonable efforts, consistent with national news-gathering standards, were employed. If they were not and the paper admits it, there is the possibility for a whopping libel judgement. Sloppy reporting is expensive. Of equal or grater importance is the fear that journalist will not have the credibility they need and deserve unless their methods are respected by the audience.

People who argue against ethical standards or moral imperatives in news-gathering tactics usually suggest that each case is so different that rules will strait jacket the reporter. They add that general guidelines are so vague that they are meaningless. I disagree. We need a theory of journalistic ethics, a fundamental framework for reporters to base their decisions on. This framework requires general understanding about ethical behaviour, whether in reporting or everyday life. It means having a clear notion about how specific journalistic dilemmas ought to be handled. This general ethical understanding does not mean that rules cannot be modified or tempered to meet particular situations. We need a thoughtful policy that serves as a conscience for individual journalist and their organizations. Such a policy should spell out standards of conduct for information gathering. One minimal standard, we think, is that journalist should obey the law. In most instances this principle means they should not lie, steal, or cheat. They should not wiretap or break into places not otherwise open to them. In rare instances, a right-thinking reporter may want to be civilly disobedient, to deliberately break the law as a matter of principle because it will lead to a greater social good. In all instances where ethical questions arise, if there is not a clear answer, reporters should consider alternatives, not simply rush to judgement with the easiest solution. If the decision runs counter to conventional wisdom and standard ethical codes, there ought to be a clean and compelling rationale for making it.

In most instances it is regarded as ethical to reveal one's sources in a news story. This strengthens the credibility of the story and ties information to attributed sources. If revealing names will put sources in great danger or make them reluctant to talk, a different decision may be appropriate. If it is determined that a source benefit, clearly agreed upon and understood by the reporter's supervising editors os that they can defend the actin later. And the reporter, if sub-ponaed by the courts, must be ready to go to jail if it comes to that.

The problem today is that many reporters do not have solid ethical training and do not have the kind of foundation necessary of ethical decision making. Again, constancy is terribly important both for accountability to one's bosses and perhaps ultimately to the courts.

Journalists have gotten in trouble for being inconsistent in recent years with regard to fair-trial-freepress codes. The press was a signatory to such codes, which list tactical guidelines for covering criminal proceedings from initial investigations of crimes to court judgements. Reporters generally agree to withhold some information in the interest of not prejudicing a jury and assuring the defendant of a fair trail. This is a social compact between the press and the legal system. When the press violates this agreement or decides onto to abide by a particular provision of the code, there ought to be a good reason (beyond curiosity seeking or pandering) to justify its action. If not, reporters and editors may have to answer in court. This happened in 1981 in a notable case in the state of Washington where a newspaper was held accountable for violation of the fair-trail-free-press code.

And this example indicates, it is always possible to substitute a "greater social good" argument or a "humanitarian" argument to explain why an individual journalist or publication may deviate from an accepted rule. We believe such exceptions should be justified on the basis of devotion to the public interest, rather than petty or self-serving reasons.

Similarly it is quite appropriate to reconsider rules the are regarded as journalistic conventions or articles of faith. Printing he names of persons accused of rape has been mentioned. This practice would seem potentially unfair both to victim and accused. The press usually prints the name of the accused. But is it really necessary? The reasons for printing names has to do with keeping the courts open so the they do not become secret tribunal. Thus, we know who is being tried, for what, and why. But as long as the courts are open to the press and to spectators, why not defer printing this material until the trail is over? No great social good is done by heralding names of victims or accused persons in advance of trial with some obscure exceptions.

Some newspapers have abandoned the practice of printing names of persons in civil litigation cases where the truly important story is the effect of the decision on similar cases in the future. If one person is suing another to establish a legal principle and if revealing names would prove embarrassing, it may serve no purpose to do so. Some wise editors are changing their policy in this area.

Consistent and universal standards of reporting with necessary escape clauses for unusual or unique situations will do much to enhance journalistic practice in America. Such standards, if widely known land the press can virtually guarantee this with adequate coverage) will do much to strengthen public confidence in the fairness and completeness of reporting. It will also have real advantages of individual newspapers and broadcast stations in an increasingly litigious society. Haphazard, thoughtless conduct that meets no standard but blunders along willy-nilly is neither appreciated nor rewarded by the courts. One of the most effective ways to put the journalistic house in order is to establish coherent policies and consistent practices. This the essence of professionalism performance and distinguishes competent from rank amateurism.

11

News Sources

Some of the best stories appear to come from nowhere — out-of-the-blue accidents, resignations, and catastrophes so startling that the essential facts alone are enough to make major headlines. Journalists can do nothing to influence whether such stories exist; all we can do is produce the best-researched and written versions of them. A lot of other good stories, however, depend on journalists for their very existence — stories which start life as lesser incidents but are transformed into the startling by the discovery of some hitherto hidden aspect; and true off-diary stories, unknown to the public until a journalist discovers and reports them.

There is nothing accidental about this process. Good stories like these do not come out of the blue; they come from successful journalists knowing where to look and doing certain things right — which is why they come up with far more of such stories than ordinary journalists. The apparent mystery of where good stories come from is not a riddle at all. It is a matter of having solid working practices, plus knowing where to look — and where not to.

Best Reporter

The best reporters get the best stories because they have sharp news instincts and they know where to look, who to talk to and what to ask. The details of these are covered in the next three chapters on sources, research and questioning. But there are other, perhaps less obvious but just as vital, reporters' habits which consistently produce good stories.

Determination is perhaps the biggest difference between the ordinary and the good reporter. A classic example, all the more relevant for its everyday nature, is the story found by Derek Lambert, then on a trial with the *Daily Mirror*. It seemed at first like a routine murder case: a Polish man had been found stabbed in the basement of a seedy lodging house in Manchester and Lambert was sent out to find out what he could. It did not look very promising. The neighbours knew (or were saying) nothing, the policeman guarding the murder scene would not speak and, when Lambert went to the police station, he was told they could not add to their earlier brief statement.

It is at this point that the ordinary reporter would have headed back to the office and reported there was nothing much in the story; and indeed that is what Lambert's rivals did. He, however, was not an ordinary reporter. He hung around, determined to get more, hoping to grab a few words with an off-duty policeman. After a while he saw detectives emerge and get into a car. Hoping they were working on the murder, he returned to the scene. There he saw two men in suits knocking on doors. He introduced himself to the detectives and got talking about the case. The dead man, they told him, was a police informer who had been run over by a car and then stabbed. Lambert had his story and soon he was dictating it to his office. It began: 'Police were last night investigating the mystery of the man who was murdered twice.' It made front page lead and secured a job on the *Mirror* for Lambert.

The Punctuality

The best reporters do not, unless they cannot possibly help it, arrive late and breathless to cover an event. They tend to arrive early and, if they have time, hang around afterwards. By doing this they get a feel for the event and its characters hear things, observe useful detail, speak to people and ask questions. Whatever the event — whether it is a court case, public inquiry, political meeting, campaign launch, release of a report — the best stories are often found not in the public part of the event, but in the time spent before and after chatting to those involved. After all, most non-journalists have no idea what makes a good news story. It is only when they are talking informally before or after a meeting, interview or whatever, that they may mention something which is a far better story than the one you originally came for.

Role of Luck

To be lucky, you have to put yourself in the position where good fortune can occur. This is partly a matter of persistence, partly an instinct for where the happening part of the story is and, especially on the big stories where there are many reporters on the same case, partly a matter of not following the mob. In 1981, the Pope was shot and journalists from all round the world were sent to Rome. Among them was John Edwards of the *Daily Mail.* Like quite a few others, he arrived in Rome at 11.30 p.m., but instead of going straight to his hotel like the herd, he wanted to get on the story straight away. But where to go? St. Peter's Square was full of nuns praying for the Pope's recovery. The police were not talking beyond a terse statement and so Edwards thought he would go to where the story was still developing-the hospital where the Pope was fighting for his life.

Amazingly, when Edwards arrived at the hospital at one in the morning, he found that he was the only reporter there. More to the point, there were no police to bar his way. So in he went and after walking around for a while he found a waiting room where he could sit and watch and judge the situation. He dozed a little and then, at around 6 a.m. there was the sound of doors opening, footsteps and voices. He saw six surgeons, their gowns covered in blood, walk into the waiting room and go on to a balcony. As they smoked and took in the early morning air, Edwards could see they were smiling. He approached them and got lucky. These people had saved the Pope's life and several spoke good English. They were pleased with their night's work and talked freely. They even drew pictures in his notebook of the incisions they made and described each step of the operation in detail. Not surprisingly, Edwards later described this as the best story he ever wrote.

Some of what the inexperienced thinks of as the mysterious instincts of good reporters are, in fact, quite straightforward calculations. One of the key ones used by successful journalists is the train of thought that runs something like: what is the best this story can be? If I considered all the possible scenarios and facts, what would be the strongest intro I could write? This calculation is often just as useful in telling you which stories are not worth pursuing, as revealing the ones that are.

Regular/ Relationship

Good reporters keep up a regular relationship with contacts and do not just ring when they need them. They cultivate them by going to meetings they would otherwise not attend and occasionally pass information to them. The upshot is that the contacts remember them when they have a good story. Less regular contacts also remember the reporters whose work has proved fair and accurate. And a source that trusts a reporter can assist in all kinds of ways. A governing party politician whom I knew was instrumental in smuggling into Iraq one of the *Observer's* top foreign news experts so he could investigate reports the paper was receiving about atrocities committed against the Marsh Arabs by Saddam Hussein. Without my relationship with that politician, her trust in the sincerity of my paper, her contacts with rebel groups in Iraq and their bravery, we would not have been able to get inside southern Iraq and the world would not have heard about these atrocities. The reporter, Shyam Bhatia, won foreign correspondent of the year for his work.

Permanent Interest

People can sense, just as you can, when a journalist is merely interested in them for the sake of a one-off story. Good reporters have a sincere interest in issues and the people involved in them — and it shows. They profit from this. In 1968 after Soviet dissident Aleksandr Ginsberg was jailed following a closed trial, his wife Ludmilla called a press conference. The night before it was due to be held, all the nearly 100 Western correspondents in Moscow were contacted by the government press department and warned that 'severe measures' would be taken against those who attended. The following day only four had the courage to go to the Ginsberg apartment, among them Raymond Anderson of the *New York Times.* A few months later, in July 1968, Anderson was given a document by a friend, who had received it from Andrei Amelrik, a dissident historian. Inside the package was the now-famous essay challenging the Soviet system written by Dr. Andrei Sakharov. After a few more adventures and inquiries, Anderson established that the document was genuine and he sent it out secretly for it to make headlines around the world.

The phrase 'follow-up' is not a terribly glorious one to many reporters, carrying connotations of being asked to tidy up a few loose ends or dress up some hand-me-down story into something that appears fresh. As applied by a lot of papers, this is true. But there are also many stories which when followed up, bear richer fruit than the original. Good reporters sense these by thinking what is — or may be — missing from the whole story. An old lady, for example, once died unnoticed in her home in the north of England. The coroner, remarking on the contrast between the visible signs of this (milk bottles on the doorstep, etc.) and the indifference of her neighbours, said that the old lady might still be alive it' neighbours had paid attention to her or taken the trouble to visit.

The *Daily Mirror* sent Derek Lambert to investigate for a possible piece on the woman who died ignored by her comfortable neighbours. He went from house to house, collecting a few scraps of information, but mostly finding blank looks and shrugs of the shoulders. Finally he came to one neighbour who talked a little. Just as Lambert was turning to go, the man said, 'Mind you, that coroner's got a right cheek, hasn't he?' Lambert asked him what he meant (always a good question). 'Well,' said the man, 'the coroner only lived up the road.' He had been one of the woman's neighbours he was criticising. Lambert knew then he had a good story — the tale of the coroner who criticised himself in court, but didn't realise.

Comedians and good journalists have a lot in common. Both find productive ideas by turning things on their head, by inverting a situation (or a phrase) in order to examine it and so deliver the unexpected. Successful reporters get a lot of good ideas by looking at things from an unusual perspective. When John Tierney of the *New York Times,* for example, was sent to do a piece on women who sign up for self-defence classes (a pretty tired idea at best), he did an article not on the women, but on the 'model mugger'- the pretend rapist in a padded suit who took all the punches and kicks.

There are, however, limits to reporters' inventiveness. There was, for instance, once a reporter called Maurice Fagence on the *Daily Mail.* Never the best time-keeper, he was so spectacularly late one day that the newsdesk punished him by sending him to cover a story they assumed would be a long trip for very little copy — a pigeon show in Birmingham. Not to be outdone, Fagence smuggled into the show a cat under his coat so he could write an intro about who put the cat among the pigeons.

Making connections is what good reporters do when they take a couple of hitherto unassociated stories, or facts, and make a link. This is what Willi Gutman, a newspaper librarian who fled Hitler's Germany, called 'scoop by interpretation'. It is one of the reasons why those who criticise newspapers for 'feeding off each other' are wrong. Many good stories come from a journalist spotting a small item in another newspaper, investigating and finding there is a lot more to the subject or issue than the first paper thought. And many important stories have only been fully revealed because individual papers working on them independently found different pieces of the jigsaw which *collectively* completed the picture. The investigation of the Watergate scandal in America in 19 73-74, which led to the resignation of President Nixon, was a classic case of this.

It is difficult to stifle a yawn when you see the cover of most official reports. But in some of them, perhaps buried away on page 94, is the real story. It may even have been put there deliberately, in the confident expectation that most journalists cannot be bothered to read that far, or that closely. Too many reporters, when confronted with a thick report, will look only at the summary pages. If you have time, read the whole report; if not, then look in the places most likely to produce good material — the submissions from criticised parties, the evidence given by the aggrieved and the case histories section.

Reading reports thoroughly can repay enormous dividends. In the early 1990s, Eileen Welsome, neighbourhood news reporter for the *Albuquerque Tribune, was* leafing through a declassified document about radiation experiments on animals towards the end of World War II. In an obscure footnote at the bottom of one page, she found a reference to 18 people who had been injected with doses of plutonium so that scientists could study the effects of radiation on the body. She began researching and in November 1993 published a three-part series. A month later the US government called a press conference and admitted all. President Clinton ordered an inquiry and lawsuits from victims families came in. The following year, Welsome won a Pulitzer Prize.

The Objectivity

The most successful intelligence agent I have ever met was a big, fat, jolly, apparently simple-minded soul whose cover was that of a professional wrestler. Large amounts of foreign travel aside, he was almost the last person you would expect to be a spy; which was why I had no idea of what he really did until after his death. I thought he had taken one too many sizeable bangs on the head.

Successful journalists know that judging people by their appearances and occupations is a good way to make mistakes and miss stories. Some of the least reliable sources look the tiniest, and some of the best ones look like bums. This does not mean you have to spend hours with the parade of lunatics, paranoids and obsessives who regularly plague newspapers with their tales of being followed, transported to outer space or persecuted by the government. But it does mean making a judgement based on what they say, rather than on how they look. After all, a journalist at the *Daily Mail* in the early 1930s once returned to the newsdesk from attending to a shabbily dressed visitor in the lobby. He said the man was an obvious lunatic who was muttering something about transmitting moving pictures. Three days later several rival papers reported the invention of television by a man called John Logie Baird — the name, of course, of the 'shabbily dressed lunatic' in the lobby.

This is hardly a devastating insight, but it is commonly overlooked. The quality and range of ideas is one of the things that makes the difference between news pages crackling with interest and those that are so limp and wet you could not use them to start a fire. You should therefore have a file where you can jot down ideas, plus cuttings from papers and magazines that might make a future story. If nothing else, it should encourage that other habit of successful journalists — reading a lot of newspapers and magazines. Apart from keeping them up to date and in touch with what the opposition is doing, it also maintains their general knowledge — something else they are conspicuous for.

Other Contacts

Most journalists think too narrowly when it comes to sources. But if you look at national quality newspapers, which have the pick of all that is available on any day, you find that the sources of their stories are not nearly as conventional as people imagine. The *Independent*, for instance, would have in a typical issue 3 3-3 8 domestic news stories, not including briefs or Parliamentary reports. An issue in December 1999 had 36 stories, sourced as follows:

Government depts or agencies	10
Off diary (contacts, observation)	5
Courts, inquiries	5
Universities	3
Pressure groups unions, etc.	3
Political sources	3
Specialist press	2
Commercial companies	2
Consumer magazines	1
International organisations	1
Police	1

Other issues of the paper show slightly more police and political stories and fewer from courts, but otherwise these proportions do not vary markedly. This means that half the stories consistently come from unofficial sources. If the government stories include only those which are official announcements, as opposed to stories obtained by personal contacts, then unofficial sources regularly account for something like 60 per cent of stories. This shows the importance of building up contacts and, in particular, of opening up your mind to unconventional sources and subjects. Here are some suggestions of the less obvious places where good stories can be found.

Whether it is pioneering medical research, a study of your region's wildlife or an investigation into why men wear certain colour ties, academics undertake studies that no novelist would dare make up. Some of them are highly specialised, but a lot will have general interest. For example, a space research institute outside Moscow has been studying for years what personality types are truly compatible so that the people they put together in the Mir space station will not begin fighting as soon as they leave Earth. Written for the general reader and applied to how people get on inside homes and offices, rather than a space ship, you would have a story that should interest anyone.

If you have the expertise to read specialist journals, they can be a lush hunting ground for off-diary stories. Your country's underground press is also worth reading regularly. The reporting in such publications is often unbalanced, but it is often the product of contact with unconventional sources. Some of the best stories first surface in such papers.

In 1998, Maciej Zaremba, a Polish-born journalist writing for Sweden's largest paper Dagens Nyheter, uncovered the full story of how Sweden had forcibly sterilised more than 60,000 women between 1935 and 1976. Working with a researcher called Maija Runcis, who had access to the archives of the State Medical Board, Zaremba discovered that, contrary to common belief in Sweden, the sterilisations had never been voluntary. Girls who fell behind at school, were labelled promiscuous or had otherwise fallen foul of authority, were defined as 'undesirable', removed from their homes by state officials, placed in institutions and were only released if they would be sterilised. The story was published all over the world and the Swedish Government set up an inquiry. And where did Zaremba first stumble upon this story? In an obscure book written by two Swedes but published only in the US.

These are not magazines written for an academic audience, but for ordinary people with special interests. Reading such magazines allows you into worlds (like that of the treasure hunter or vegetable grower) which you would never normally enter. And in almost every issue you can be sure that there is a story which, properly handled, would be of interest to the newspaper reader. A computer magazine might have a story about a new computer virus that is threatening commercial data systems; a car magazine one about a new auto-theft racket; a sex newspaper might have an advertisement that leads you to investigate child pornography; a gardening magazine a story about how used bank notes are being pulped to make fertiliser.

There are thousands and thousands of international organisations pumping out reports, statistics and data, holding conferences and seminars and staffed by experts — yet they never hear from a general newspaper reporter from one year to the next. This is a great shame. Organisations like these are one of the great untapped sources of stories. And not just stories about global problems. Much of their work involves studying or working on specific problems in particular countries. Go to a library, look up the organisations covering your area of interest and make contact or visit their website. The United Nations, for example, has bodies dealing with women, disasters, children's welfare, health, disarmament, training, economic development, human settlement, the environment, oceans, trade, refugees, peace-keeping forces, population, food aid, food growing, atomic energy, civil aviation, labour, shipping, telecommunications, industry, copyright, meteorology-indeed almost every subject under the sun.

Journalists who do not read the classified advertisements in any paper they can get their hands on are missing one of the best sources of human interest stories there is. After all, this is where the parts of the human race that are not journalists often communicate with strangers. For instance, on 2 May 1962, the following ad was placed in the San Francisco Examiner's classified columns by a Mrs Gladys Kidd:

I don't want my husband to die in the gas chamber for a crime he did not commit. I will therefore offer my services for 10 years as a cook, maid or house-keeper to any leading attorney who will defend him and bring about his vindication.

One of the city's most famous lawyers, Vincent Hallinan, saw the ad and contacted Mrs Kidd. Her husband was about to be tried for the murder of an old antique dealer after his finger-prints had been found on an ornate bloodstained sword in the victim's shop. During the trial, Hallinan proved that the dealer had not been killed by the sword. He also established that Kidd's prints and blood found on the sword got there because he once fooled around with the sword while out shopping with a friend. The jury found Kidd not guilty and Hallinan refused Mrs Kidd's offer of servitude. There are countless lesser examples of stories found in the classified sections: from the woman in Russia so poor that she was trying to sell her son to the exotic animal smuggling ring that was advertising rare pets, and so on.

These are an endless source of stories. The anniversaries can be simple births and deaths, major historic events or more unusual, social anniversaries like inventions of household objects, or other landmarks of everyday life. Nor do anniversary stories have to be light. Researching the five-year anniversary of a major news story for a background piece can often turn up some buried report, neglected group or something else that makes a good hard story.

Other productive areas are: specialist branches of police and other emergency services (especially those dealing with fraud, computer crime, art and antiques); obscure government bodies (such as ones dealing with public access to landed estates in return for lowered death duties, managing the assets of the mentally infirm, etc.); investments promising very high yields; any get-rich-quick or 'can't fail' business scheme; loan companies (especially those which target the less well-off); newly released public documents; and pressure groups or self-help groups operating in unusual areas. You come across many more if you keep your eyes and ears open. Look for the incongruous, the things which don't seem to add up, the things which need explanation. My first major story was about homeless people on the streets of the city in Britain where I lived. It was the result of noticing them late at night in doorways and parks and asking the basic reporter's questions: who? why? etc. The series I wrote led to a great number of people approaching me with stories and to my news editor giving me better assignments.

Insignificant Items

If successful reporters have a trick, apart from hard work, it is knowing the stories that are unlikely to be good ones and staying well away from them. They know that good stories don't, except in very rare circumstances, come from commercial press releases, routine press conferences, most of the mail that arrives at your news desk, or from people who call you up and say 'Have I got a story for you!' Neither do they come from surveys with small samples, surveys that dress the blindingly obvious in the language of science, surveys purporting to identify new social groups, stories that are purely about what people are saying, or from events concocted purely for the benefit of journalists, like photo-calls, press launches or stunts. And, above all, they know they don't generally come from row stories.

Row Stories : These have become the great contagion and con-trick of journalism. Legitimate when reporting serious criticisms of official action, genuine or sharp disagreements among those who can influence an outcome, row stories are more commonly seen in a form where the 'row' is nothing much more than a figment of the reporter's desire for some phoney drama. Something happens, or something is said, and a reporter phones some known and convicted loudmouth who obliges by condemning, deploring or calling for an inquiry. This journalistic equivalent of shooting fish in a barrel is then topped off with a headline about 'Row over...', Fury over...', or even 'Furore as...'. The result is stories that are blindingly predictable and have reality only within the pages of a newspaper.

Another common form is when a 'row' angle is written onto a story in an attempt to 'freshen up' something that has happened or been announced earlier in the news cycle. The predictably opposed are asked for a comment and their disapproval is then reported in the intro as 'A furious row last night erupted over...'.

This, quite apart from the hyped-up language of 'erupted' and 'furious row', is a complete non-angle. As an intro, it weakens the story rather than strengthens it.

The ultimate test of 'row' stories is, however, this: have you ever heard readers discussing a 'row' story in the terms as presented in the paper? There are two kinds of journalism. There is the journalism that is trying to tell the truth and there's the journalism that treats the news as showbusiness.

Various Approaches

Medieval Christians believed that those condemned to hell had to endure the eternal torture of alternating extremes of intense heat and terrible cold. This bothered theologians greatly. If that was so, they puzzled, would the wicked and the damned have one exquisite moment as cold turned to heat? Would their thawing souls have a fleeting moment of ecstasy? And where, they wanted to know, was the punishment in that?

Similar hair-splitting debates go on every time someone tries to define the difference between a news story and a feature. A lot of journalists think that news reporting is always arid, dry and impersonal, whereas features are rather jolly free-form things. They see the reporter as an earnest collector of 'facts' and the feature *writer* as someone who wanders around thinking of fine phrases which save them the trouble of doing much research.

At the extremes - say a report of 68 people dying in a fire on one hand and a gardening advice column on the other - there is not much danger of confusing the two. One is a news report, the other plainly a feature. But in between these two extremes are the vast majority of stories and at what point does a news story become a feature? When it reaches a certain length? When it lacks a certain amount of facts? When it deals with certain subjects like life-styles and relationships that really interest people? When it ceases to deliver fresh information in stories with news pyramid structures?

The truth is that trying to make distinctions between news and features does not get us very far. In fact, it is positively dangerous. It produces narrow thinking which can restrict coverage of news to conventional subjects and puts writing it into the unimaginative straitjacket of a formula. With features, it encourages the insidious idea that normal standards of precision and thorough research don't apply and that they can be a kind of low-fact product, instantly recognisable from their lack of capital letters. The opposite, of course, is the case. Most news pages could benefit from a greater sense of adventure and a more flexible approach to stories. Similarly, most features sections cry out for sharper research and less indulgent writing. There is no great divide between news and features. Best to think of it all as reporting.

Having jettisoned this rigid thinking, you can then appreciate that there are an almost infinite number of ways to write, supplement or follow-up a story (whether it appears on news or feature pages). Some of these approaches are relatively common, some are not. Some make sidebars or panels, some separate pieces paired with the main report, others can appear on comment, feature or analysis pages. All of them, if used judiciously, can bring variety and life to pages.

Colour Piece : An article describing a scene or event which throws light on some of the themes or people involved in the main story. Often regarded by writers as convenient camouflage for their own opinions, colour pieces are at their best when precisely descriptive. The most telling often alight on some detail and use that to symbolise the wider situation. The effect of this, however, can be destroyed by making heavy-handed analogies. The best approach is usually to provide the detail and trust the reader to see its significance.

Fly on the Wall : The journalist as observer, pure and simple, asking no questions; merely watching, recording and noting the behaviour, speech and interactions of the subject(s). The published report will probably use a lot of quotes and verbatim exchanges between people. This type of piece is commonly written on some place or institution which is exotic to your readership.

Behind the Scenes : This has similarities to the above but differs in being an explanatory, rather than observational, piece. It should describe how something works. This approach is often best on subjects that readers take for granted, but in reality know very little about. How, for instance, does a national railway timetable get planned? How does a credit-rating agency work?

In Disguise : The journalist assumes the role of the subject to see how people react. This can be done for two reasons. First, for fun, such as dressing up as a priest to see how this affects people's behaviour (a London journalist recently did this, and in addition to just wandering around in his disguise, also went into bars and nightclubs). Second, it can be done for a serious purpose, such as taking the role of a homeless person to see what treatment is available. Several years ago a reporter roamed America posing as an HIV sufferer to write about people's reactions when he slipped this 'fact' into conversations.

Profile : Normally a study of a personality at the centre of a story, but it can also be the portrait of a place, organisation, religion, etc. It can be a report of one encounter with the subject, or gather many views and give a rounded portrait.

Interview : Can be either written as a story, with context, background and comments, or given as a verbatim, but edited, account of the interview. If the latter, the questions should not be too long, should be more carefully phrased than usual and any editing of the answers should be made clear with ellipses (...). The subject needs to speak well and interestingly, as there is no scope for making good this deficiency with entertaining commentary from the interviewer.

Factboxes : Simple lists of facts associated with the story, or previous instances of the event at the centre of your story. These are usually blobbed or given by date, rather than written through as a single piece.

Chronology : Relates 'the story so far' in short items, with each usually starting with the date in bold, followed by the development at that time. Often best written in punchy, abbreviated language shorn of definite articles, etc.

This is most appropriate when the subject has been around for a long time and is suddenly thrown into prominence by events. This will also work well on familiar subjects whose history is not broadly known. Works best when it is a true history and not merely a summary of the last few years' developments.

Full Texts : When you have a story which deals with an important speech, statement or document, it is worth thinking about running the complete text. My testimony

Personal experience written by a journalist after interviewing the subject, or written by the subject him or herself. The latter method always has the edge, as it provides the unmistakably untidy and honest tones of a real person speaking, compared to the smoothed-out sentences of the paper's journalists.

Backgrounder : A piece explaining the recent past of the issues or themes at the centre of a story. This gives a sense of such developments being part of a continuing process, rather than unprovoked eruptions of fate. Writing such pieces is often an object lesson in the kind of material you should be routinely including, albeit in a shorter form, in everyday reporting.

Analysis : A piece examining the reasons why something has happened, or not happened. Even if you are an experienced reporter, this is best done after consulting experts rather than off the top of your head.

Vox Pops : Short verbatim quotes from people you have telephoned or stopped in the street for their reaction to the story. Often fails because the questions are so predictable (e.g., variations on 'Do you think murder is wrong?'), too facile to get anything more than a knee-jerk response, or the responses are too prosaic. Ask questions that elicit replies that give personal experiences or highly individual reactions. And don't go back to the office until you have a good variety of responses.

Experts' Round-up : The same as the above, but with specialists rather than members of the public. The same precautions apply.

Opinion Poll : A poll of people's views carried out by an accredited research organisation. Having your own staff carry out the poll is not a good idea. The results will be unscientific and therefore meaningless.

Review : Just as you review films, plays or new cars, so you can review other things, such as a new health service, museum, newly opened historic house, park or any other public service. A refinement is to go with someone at whom the service is aimed (such as taking a claimant along to test a new welfare service), and writing a review based on their experiences.

12

Basic Elements

Here, we discuss newspaper reporting and the main components of a news report-the body and the lead. The news items that appear in newspapers are also called news stories. In literature stories may not have their basis in actual events, but a news story is always based on facts. History is also based on facts but it deals with things of the past while news stories are on current events. Further, a news story is normally written in inverted pyramid style, that is, the most important facts come first followed by other facts in order of significance.

The inverted pyramid style has developed in journalism over the years. It helps the readers who don't have enough time to read the whole story. It also helps sub-editors who can easily discard as much of the story from the tail without affecting its readability.

London, May 1 (PTI)-The British Government today rejected the plea of Sikh separatists for recognition of Khalistan which they had proclaimed in Amritsar three days ago.

A foreign office spokesman said the unity and territorial integrity of India were central to peace and to the well-being of the whole region, when asked about reports that the separatists had appealed to Britain and certain other countries to recognise 'Khalistan'.

Past elections in Punjab had demonstrated that the people did not support secession. Therefore, the question of recognising 'Khalistan' did not arise, he added.

No UK Recognition for Khalistan which appears in bold type is the head line. It is put at the head of the story and gives an idea to the newspaper reader about the subject of the story.

London, May 1' is the date line. It tells the reader the place and the date of the news story.

(P.T.I.) is credit line. The newspaper has published this story which was supplied by news agency Press Trust of India and by putting "(P.T.I.)" the paper acknowledges the source of the story and this gives the credit to the news agency.

Sometimes the name of the reporter or correspondent appears below the headline with a By or From. For example, "From V.S. Karnic" or "By Kanwar Sandhu". It is termed by line.

The first paragraph of the story is called intro or lead. In the above example, "The British Government today rejected the plea of Sikh separatists for recognition of 'Khalistan', which they had proclaimed in Amritsar three days ago," is the intro.

The rest of the story is called body of the story. Intro gives the most important information which is contained in the story and therefore it is the most crucial part. It should contain highest quantum of news value. A good intro is prerequisite of a good story. The proverb-Well begun is half-done-goes very well in this case, you really do half of the work on a news story if you write a good intro. They body of the story will automatically follow in the inverted pyramid style.

Basic elements of a news story can be found by asking and trying to find answers to six basic questions popularly known as he five Ws and one H. The five Ws are-What? When? Where? Who? and Why? and the H is How?

There was a time when journalists were supposed to answer all the questions in the intro. But slowly it was discovered that it resulted in over-crowding of the opening para, loss of clarity which at times confused and irritated the reader.

There is no hard and fast rule about these Ws and H and their inclusion in the intro or lead. A story may not have answers to all of them but all these questions should be asked to identify the basic elements of a news story. Then, according to news value, the most important element should come in the intro.

An intro may be in reply to one or more or all of these questions, but there should be no compromise on clarity of expression. If a reader has to look over a sentence a second time to understand it, then it cannot make a good intro or lead.

The Key

A test for elements of news and their proper order could be provided with four letters from 'news' as keys:

N for news worthiness-does the story contain news values?

E for emphasis-does the intro contain the most important and interesting fact?

W for the five Ws and the H-do their answers exist in the story?

S for sources of information-does the story identify or imply the source where it is necessary?

The Intro

Newsmen deal with a very wide range of subjects and everybody has his own way of presenting things. Therefore, there are innumerable ways of writing intros and leads. This variety is obvious to everybody who reads newspapers carefully as the same news story is presented in different ways in different newspapers, while the same paper presents different stories in different ways. Any two reporters doing the same story will write it differently and this explains the variety.

There are various ways to classify intros or leads depending on different criteria. Based on the number of incidents involved, the intro could be simple or complex.

(i) Simple lead involves a single incident. Even if the event may have several different incidents, the intro takes account of a single incident. Simple lead is very common in newspapers and should normally be favoured as it is easy to write it clearly. For a complex event like police action in the Golden Temple Indian Express, Chandigarh, gave a simple lead:

Express News Service

Chandigarh, April 30. The Punjab Police and paramilitary forces entered the Golden Temple complex at Amritsar this afternoon to clear it of "terrorists, separatists and anti-national elements.

(ii) Complex lead involves more than one incident in the intro. It is normally used when similar or related incidents are clubbed together in one story. One has to be careful with this kind of intro as it is normally long and a times confusing. Various incidents of violence in Punjab have been clubbed in this complex lead (Indian Express, Chandigarh):

Express News Service

Chandigarh, April 30. Three persons were killed and two others injured by suspected terrorists during the last 24 hours while a petrol pump and two liquor vends were looted in Faridkot district. Among the killed is a brother of a Deputy Superintendent of Punjab Police.

Two armed terrorists gunned down Rajiv Kumar a dispenser at Pakhoke village near Taran Taran and injured seriously Daljit Kumar. Both were travelling in a tonga. They were made to get down and shot at. Jaspal Singh, a brother of Mr Sukhdev Singh, a DSP posted at Batala, was also killed by the terrorists.

According to a report from Moga, four car-borne armed persons today looted a petrol pump, and two liquor vends at three different places in Faridkot.

It appears from the intro (the first paragraph) that all the incidents took place in Faridkot district while the second and third paragraphs make it clear that three different districts were involved. Taran Taran is in Amritsar district while Batala is in Gurdaspur district. A little more care was needed to avoid this mistake. In the following example care has been taken to avoid a similar mistake:

Substantive Clause Intro

New Delhi, April 10 (PTI). Despite adverse agro-climate factors, foodgrains production in 1985-86 was likely to touch 150 million tonnes, the Agriculture Minister Mr. Bata Singh disclosed today.

Conditional Clause Intro

New Delhi, May 2. The Minister of state for agriculture, Mr Yogender Makwana, has assured the Rajya Sabha that the government would take prompt action if charges of bunglings against any of the NAFED officials were found to be true.

Present Participal Intro

United Nations, April 30 (UNI). Calling the United Nations' current financial crisis "Yet another" challenge to multi-lateralism India has asked members to defeat those trying to weaken the world body.

Past Participial Intro

Cherrapunjee, April 27 (UNI). A large number of people here were disappointed today as President Zail Singh cancelled his Cherrapunjee visit due to inclement weather.

Prepositional Phrase Intro

Dhaka, March 11 (UNI). In the backdrop of the political imbroglio in Bangladesh, the leaders of the two major Opposition alliances held an unexpected parley last Sunday at an undisclosed venue to discuss the launching of a movement to make the government of President H.M. Ershad concede to Opposition demands to ensure free and fair elections.

Intros or leads can also be classified according to the elements of the news (five Ws and H) that dominate in the lead:

Who Lead

Hoshiarpur, May 3 (UNI). The Punjab police chief, Mr. J.F. Ribeiro on Saturday said maintenance of law and order in the state was not an easy task.

What Lead

Bombay, April 27 (UNI). M.V. Jhansi Ki Rani, a 76,600 dwt bulk carrier owned by the Shipping Corporation of India (SCI) ran aground at Fredrick Reef, some 500 km off the Australian east coast around 2 p.m. yesterday, a delayed report reaching the SCI's headquarters in Bombay said. No casualties were reported.

Where Lead

Sonepat, May 3. Rail traffic on Sonepat-Delhi junction of Northern Railway remained disrupted for about five hours following the derailment of two bogies of a goods train near Ganara railway station, about 1.6 km from here early this morning.

When Lead

Ahmedabad, April 10 (PTI). Since Vedic times, ancient Indian astronomers observed and carefully studied rare celestial phenomena, including comets, according to Mr Parmanand Desai, executive director of the Vedhshala (astronomical observatory) in suburban Naranpura here.

A close study of some of the not so well-known Sanskrit works cast new light on comets, the "old faithful visitors" to the solar system he said.

How Lead

Jayaprakash Pattan (Pune) April 29 (UNI). Janta Party's national council meetings plunged into turmoil this afternoon when Swami Agnivesh staked his claim for party presidentship after Mr Chandra Shekhar was unanimously re-elected.

As the confusion in the Ashoka Mehta Shamiana-the venue of the meet-came to an end, election returning officer Bapu Kaldate, owned up his mistake in declaring that he had received only the nomination of Mr Chandra Shekhar and announced that the election would now take place tomorrow morning.

Another classification is possible on the basis of variety of presentation in the intro.

Astonisher: This intro is of moderate length, from twenty-five to thirty-five words, and tries to arrest the reader's attention by presenting the unexpected but not of world rocking importance.

Express News Service

Ludhiana, April 29. As many as 27 persons were killed and another 26 were injured when two Punjab Roadways buses collided head on the Ludhiana-Malerkotla road near Gopalpura village this morning.

Cartridge or Capsule: This lead is brief and goes right to the point and presents news with high concentration of news value.

Express News Service

New Delhi, April 29. Six cases of AIDS disease (Acquired Immuno Deficiency Syndrome) have been detected in Tamil Nadu. Punch: Milder than the astonisher or cartridge, its length is somewhere between cartridge lead and the astonisher lead. It is useful for presentation of news that is not inherently exciting or sensational.

Lusaka, April 28 (Zana-pool). Woman are under represented in and misused by the mass media, a study on women in the media has shown.

Historical or literary-allusion lead: It draws some character event in history or literature in relation to an event or person in the news.

Question Lead: It fits with unusual or routine stories that need an informal tone as well as with those that deal with matter of universal interest.

New Delhi, May (UNI). What accounts for the phenomenal rise of the marwaris in the industrial field?

Geographical factors and the social set up have been responsible for drawing the best from the community, says a recent study. This study on Industrial Entrepreneurship of the Skekhawati Marwaris, was made by Dr. D.K. Tanket of the department of business administration in the University of Rajasthan.

Marwaris, particularly those from the Shekhawati region of Rajasthan, are 'unsurpassed by any other community in the world, Dr Tanket says. The region at one time accounted for 60 per cent of investment in the private sector.

The dry climate of the region compels the people to wage a continuous struggle against the vagaries of nature. Entrepreneurship springs out of adversity, the study says.

Direct Quotation: When the lead is using a direct quotation it should be short and eye-catching.

Bombay, April 20. "1 have no other friends except those that are strictly political," said Mr Pranab Mukherjee to Mr Pritish Nandy in an interview in the Illustrated Weekly of India issue April 27-May 3).

Indirect Quotation: Instead of using the speaker's actual words, the reporter can say what the speaker said in his own words. Credit must be given to the speaker in the intro. Compared to direct quotation more information can be given in this variety of intro.

S.S. Barnala over the telephone this morning and congratulated him for the prompt action taken in flushing out terrorists and other anti-national elements from the Golden Temple complex in Amritsar.

Contrast Lead: It attracts readers' attention by comparing extremes. Here is an interesting example:

Express News Service

Jammu, January 22. The "darbar move" of the secretariat and

other government offices has been in vogue in Jammu and Kashmir from the times of the Maharajas.

Mr. G.M. Shah has now introduced the "darbar move" of the detenus as well. That is how a state government employee at Kud put it to ENS on Tuesday.

He was referring to the winter "move" of the detenus from the tourist bungalow at Kud to some warmer place.

Direct Address Lead: It speaks directly to the reader or an interesting subject or one with a universal appeal.

Dallas, April 27 (Reuter). Living in Dallas may be hazardous to your marriage. A new book of statistics about 785 international cities, reveals that Dallas is he divorce capital of the world with 84 divorces per 1,000 people.

Descriptive Lead: Also known as situation or picture lead, it tries to paint a word picture of an interesting person place or thing to help create mood for the story.

Lucknow, April 10 (PTI). One could hardly see any crossing or eye catching spot or an electric or telegraph pole in "Kumbh Mela" are at Haridwar, where something or the other was not written in the form of a banner or a hoarding or a poster concerning what one could do to improve prospects of child survival and development, as part of a campaign launched by UNICEF.

Parody Lead: It attempts to play on words, using widely known proverbs, quotations, song titles, currently popular sayings book titles and other expressions to help establish immediate identify with the reader and to bring a bit of sparkle to what otherwise might have been a outine story.

Bangalore, May 2 (UNI). Comet Halley has said 'au revoir' after more than eight months of its tryst with the solar system.

Prof. K.R. Sivaraman of the Indian Institute of Astrophysics (IIA), coordinator for the country's Halley observation programme, told UNI that the comet was now moving away from the solar system.

One-two-three\one-two-three-four lead: This kind of intro is rarely used now. But it is useful in giving the salient points of an important programme or putting important budget provisions. In this kind of intro a general statement is followed by various important points with numbers (1), (2), (3), (4) or letters (a), (b), (c), (d), and so on.

Staccato Intro: It consist of short clipped words, phrases, sentences, sometimes separated by dots or dashes. It is casually disruptive and should not be used if the facts of the story do not justify it.

Mid night an old Yamuna Bridge ... a scream ... a shot ... a splash ... a second shot ... a splash.

This morning Delhi police recovered bodies of a couple... Miscellaneous freak lead: This type of intro has a novel approach in sentence structure and presentation, in order to catch the reader's attention.

Express News Service

Nagpur, October 27. It's Kapil Dev, of course. All the idle speculation on the choice of a captain for next month's visits to Sharjah and Australia after the setbacks in Sri Lanka were set at rest by the selectors, here, this afternoon. And it took them only five minutes to decide to retain Kapil Dev for the job.

The formal announcement of the unanimous choice of Chandu Borde (Chairman). Hanumant Singh, Kripal Singh, Amber Roy and Manmohan Sood was made by the Indian board secretary. Ranbir Singh Mahindra. And it surprised nobody. Chairman Borde said that no other name was discussed." There was no difference of opinion any rumours of dissensions on the issue are false."

Many of the above leads actually summarise the story and therefore they can be described as summary leads.

With interpretative news stories becoming more and more prominent in journalism interpretative leads are also becoming common in newspapers.

Interpretative leads normally do not quote any body and begin with a statement from the writer of the story. The interpretative lead gives the assessment of the reporter or special correspondent based on facts of the situation. Here is an example:

Express News Service

Washington, May 4. The future of India's entire national television network and its two way telephone system is under enormous strain. For the launch of Insat 1-C the only back up satellite for insat I-B (itself the only satellite to handle this enormous Indian workload for the last 30 months) is now postponed indefinitely.

India has abandoned all plans to launch insat 1-C through the US space programme following the unexpected explosion of the US space rocket Delta over the Atlantic on Sunday night...

Thus we see that all sorts of composition can be used in an intro. Its contents must have highest news value in the story. It must be easy to read and understand.

Body of News

After the intro is written the body of the story will follow in the logical order of inverted pyramid style.

Mention of the source in the lead is inescapable, when the news point is controversial or, in any case, not indisputable. But where the fact is unchallengeable, the opening paragraph may give the straight news, bearing the source for mention in the next

In such cases, one should avoid starting the next paragraph with: "This was announced (or stated) here today by Such a sentence just after lead arrests the momentum of the story. The second paragraph can go straight to the next important point of the story, bringing in the source in an easy manner, so that the story is kept moving smoothly.

In the body of the story choice of apt words is essential to ensure precision and better readability. The body should be concise and shorn of all verbiage. It should take notice of all material points concerning the news event, elaborate or background them where necessary, but should not be burdened with dispensable details.

The Language

The language of news story should be simple and familiar to be understood by the average reader. Simple and direct sentences are more effective than long, involved ones. The simple style is also easy to translate if copy is used in some sister publication in a different language. In multi-language societies like India this is a significant advantage.

It is not enough to collect news. It must be put across. Meaning must be unmistakable and it should be succinct. Readers do not have time and newspapers do not have space for elaborate reiteration. Every word should be understood by the ordinary man, and every sentence must be clear. There must be no abstractions.

Some people are proud of writing long sentences with many dependent clauses, with subjunctive and conditional, with exclamations, and interjection, quotations, allusions, metaphors, long images, Latin terminology, subtlety and conceits. They presume that the reader has enough time and has old classical education and has not to work for his living.

One must always keep in mind that a sentence is more likely to be clear if it is short, communicates one thought or closely related ideas. The length of sentences with too many ideas is not the cause of the disease but it is often a clear symptom where the ideas in a sentence are complex they cannot intelligible be presented in subsidiary clauses separated by a mere comma. A full stop in such cases proves a great help to clarity.

The prefixing of a subsidiary clause with one or more ideas in advance of the main idea often produces a long confusing sentence. Opening a sentence with a subsidiary clause has special difficulties for the reader if the two ideas go in different directions.

The sentence carrying the most important thought should be given immediate identity of its own.

This does not mean that newspapers should use only simple sentences. Economy of space as well as rhythm requires all kinds of sentences to be used. For example, it may be wasteful to introduce a complete subject and predicate for each idea. A subordinate clause in a complex sentence can express better precisely and economically than a series of simple sentences or compound sentences joined by 'and', etc. The crux of the matter is-have something to say and say it as clearly as you can.

Unfamiliar words and jargon (expressions peculiar to various fields of special knowledge) should be avoided as far as possible. The choice of words should be simple and elegant. Unfamiliar words should be explained in simple language.

Latin and Greek expressions appear in law, medicine, biology, etc., and some of these expressions have become part of the English vocabulary through usage. If these are readily understood, they may be used without any explanation, but if the Latin or Greek expressions have a popular English equivalent that should be preferred.

In other cases these expressions if used, should be accompanied by an interpretation or an explanation for the benefit of the lay reader. Mere fashionable use of foreign expressions should be avoided, profanities or obscene or vulgar language should be totally eschewed. They should be cut out even from direct quotations. Slang, though not in such bad taste as obscenities, should also be avoided, even in portions quoted. Colloquialism in also best avoided except in quoted texts.

Preference should be given to the active voice sentences in the passive voice have a deadening effect. Vigorous, economic writing requires a preference for sentences in the active voice. One should always prefer "The directors will meet next week" to "A meeting will he held by directors next week."

Official reports are full of the passive: it was felt necessary, in the circumstances it was considered advisable etc. In officialsense the language is polluted by viscous verbiage, meaning is clouded by vague abstraction, euphemism, conceals identity and heavy words weigh the mind down. It does not rain, in officialese, but precipitation is experienced. However, in certain circumstances the passive voice is useful, especially where he deed is more important than the doer. "A general strike has been called for tomorrow by... to protest against is better than: "The... has called a general strike for tomorrow in protest against..." All names in the copy should be properly identified as far as possible. Where the subject of a copy has multiple identification, that is, if he or she can be identified in more than one ways, the most pertinent among them-as a rule the office or position of consequence he or she currently holds-should be mentioned in the first instance, the , others being suitably mentioned in later parts of the copy. Where the subject does not hold any office currently, he or- she would of necessity have to be identified by the former office.

Adjectives and epithets retain their significance only when used in proper context and sparingly, chosen carefully and used aptly. They add colour to a news story and improve its quality. On the other hand, they can mar a story when used needlessly. Further, in view of objectivity no adjective or any other expression that smacks of bias, involves a value judgement should be used. Language should be used carefully to avoid any value judgement when it is not intended. For example, while reporting police firing one can say. "They police had to open fire,.." or "...was forced to open fire". The correct way to give a factual narration is, "The police opened fire". But when a minister or an official states that the police had to open fire, it may be reported as such with attribution.

Quotations should not be over used and must be restricted to more telling portions. Sometimes a couple of words within quotation marks are more effective than a whole sentence. It should be remembered that excessive use of quotations can spoil a copy. In reporting statements or speeches the safest verb is "said". There is no harm if it appears repeatedly in a copy. In appropriate circumstances, an occasional charge from "said" should be considered.

Verbs that substitute "said" are : observed, remarked, stated, averred, declared, affirmed, pointed out, told, informed, opined, confined, admitted, accepted, conferred, alleged, denied, rejected, repudiated, refuted, argued, contended, disclosed, revealed.

"Remarked" may be used with any ordinary statement, but "observed" and "stated" may be used only where there is really an observation or a statement. They are not to be treated as normal variants of "said."

"Averred" is legalistic in use and it is better to steer clear of it. "I declared" is acceptable subject to the condition that the person making the concerned declaration is competent to do so. "Declared" must be backed by the strength of authority, not in an absolute sense but in relation to the concerned statement.

"Affirmed" has an element of "firmness" in it and is stronger than "said". "Asserted" is stronger still. The use of these verbs, if at all, should be restricted.

"Opined" sounds pedantic and therefore should not be used except as part of a quoted passage.

"Told" and "informed" cannot stand by themselves "Told" or "informed" whom? "Told newsmen or a conference or informed parliament would be correct, but not, "Mr ... told that..."

"Pointed out" may be used only in relation to a universally accepted proposition or an incontrovertible fact, and not in relation to a matter on which views differ, or are likely to differ. Since it is not always easy to determine what is a universally accepted proposition, the use of "pointed out" is best avoided.

"Accepted," "refuted" and "confessed" should too be avoided. "Admitted" is admissible in the coverage of court proceedings.

The words "denied", "rejected", and "repudiated" may be selected on the basis of how strong a denial or contradiction is- "argued" and "contended" should be used when a serious contention is involved and not when a mere opinion is expressed.

"Alleged" can be used with reference to a statement which

contains an allegation or a charge. "Revealed" should be avoided altogether. "Disclosed" can be used when the person has the competence to make the disclosure.

Sentences should assert. The reader does not want to be told what is not he should be told what is. As a general rule newsmen should strive to express even a negative thing in a positive form. For example, "The project was not successful", should be written as "the project failed'. Likewise, "They did not pay attention to the complaint", should be written as, "They ignored the complaint".

No sentence should contain unnecessary words and no paragraph should have any superfluous sentence. There should be the right words in the right order. Adjectives and adverbs should be used only when they add to precision and economy of a sentence.

Redundancies or meaningless modifiers should find no place in news copy. No word should have a parasite consuming space and debasing language. An accident is either unique or it is not. It cannot be "rather unique". It is like being "rather pregnant". In "widow of the late Mr..." words "the late" are redundant since "widow" presupposes that the husband is no more. One should not write "at 9 a.m. in the morning". It should be either " a.m." or "morning".

Repetition is always needless, at times it becomes irritating. A peculiar journalistic problem is repetition of source. It has crept into Indian journalism through Associated Press (AP) news agency copy. Once the report has identified the source of the information there is no need to keep parading it. Only if identity is in doubt should it be repeated.

The grammar of the language applies to newsmen as it applies to others. On finer points of usage the style book of the newspaper or news agency should be adhered to. Many newspapers have not developed style books. They can make use of Press Trust of India Style Book with modification to suit their specific requirements.

13

News Selection

Newspapers fascinate people from all walks of life, but very few have the time or the patience to study the organisation, production and presentation of news. Most people look upon the newspaper, as a comprehensive presentation of news. Most people look upon the newspaper as a comprehensive presentation of all the important events in the past twenty four hours. Some newspapers have mythologised this concept by claiming that they print 'all the news that's fit to print. Apart from the fact that no newspaper can print everything that is worthy of printing and people's attention, there is another implication in this claim: news judgement. The newspaper organisation decides what is fit and what is unfit to print. Selection is inevitable. According to Walter Lippmann.

Every newspaper when it reaches the reader is the result of a series of selections as to what items shall be printed, in what position they shall be printed, how much space each shall occupy, what emphasis each shall have.

Traditionally, the newspaper has been looked upon as a platform of public opinion, a vehicle for moulding public opinion and an instrument to fight oppression and tyranny of the rulers by bringing to light their misdeeds.

Historically, the press has played an adversary role vis-a-vis the government and championed the cause of the people, particularly the middle and upper classes. The role of the press in freedom movements in all countries has been a very significant one.

But the modern newspaper is a different product from a different organisational structure playing a totally different role. Ever since the business and commercial class began to extend its influence on government, the newspaper's attitude to its own role in society had to change. The new commercial newspaper had to depend on the support of the commercial class since it was the product of that class. Its adversary role against government took - a new turn. The newspaper had to become a vehicle for the criticism of those actions of government which went against the interests of the commercial class. Any action by government which smacked of interference in the free trade philosophy of the merchants, industrialists and financiers was jealously watched by the press and criticised vehemently. Somehow people's interests were taken by the new press as identical to those of the commercial class. This was a phenomenon that occurred in the early part of the 19th century not only in the economically advanced countries but also in their colonies. It is still continuing in both the 'developed' and the 'developing' sectors of the world. In erstwhile colonies, the bulk of the press is still in the hands of the entrepreneurial class that uses the newspaper as an instrument to safeguard its financial interests and to prevent or forestall movements, if any, to change the existing economic order. In the advanced countries, the press is in the hands of powerful media conglomerates which have strong banking and financial ties with multinational corporations.

Sorting Process

No newspaper anywhere in the world can print all the news that comes to it from various sources. Severe selection processes are thus inevitable. This section discusses first, the selection of news in general, and then turns its attention to the selection of foreign news in the light of certain major concepts associated with the making of news.

Economic considerations of total space, size and advertisement content put constraints on the amount and types of news and feature materials that go into the newspaper. The dependence of the modern press on the business world can be seen from the heavy advertising content of the modern newspaper. Even the New York Times which is acclaimed by many as the best newspaper of the United States has a 60 to 75 per cent advertisement content on any given day. All the front-ranking newspapers of the world have similar quantities of advertising in them.' Whether newspapers change their editorial policy or news content according to the dictates of industrial giants who are heavy advertisers is open to, dispute; but it is only logical to assume that advertisers as a group do exert an influence on the large circulation press because the press depends on their support to survive the mounting costs of high technology currently being used by it. Another important factor is the crucial interlocking between the news and information industry and other unrelated industries. This is especially true of the big Indian newspapers such as the Times of India, Statesman, Hindustan Times and the Indian Express. These newspapers are connected with vast industrial and business empires such as the Tatas, Birlas, Goenkas, and others. Directors of huge cement, jute, steel and rubber companies guide the destinies of some of these newspapers. The giants among the American newspapers are also connected with giant industries, a fact well brought out by Dreier and Weinber.

In addition to economic considerations, technological imperatives affect the nature and quantity of news, particularly foreign news, in a modern newspaper. In their bid to bring the latest news in competition with the electronic media which are naturally much faster, the newspapers have spent huge sums of money to install the latest electronic machines and computerised systems of news and picture transmission. They also depend heavily on the satellites and the global wire services. This situation affects the content of newspapers to a great extent, because what is electronically transmitted gets priority. The newspaper editors listen to early morning news bulletins from the broadcast media and then follow up the leading stories-from the wire-services.

The wire services play an important role in the selection process in all news organisations that have installed teleprinters. Whatever comes off the wires is considered more urgent and important than reports coming through other sources. In fact, half a dozen major wire services in the world-Associated Press (AP), United Press International (UPI), Reuters, Agence France-Press (AFP) and TASS-determine the type and quantity of the news content in the newspapers of both rich and poor countries. This is particularly so in the case of foreign news. Since newspapers are in the business of producing under pressure, they find it very convenient to adapt readymade wire service reports and meet the deadline. Moreover, most newspapers cannot afford to station their correspondents in major cities that provide most of the news. Heavy dependence on the global wire services is the characteristic of all newspapers. Diversity in news is likely to suffer from the practice of all newspapers depending on the same wires.

The Production

The very nature of newspaper production imposes certain constraints on the product that reaches the audience. Lack of time and stall imposes restrictions on the selection process and hence on media content. Indepth reports have to wait; what is readily available will form the top story since immediacy is a primary consideration of news organisation and news workers. This will put severe constraints on completeness journalists are sometimes torn between two equally opposing forces: the desire for completeness which may delay the transmission of messages, and the desire for immediate release which may affect completeness. If a large enough staff is not available for research, a story may be 'killed' or delayed indefinitely, or alternatively, the story may be reproduced verbatim from another source more readily available. Most of the time, the wire services determine what stories go into the day's newspapers. Since this is the age of computerisation in newspaper production, standardisation becomes inevitable.

But, are technological reasons the sole determining factors is selection? Are there sociological, organisational and hierarchical factors exerting a decisive influence on the selection process?

In order to understand the sociological, organisational and hierarchical factors exerting a decisive influence on the selection process?

In order to understand the sociological aspects of selection, some theoretical matters connected with the definition of news, function of news organisations in society, structure of news organisations and the decision-making process have to be examined.

First, a look at the process of communication itself. There are four components in the process: the communicator, the message, the channel and the audience. Theorists use four other equivalent terms: the encoder, the symbols, the media and the decoder. The communicators and the audience interpret the message properly only when they have the same frame of reference. Those who produce and present the messages and those who receive them should have the same symbolic frames of reference for proper understanding or communication to take place. Normally those messages which are out of the symbolic context or experience of the audience will be left out by the communicators.'

In his case study of selection and communication in a television production, Elliott identified seven distinct stages:

> programme ideas and outlines; researching and collect on of programme material; programme material; selection of programme material; detailed outlines and scripts; cuts and adaptation; and programme recording-in that order.

If we transfer this model to a news report production, we can identify the following major steps:

1. Selection of an event to report, or an idea to convey. This may be done by the reporter or a source outside the news organisation. For example, a government or private source

may contact the news agency or newspaper organisation, or its representatives with a ,story' for possible inclusion in the next issue of the paper.

2. The report prepared by the reporter or outside person.
3. The report goes to the receiver's desk for selection.

   It is here that the fate of the report is decided. The selector here is usually referred to as 'the gatekeeper'. From here the report may go in toto into the next issue of the paper or it may be totally rejected; sometimes it may be modified a little through further consultation with the reporter and the source, or without any such consultation. Cuts, additions and alterations are made here.

4. If the report goes into the paper in part or as a whole, it reaches the fourth selection stage, namely, that of the audience. The audience may or may not see it. It depends on the positioning of the report, the audience's interest in the subject matter, the size of the headline used, and the relevance of the report to the conditions of the time.

In all the above stage, sociological factors affect the selection process.

A closer look at the four stages is important here.

The communicator is not just the sender of a message. Whether he be a reporter, special correspondent or an outside informant, the communication worker has grown up with certain impressions and value judgements about the socio-economic, cultural and political significance of an occurrence. His impressions are not substantially different from those of his compeers and colleagues the media organisation, and ultimately, they are the sa as those of the top management personnel who control the medium. There are some exceptions to this general rule. Some newsmen have left their organisations precisely because of the incompatibility of their vie with those of their organisations. By and large, however the selectors in all stages have certain common bonds selection philosophy which is unwritten, yet visible actual operation. Communication is part of the to socio-economic and political structure prevailing in country. Culture is again manipulable by those who control the ingredients of its social structure: means production (technology), marketing, finance capital and employment capabilities.

In the first step of selection, therefore, the selector leaves out certain aspects of reality (which is one, holistic, and integrated, although consisting of several aspects). He does this either intentionally or unintentionally, probably because of a set pattern of selection in his mind conditioned by his past education, cultural upbringing, his country's national and foreign policies, his social class, or his corporation's economic objectives. The modern newspaper organisation being a huge, capital-intensive, highly centralised and high technology-oriented corporation, stays in business to make profits. Therefore, those who work for it will have to select a story that will sell. Is there any coercion on the selector at this stage? Perhaps not journalists are by nature free spirits who wish to do their job unhindered by their own bosses or by pressure groups or by government. However, as Gans says, journalists, despite their resentment of bureaucracy and toeing the hierarchical or organisational executive line, are in fact, part of a well-formed bureaucratic set-up that 'suggests' rather than 'orders' -specific tasks.

Senior executives in a news organisation exert a certain amount of pressure on the newsmen because like any other business or social organisation, the press is hierarchical in its structure. But the whole hierarchy is conditioned by the socio-economic and political climate prevailing in the country. It is I relevant to quote Gans again as he studied newsroom decisions by participant observation. He writes:

> Because news organisations are assembly lines on which people must work together to manufacture a product against a deadline, they almost always generate conformity. Few top editors are either sufficiently powerful or Machiavellian to manipulate the pressures for conformity ... [Yet] they resolve uncertainty, decide which selection considerations have priority, set tones and some precedents, which

> then require conformity. Senior editors do much the same in their sections (1979-98).

Informal methods failing, formal authority is used to bring the 'deviant' reporter back to the organisational policy track. In fact, 'deviations are discouraged or prevented by six factors', according to Warren Breed. They are:

> the use of formal authority and sanction, with the possibility of giving controversial stories to 'safe' men to handle' desire of newsmen to get on in their careers, the lack of any alternative group allegiance to support deviance; the gratifications of remaining in the in-group and finally handling news according to policy becoming a value in itself.

The policy, according to Breed who studied the role of news selectors or 'gatekeeper' in detail, is usually to protect property and class interest.

The First Step

The communicator in the first step is, therefore, news organisation, he is still under the influence of the business or government organisation he works for, whether or not be admits it. This factor of corporate influence over selection is of vital significance in modern media organisations because of the trend towards concentration and centralisation of mass communication technology, production, and ownership; and the interlinkage between organisations and out side organisations including some government agencies. As mentioned earlier, communication industries in both rich and poor countries are under the tight control of either huge conglomerates which, have multinational connections or multinational corporations which have direct or indirect control over several media in many countries. This is the age of monopolistic communication practices.

In the second stage of selection, that is preparation of the report, words or pictures are selected in such a way that those aspects of reality selected in the first step are presented effectively. Again, the reporter's subjective decisions play a role at this stage.

In the third stage, when the message reaches the receiving end, that is, the media organisation, the decision-makers there begin their selection. The message goes through the 'gatekeeper'. Kurt Lewin was the first to introduce the term 'gatekeeper' in 1947 with reference to the people in a news organisation who watched the flow of news. David Manning White and Warren Breed popularised the idea. According to Breed, the policy of a publisher gets translated into action by the 'gatekeepers'. McQuail found that the 'gatekeepers' had the power to decide if an item would have to be changed before it was transmitted. At this stage, major decisions are made regarding the selection of stories for the day's issue the decision-makers go through the stories selected by reporters and judge wire service news stories. The decisions are usually made at the afternoon editorial conference where each section editor brings in what he has chosen for inclusion in the next issue. As Lippmann observed, there are no written rules on decision-making, only conventions.

Some scholars have given more importance to the decision-making process at the first step, namely, the news gathering stage. For example, Bass considers the news gathers' decision more important than the news processors' decision. The news gathers, according to him, consist of the writers, reporters, bureau chiefs, and city editors; the news processors include editors, copy readers and translators. But this does not deal with the organisational and sociological imperatives exerting influence on the climate of the news gathering and selection process. For an understanding of this influence, we have to refer to some other studies based on the content of news media.

In their classic study of a demonstration against the Vietnam War, Halloran and others showed how events were selected for news reporting in terms of their fit or consonance with pre-existing images. In other words, the news of the demonstration confirmed earlier ideas. Their conclusion was:

> The more nuclear the news item and the more uncertain or doubtful the newsman is how to report it, the more likely it is to be reported within a general framework that has already been established.

Four other factors were cited by Halloran based on the findings of Galtung and Ruge as vital components of news value: reference to elite persons; references to elite states; personalisation or personification; and negativism. Do media select top people and top nations more frequently than others? Is news reporting person centered? Are negative events preferred to positive ones?

Another important finding of Halloran and associates was that despite he outward differences among various newspapers, all of them showed a fundamental similarity in the presentation of factors which made events news. They found little variation in the approach of the various newspapers to the demonstration against the Vietnam War.

Viewers and readers were not presented with various interpretations focusing on different aspects of the same events, but basically the same interpretation which focused on the same limited aspects-the issue of violence.... Events were not so much deliberately distorted or otherwise falsified by presentation, as selected and interpreted for their relevance to the basic and predetermined news issue.... The simple negative image built up for the demonstration story was the only image made widely available to the public by press the television news.

It is in the function of selection and interpretation that the news producers exercise, their value judgements. This function is performed with reference to a framework of ideas and symbols considered important not only to the communicators but the 'communicatees'.

Stuart Hall's comment on the process of interpretation in broadcast media is relevant to that in the mass circulated press as well:

> Every news event is already, completely, assigned to a context which explains it. The broadcaster, or his reporter and camera-man in the field, must already have such a context in mind in order to know what to film, which to select and send back to the editor, which to include in the broadcast.

If we accept this premise, we have to concede that in the process of news selection. Agenda setting is unavoidable lit-cause the recipients of communication should be provided with certain stories presented in a certain way for contextualisation. For many years, researchers have been trying (and they are still trying) to find relationships between media usage and attitude change. Agenda setting is a trend discernible in the mass media and it is resorted to by the media owners to bring about a symbiotic relationship between their priorities and their audience's supposed priorities. The ultimate aim is to find that perfect fit or consonance between the communicators and the audience which is essential to maximise sales of media products and hence profits. Through agenda setting, the media fare will synchronise, it is hoped, with 'what the public wants'.

The Readership

We are now in the fourth selection stage, namely, the audience of media fare. There have been many studies of the audience of all types of news including foreign news; but most of the studies have concentrated on how to effect behaviour modification through appropriate messages to the audience. Since a study of the effects of messages on the audience is not our aim, it is enough to mention that members of the audience select messages depending on their particular needs and interests. Newspapers are aware of their audience's selection of messages, and they hope to reach messages they consider important for the readers by placing them in special positions or displaying them distinctly. The placement of messages and their display is allied to the concepts of selection and agenda setting. Since agenda setting is linked to the fourth selection stage in the communications model, some details of that concept are worth examining.

The press, as Walter Lippmann said in his classic work, Public Opinion, fills in our unseen environment, and helps us to form our mental picture of the world on a daily basis. People exposed to the mass media do learn from them and form opinions based on that learning. Can the press steer the course of their thinking or influence their thinking process? According to Shaw and McCombs, the two researchers who studied this issue empirically, the press presents to the people should be concerned about. It may be argued that enlightened people will have their own independent judgement on all such issues: but research has shown that the press through the agenda setting process provides issues and event to think about, if not opinions to hold. The concept is defined as 'the ability of the media to influence the salience of events in the public mind. It has been derived from two important pronouncements made half a century apart-one by Walter Lippmann in 1922 and the other by Theodore White in 1972. Lippmann spoke about the power of the press in creating pictures of the world in the minds of the readers. White spoke about the press setting the agenda of public discussion.

Through the process of selection, as already explained, the media transit to the audience those national and international issues which they consider newsworthy and hence worthy of the audience's attention. Shaw and McCombs have shown that people form their individual political congnitions based on what the mass media present as salient. The agenda-setting function of the press is put into practice through the following steps:

1. daily selection of news events and issues by the wire service reporters and editors;
2. daily selection from the wire service news and issues by the newspapers' editors (gatekeepers); and
3. placement of the news and views in the newspaper by the new editor.

Placement in the broadcast media is achieved by the numerical order in which the news and views are presented. Whichever is announced first is the leading news story of the hour. In the newspaper, what the news editor considers to be more important news events will be placed on the front page. These -will not only be placed on the front page, but discussed in the editorial and opposite-editorial pages. Among the important stories on the front page, the most important will be presented in large size types, with bold letter synopsis, 'boxing', etc. Sometimes pictures are incorporated to heighten the importance of the event.

Items placed on the left hand corner catch the readers' attention first since people's eyes move linearly from left to right, except in those countries where they read from right to left. What the media emphasise through selection, placement and display go down in the audience's consciousness as salient. According to Shaw and McCombs.

The agenda setting power of the press may be thought of as a process of consensus building between those who have access to the press or whom the press regularly covers with news, the press itself, and the audience or society at large. Agenda setting represents social learning.

The above discussion shows that reporters and news editors or the maker of news have the power to select events and topics. They exercise this power on a daily basis and what the audience gets is the product of their selection. We move on now, to some more conceptual matters relating to news selection and newsmaking.

Access to the press is supposed to be the corner-stone of democracy since it ensures open debate on public issues. The freedom of the press is ultimately people's freedom to express their views even when those views are against the prevailing authoritarian forces. But, can every citizen be guaranteed access to the media? Is the modern, well-established, high technology press small enough to be accessible to the ordinary citizen?

Technological Progress

Technological progress has changed the structure of media organisations and the very nature of mass communication. The trend towards centralisation of the technology and ownership of the mass media has been referred to already. Big newspapers force the smaller ones out of business and multimedia conglomerates dominate the communication scene. The concentration of the media in the hands of a powerful elite minority is not conductive to citizens' access and to the freedom of the press. In the United States, newspaper monopoly exists in 95 per cent of the cities. In India, there are thousands of small towns and villages which do not have any newspaper circulation at all. Lack of access leads not only to the loss of vital information but also to the stifling of dissenting views and to a lack of diversity. Despite the argument that it is impossible for any newspaper to publish everything that comes to it, it should be recognised that the only way to ensure access is to multiply media voices through alternative media, if necessary. If the media of communication continue to depend on centralised, capital-intensive, high technology, they will remain inaccessible to the average citizen's points of view.

This is a quality often stressed by newsmen. It is closely linked to completeness, but since newspapers are mainly in the business of bringing the latest news, and not that of completing an already broached story with additional facts and figures for the edification and education of the readers, continuity is not often adhered to as an inviolable news principle. A big story of yesterday will be discontinued or inadequately treated today in order to play up today's big story which in turn will be replaced by another story tomorrow. Do various newspapers follow a pattern of omission or inadequate treatment of an already broken-in story? Are there reasons for this other than the desire to bring the latest 'big story and action news' to the readers? Are there organisational pressures or governmental pressures? By discontinuing stories or reporting incompletely, especially news about other countries and cultures and national minorities, will not distortion occur in news treatment? These are questions that have been answered to some extent by Gans and Tuchman who, like Gans, Audied the newsmaking process as a participant observer.

Tuchman gathered, over a period of ten years, relevant data on the process of newsmaking in two television stations and three newspapers. She also interviewed several news-related organisations and workers. Her main theme is that :

> act of making news is the act of constructing reality itself rather than a picture of reality.... Newswork

> transforms occurrences into news events. It draws on aspects of everyday life to tell stories, and it presents us to ourselves. By accomplishing this second task, it serves us as a basis for social action. But the process of making news is not accomplished in a void, and so a second theme is that professionalism serves organisational interests by reaffirming the institutional processes in which newswork is embedded.

Chains of Command

According to Tuchman, bureaucratic chains of command are developed in the newspaper organisation to keep p track of daily occurrences out of which particular stories are woven into news and in this process, /news worthiness' is bestowed on selected occurrences. Reporters and editors create a 'web of facticity' for the sake of news credibility, and this web legitimates the status quo. Newsmen identify some sources and institutions as the appropriate location of facts and dismisses others. When legitimate leaders are unavailable, new's organisations bestow authenticity to news into hard news, soft news, spot news and developing news. They also call some news items 'continuing news'.

But in their pursuit of more important news every day, they leave out the concept of continuity, although they may claim that a 'fair amount of coverage' is given to all stories. Perhaps certain news events are covered more frequently than certain others depending upon the importance the news organisation bestows on them.

Connected with selection, continuity and access, is the idea of objectivity. Some newsmen consider their papers to present 'objective news' and take great pride in it. Objectivity is, no doubt, an ideal worth striving for. In it are included other ideals such as impartiality, fairness, truthfulness, reality, and total detachment of the newsmen from their sources and their news. Objectivity is not an ideal that can be achieved easily or frequently. In practice, subjectivity is involved in the selection and presentation of news. Even definitions of news are subjectively derived and not scientifically or objectively tenable. At any given moment, what is newsworthy depends on the decision-makers' socio-economic and cultural background, and the political climate that prevails in his country. As members of a social group, newsmen have certain symbols embedded in their consciousness which they use to interpret reality. Very often these symbols help in the perpetuation of the existing order and systems rather than in replacing them with something different or hitherto untried.

Objectivity is usually considered attainable by reporting opposing points of view. In fact, searching for the opposite side has almost become a ritual with newsmen. But there are a thousand shades of opinion between the two sides. On specific issues, many hundreds of people do not take any rigid view based on party affiliations. Since the newsmen's objectivity is limited in scope, the differences they try to bring out from opposing camps are not real differences but artificial ones couched in terms used by opposing camps. This, can create a semblance of objectivity. The average citizens are sometimes misled by the artificial objectivity in news reports. Even in the first selection stage itself, subjectivity determines what news items and which news sources should be let into the news framework. Once newsmen realise and recognise the process of selection that goes on in their day-to-day work, they will not be as vehement in their protestations of objectivity.

An argument put forward by Tuchman is particularly relevant here. She believes that although it is wrong to accuse news workers of bias, and though it is difficult to define objective truth, it is valuable to identify news as an artificial accomplishment attuned to specific understanding of social reality. Those understandings, constituted in specific work processes and practices, legitimate the status quo.

A newspaper does not hold up a mirror to nature or to events because its reflecting scope is limited. News cannot be comprehensive because of the very nature of newsmaking. The 'reality' constructed by newsmen is not, or need not be, the actual reality or the whole reality. It is only aspects of reality which they produce and present to the public. Berger and Luckmann have discussed the concept of 'construct reality' elaborately in their work. That concept is applicable to the newspaper because, irrespective of the nature of external reality, journalists see it only through their own constructs. As far back as 1953, Kuart and Gladys Lang had shown that events covered were themselves journalistic constructs of related phenomena.

The 'medium is not the message', since the message depends on the men who utilise the medium. Communicators work in a national culture constructed out for several sub-cultures but very much under the powerful influence of the dominant group that holds economic, political and military power. This is why Gans calls news among other things, the exercise of power over the interpretation of reality'.

Similar views are expressed by Tuchman who believes that the work of the media should be evaluated in terms of the sociology of knowledge. Since knowledge is power and communication is part of the knowledge industry, those who run the media are doubly capable of strengthening their network of power over society. They, in fact, start from an already powerful position for reasons of conglomeration with other forms of production. Readers and viewers are not totally helpless if alternative media choices are possible, and if journalists try to maintain news credibility and reliability; but as McQuail has said, the media's views ultimately prevail because they have the final say on what gets into the channels and hence on access and availability.

In the interpretation of reality, the news media use certain techniques for attracting the audience, the most important of which is the technique of dramatisation. This is especially true of television news as confirmed by Epstein who studied the news manufacturing process in the three major networks of the United States. There is no doubt that the newspapers are now compelled to imitate television practices to survive the fierce competition from the electronic industry in technologically advanced countries and also in some developing countries where television is gaining strength. Most news stories open with a dramatic lead. The element of fiction in news stories is also not negligible. These news practices will continue because newsmen in the print media listen to the radio and television news bulletins broadcast early morning for lead stories in their afternoon editions, and the bulletins of the evening broadcast for their morning editions.

The Preoccupation

Newsmen's preoccupation with personalities and their tendency to personalise news are also allied to the technique of dramatisation. It is easier to dramatise an event if colourful and controversial personalities are involved in the news story. Pictures will heighten the dramatic aspects of a news event. Selection of news is influenced by picture possibility as well as opportunity to dramatise the event through well-known personalities. But who are the personalities who usually appear in the news? After studying a six-month sample of stories appearing in alternate months during 1967, 1971 and 1975, Gans found that most of the news was about affluent people; the main actors in most stories were people in the top 1-5 per cent income bracket, although most were distinguished by their geographical, racial, ethnic and religious background far more often than by their economic background. The magazines were found to universalise upper middle class practices as if they were shared by all Americans. Gans concluded that news story selection was based on availability and suitability of news and that it was the economically and politically powerful people whom journalists sought out for news stories. But drama and colour may not be the only considerations by newsmen since most often, those dramatic events and colourful personalities are chosen, who fit the socio-economic and political environment in which the media operate.

Under the influence of the electronic media, newspapers have changed the format of their pages, increasing the picture content and visual appeal of every page. One of the editors interviewed by this researcher said that he had standing instructions to use at least three pictures on the front page-one big and two small, and one picture on each inside page besides advertisement pictures. News items with picture possibilities and readily available pictures naturally find a place on the front or inside page much more easily than those without a picture. Thus, questions of immediacy, objectivity, completeness, continuity, and other values usually held in high esteem by news workers, are affected by the actual process of newsmaking.

The foregoing discussion should convince us that it is essential to look at the newspaper as a product of the, efforts of a professional group of people who have identical interests and who belong to more or less the same socio-economic, political, and cultural systems. The newspaper is not just a picture of constructed reality, but constructed reality itself to those who produce it. It serves socio-economic, political, surveillance, cultural and entertainment functions news does not simply happen. There are occurrences in everyday life in every part of the world out of which news events are woven with due attention to factual correctness, balanced judgement as far as the selected facts are concerned, relevance to the audience, clarity, contextuality, completeness as far as the chosen facts are concerned, authentic references to news sources specially selected for the purpose, the reliability of the facts selected and presented.

One of the substantive considerations among newsmen and newspaper organisations is that domestic news is more important than foreign news; however, when national interests abroad are threatened, foreign news relating to those interests becomes as important as, if not more important than, domestic news. In the study planned here, foreign news presentation occupies the major position and hence a detailed discussion of foreign news selection is necessary.

Newspapers and all mass media disseminate information not only about events happening in their own countries but in other countries as well. The selection of foreign news is stricter for several reasons, some of which are discussed here.

The Completeness

Normally, only about one-third of the total space in a commercially successful and profitable newspaper is devoted to news. The rest of the paper is taken up by advertisement matter of one kind or another. And the bulk of the area devoted to news (called newshole) goes for metropolitan, state capital, large town or newspaper town and suburban news. A sizeable portion is cut out for regional and national news. It is the remaining space that is devoted to events occurring in other countries. Completeness, continuity, objectivity, access, authenticity, and other qualities expected in domestic news presentation will suffer heavily in the case of foreign news because of the pressure on space.

In an investigation of the reasons why newspapers rejected most of the foreign news that flowed into them through the wire services, Casey and Copeland found that 20 per cent of foreign news copies were rejected by American newspapers for 'lack of space', 35 per cent for lack of appeal or interest to readers, lack of news value and significance; 16 per cent because of loss of timeliness and 27 per cent for various technical reasons. They also found that large metropolitan papers allotted proportionately more space to foreign news than did non-metropolitan papers. The International Press Institute study of 93 US newspapers during four separate weeks between October 1952 and January 1953 during the Korean war concluded that the average proportion of foreign news material to text space was little more than 8 per cent.

Sunwoo Nam hypothesised that the flow of news reflected the power configuration of world politics and depended on the political alliance and functional proximity of the reported country, rather than on geographical proximity or any other factor. He also expressed the view that the bulk of foreign news is not meant for the general public, but to help specialised audiences, decision-makers and foreign affairs experts in the functions of surveillance. According to his argument, the press in developing countries reports more foreign news because the press in these countries is elitist. Markham and Hart expressed similar views in their studies of the South American press.

Smith indicated that the growth of a country's interest in international communications is directly proportional to its military, economic and political interests in international areas. Gerbner has indicated that the modern mass media are the cultural arm of modern industry and business. A study by Onyisi under Gerbner's supervision concluded that the southern part of the African continent received the most attention in the United States media because the multinational corporations with headquarters in the country had strong economic interests concentrated in that region of Africa. This relationship had already been studied more elaborately by Schiller in the case of the United States and he concluded that the American mass media were part of an American industrial and military complex. Abu-Lughod found that the degree of international coverage in a country's media depended on that country's dependence on other countries. He also hypothesised that the United States received a disproportionate amount of 'big power' coverage because several countries depended on it.

Lent has pointed out that 'national interests, crisis reporting, foreign censors, and a shrinking corp of correspondents' constrain international coverage in the US media. Gerbner and Marvanyi have graphically represented the many worlds of the world's press after making a multinational comparative study of foreign news coverage, confirming that coverage depends on the big power configuration that dominates the modern world.

But Elliott and Golding have pointed out that foreign news like domestic news is developed by the media organisers as a marketable commodity throughout the world. According to them, the culture to which news, and other aspects of the international system contribute, is not related to any single society or social structure so much as to that network of economic interests and organisations that is international corporate capitalism. Increasingly the growth of the international media system enables the news media to play broadly the same ideological role at an international level as is already apparent nationally in particular developed countries. The international media system is one mechanism by which developing countries are brought within the common cultural hegemony of western capitalism.

Role of Agencies

Heavy dependence on the global wire services has been cited by some as a determining factor in the selection and quantity of news from other countries. The IPI study, already referred to, found that the news agencies were the paramount source of international news and that the coverage by the news agencies centred heavily on the major countries of the world. To Hachten, the flow of news concerning less developed countries seemed to be more, closely related to the use of a world news agency than to geographical proximities or language similarities.

Most newspapers of the developing countries do not have the economic capability of stationing their own correspondents in foreign countries. In developing as well as developed countries, it is the big chains and conglomerates that have their own wire services staff and special correspondents in other countries. All the rest depend on the big news agencies of the world. This leads to verbatim reproduction of news agency reports, sometimes including spelling and other errors.

Foreign news in most countries' newspapers is likely to have more or less the same content as far as a particular news story is concerned. There may be differences in the stories selected, but not much variety in the presentation of individual stories.

The history of the development of the news agencies have a great impact on the process of foreign news selection and reporting.

The history of colonialism had an equal impact on the growth of the international news media. Towards the end of the nineteenth century, the newly established European news agencies concluded a series of cartel agreements by means of which they divided the world between the, according to the prevailing imperial spheres of influence. These first links in the international media system set a precedent for much that was to follow as the media in developed and developing societies alike became progressively more involved in corporate capitalist economy.

Colonial news agencies are still strong in erstwhile colonies, and several of their reports could reflect the national interests of the countries in which those agencies originated. They reflect their

national ethnocentrism which paves the way toward cultural imperialism. They reporting of an event in a developing country may be influenced by the world's leading wire services, all of which are headquartered in the developed countries. The wire services' reports, thus, could lead to distortion and omission of vital aspects of the events, since they tend to interpret the event from their own national and global economic interests.

This leads us to the fourth factor that influences the selection, presentation and quantity of foreign news.

Quality of Foreign News

As mentioned earlier, domestic news becomes foreign news depending on the foreign policy actions of a country. When millions of refugees from East Pakistan fled to West Bengal, and Bihar their plight was first considered a foreign problem, but the stern action taken by India against Pakistan made it domestic news in India. Similarly, news about a country's nationals in other countries, although strictly news of foreign origin, becomes domestic news because of special domestic links with the nationals residing abroad. With the deep involvement of the United States in Vietnam, the latter country became domestic news in the US media. Afghanistan has now become well-known in the US and the USSR, after the latter's troops marched into that country. The conflict in the Falkland Islands became national news in the British news media. Thus, foreign news is not wholly foreign; it is in a way domestic news extended to a foreign country.

Several researchers have found that three types of countries dominate foreign news in a country's newspapers: its closest or most powerful allies; its chief foes and their allies; and the rest of the world when something extraordinary occurs there. Gans, for example, fund that most foreign news in newspapers in the USA was about England, France, West Germany, Italy, Japan, Israel, Egypt, the Soviet Union and mainland China. He observed that:

> Foreign news deals either with stories thought relevant to Americans or American interests; with the same

> themes and topics as domestic news; or when the topics are distinctive, with interpretations that apply American values... often limit themselves only to the most dramatic overseas events. In addition, they tend to follow American foreign policy, even if not salvishly.... Foreign news adheres less strictly to objectivity than domestic news; but... the values it applies are not very different from those that appear, less explicably, in domestic news.

This observation is not only applicable to the US, but to India and other countries as well. In fact, major newspapers of all countries toe the official foreign policy line most of the time.

Issues of nationalism and patriotism might motivate the media to conform to their national government's foreign policy. It is difficult to find consistently favourable reports about socialist countries in capitalist countries' newspapers (unless there is a very special relationship between them) and vice versa. Similarly, it is difficult to find reports, not to mention favourable reports, about enemy countries in a nation's news media unless the government itself wants certain information to be passed on to the people in order to alert them.

Since foreign policy is a major determinant of foreign news selection, most economic and political developments are seen in terms of the East-West ideological conflict or of the Cold War. Smaller countries are usually ignored unless news about them has some relevance to the newspaper's country. Some major countries are seen as allies or foes. Favourable reports about allies appear in the country's newspapers despite the existence of some very grave threats to human rights in those allied countries. Reports about Latin American countries in newspapers of the US are examples of this. Every foreign news event is likely to be interpreted in relation to either the US or the Soviet Union by most newspapers of the world. 'The daily task of constructing the segment of international reality takes place in a particular kind of setting, both institutional and social', says Cohen. His views about the selection of foreign news are relevant to our discussion:

> Effective decisions are made... at a number of different points, although the general news editor and the telegraph editor, who preside over the bank of news tickers, together with whatever assistants they might have, make the major decisions involving selection and layout. These men do not, of course, start the editorial process de novo each day; they approach the task with an experience and a perspective that have both long and short term components. Over the long term, particular classes of stories preempt the leading news spaces-economic reform, war, international political competition... In the short run, the editors carry in their heads the knowledge of what the news has been over recent days and weeks. Hence, they come to their tasks every day with half-formed and unarticulated notions of what the news is apt to be like.

Cohen agrees that no newspaper can 'shovel out to its readers as news the total stock of information and stories that it receives/ but he points out that :

> priorities and not absolutes determine the amount of... foreign affairs news. Foreign news has to compete with other types of news for getting into the paper. Space allocations are not made every day, but as part of a long term policy, which will be changed only by the top personnel. The selection of all types of news is done by editors on the basis of prior decisions on what the readers will buy.

However, it is not always the sales angle that determines the selection and presentation of foreign news. Political or ideological considerations, global economic interests, military strategies, patriotism, national security interests all these exert a decisive influence on the selection of foreign countries and themes for presentation to the newspaper readers. Journalists often willingly cooperate with government when national security is threatened. As Cohen observes, 'personal friendships between government officials and newsmen are common, extending right up to the Presidential level'.

Occasional Conflict

There may arise an occasional conflict between senior government officials in charge of foreign policy and some journalists who go wrong in their facts. But by and large, there develops a symbiotic relationship between the foreign news correspondent and his country's local embassy officials and this leads to reporting of events from the official point of view. Sometimes, conditions ripe for revolution in a far-off country, or the true facts of a revolutionary movement may miss the attention of the correspondent who hastily accepts embassy hand-outs for transmission to the newspaper's headquarters. The newspaper organisations are willing to cooperate with the government by resorting to self-censorship on matters of national security or safety of citizens abroad. Several instances can be cited from the reporting of the Vietnam war or the Indo-Pakistan war where , journalists as citizens cooperated with the government. Gans even goes to the extent of saying that journalists occasionally report news from distant countries based on slender evidence.

The intimate cooperation between journalists and government has been discussed by Cohen:

> Stories about foreign aid, Christmas food packages, disaster relief packages, etc., illustrate how the press as a system of communication has become an integral part of the battery of instruments by means of which American foreign policy makers try to influence the expectations and the behaviors of other peoples and governments-friends and allies as well as potential enemies and countries with wandering affections.

The mass media's supply of international news is an important factor in everyone's picture of the world. But foreign policy influence on the press affects the public's attitude towards, and image of, the people in other nations. According to Petersons, there is a correspondence between public opinion and official attitudes with regard to foreign policy.

In the formation of national images of international events and personalities, the transnational news agencies play a dominant role. They also play a role in educating the people of poor countries about rich life-styles. There is a view among researchers that after constant exposure to media fare from rich, technologically advanced countries with multinational economic interests, people of the poor, developing countries learn to identify whatever news they receive over the international news agency channels as relevant to their own circumstances. Himmelstrand and Hedman believe that 'in the long run, people's definition of news will become the same as the supply of news, as they will demand the information they are used to receiving from the news agencies. One might say the news agencies create their own demand'.

It must be stressed that the multinational agencies are under the strong influence of their own national government's foreign policy when they report foreign countries.

How newspapers change their attitudes to countries on the basis of changes in their own countries foreign policy has been documented by Sahin, Kreisberg, and by Lynch and Effendi. These three studies were based on the pattern of reporting in the New York Times over long periods of time. Very little news, for example, appeared about China in the US papers during the two decades following the Chinese revolution. But once President Richard Nixon broke the ice, the newspapers began to turn more frequently to China for news.

There is some merit in the argument that foreign news is meant primarily for the benefit of foreign policy formulators and top echelons of government, and that the average citizen is not deeply interested in foreign affairs. Much of the foreign news published may not be read by ordinary citizens. Some theoretical support to this view has been derived from the oft-quoted 'nature of news' theory of Schramm. Schramm's assumption is that by its very nature, foreign news cannot occupy any significant proportion of the newshole since it may not given immediate reward to the average news consumers. For immediate reward, the average reader turns to soft news: sports, crime, disasters, adventures, comics, movies, other entertainment, society, human interest, scandal, gossip, sex, psychological questions and answers and the like. They also turn to personalities, especially colourful personalities, such as kings, queens, dictators, ruthless tyrants, movie stars, mavericks, controversial figures such as racists, atheists, sex therapists and others, who generate more heat than light for the average reader. Then why does foreign news appear regularly in all newspapers? How much foreign news does appear? What countries and themes are more frequently reported?

Past research has indicated that 'prestige' or 'quality' newspapers devote somewhere between 10 and 30 per cent of their newsholes to foreign affairs. The 'popular' newspapers do not report as much foreign news as do the 'quality' ones. Do newspapers of different press systems have different approaches and attitudes to foreign news reporting? A comparison of two press systems operating in widely different environments may yield answers to the above questions, and clarify some of the conceptual matters discussed in this chapter.

The Susceptibility

While the lead should arouse the reader's interest, the body should sustain it. The body should flow-smoothly and logically from the lead. It should expand each of the points mentioned in the lead and, as far as possible, in the same order. The body should be as complete and as tight as possible. It should provide all the relevant information within the shortest space possible. The essence of good journalistic writing is brevity and simplicity. Do not use two words where one word would do. And do not use a complex or long word where a short word would do. Eventually, you should reach the point at which, choosing the story structure becomes second nature to you. This will, of course, come with experience and practice. You will then begin concentrating on the more creative and experimental aspects of writing.

A good reporter will spend a great deal of his time not sitting in the office but visiting places and meeting people who are potential sources of news. He should always keep his ears and eyes open. He should know where to go for the facts he needs for the story, recognise news when he encounters it, select the vital points for inclusion in his story and discard the inconsequential details.

Various Types

Let us now turn to different types of reporting such as objective, interpretative investigative and crime reporting.

Reporting of news, unlike editorial writing, is often described as a coldly impersonal job. A reporter is essentially a story teller and he should tell the story in an objective and truthful manner, without lacing it with personal opinions or subjective comments. He should be fair and impartial and present both sides of the story.

Complete objectivity is a mere concept. The reporter is a human being, not a robot, and he has certain ideas, feelings, attitudes, opinions and prejudices. However, a good reporter should try to rise above them and tell the facts as he has collected them in his search for truth.

No responsible reporter would behave like the notorious American journalist, Janet Cooke, who won the prestigious Pulitzer prize in 1980 for a story about drugs which was later proved to be fictional and fictitious. The journalist committed a deliberate fraud by dramatising a fake scene in which an eight year-old boy is injected with heroin supplied by the lover of the boy's mother.

Nearer home, the story of "mass rape" at a students function in a Madhya Pradesh town, published in a national newspaper was found to be baseless. When the report appeared on the front page of the newspaper it caused a sensation. The Editor asked a reporter to investigate. On arriving in the town the reporter first questioned the reporter of the news item, who insisted that the mass rape did take place. By , way of corroboration he produced a number of eye-witnesses. However when they were cross-examined and asked specifically to reveal only what they had seen, and not what they had heard, the investigator soon realised that the reporter had written the story on the basis of a bazar gossip and field it without verifying the facts. All that had happened was that during a function to celebrate the annual day of a local college, a portion of the shamiana came down, the electricity got cut off and a few students entered the women's enclosure and molested some of the girls.

There is this apocryphal story of a cub reporter, who, on his, first day at work wrote a piece with a cocksureness which was misplaced. On reading the piece, the editor advised him to be cautious and a little circumspect when writing about sensitive issues. The press, the editor reminded him, must not ordinarily violate the various laws on the statute book concerning libel, national security and parliamentary privileges.

The next day the cub reporter submitted a story which ran as follows:

> "Mrs. Gulab Paniwala alleged wife of Mr. Rakesh Paniwala, who claims to be the mayor of Shangrila, gave a cocktail party at her house in Model Town on Monday to bid farewell to Mrs. Jyoti Jariwala, reported to be the wife of the well-known industrialist, Samar Jariwala. Among those present at the party were Mrs. Romi Puriwala, said to be the widow of the late Hansraj Puriwala, a former cabinet minister, along with her alleged offspring, Jani Puriwala..." and so it went on.

The reporter had quite clearly gone to the other extreme in writing this report which was quickly consigned to the waste paper basket.

In reporting news, you must remember that facts are sacred. You must check and cross-check the facts from different sources until you are absolutely sure of them. Only then should you write your story. The golden rule is: tell the truth.

Objective reporting is, of course, not synonymous with dullness. It means fair and impartial reporting that is free from personal bias or prejudice.

14

Various Stages

Investigative Reporting

It is difficult to define the term "investigative" journalism. Some newspapers scoff at the very idea of an investigative journalist. In one way, of course, "investigative" journalism is a redundant concept, since all stories require some kind of investigation on the part of the reporter. However, the investigative reporter is expected to dig deeply beyond the facts stated in the hard news. Though we may face difficulty in defining the term, we cannot ignore the concept of investigative journalism. Many journalism students have an ambition to become "investigative" reporters. An "investigative" journalist sees himself as the conscience of society, pursuing corruption in high places without fear or favour. In his book Press and Law (Vikas, New Delhi 1990), justice A.N. Grover has quoted from the forward of Investigative reporting by Clark R. Mollevhogg. According to the Foreword, investigative reporting has three elements: It has to be the own work of the reporter. Under no circumstance should it be of others. The subject of the reporting should be such that it is of importance for the readers to know; and There must not be any attempt made to hide the truth from the people.

Investigative reporting has made great leaps in western countries. In India, it is still in its infancy. Most Indian newspapers do not have, or do not allocate, the manpower and funds necessary for a first-rate investigative job.

Attempts at investigative reporting, to quote one eminent Indian editor, are like drilling for oil. A fair amount of wastage of effort has to be taken for granted. But when the oil is discovered and becomes marketable, the sense of achievement is usually more than in any other sector of journalistic enterprise.

The best example of investigative reporting in our times, was the Watergate story which led to the disgrace and downfall of U.S. President Richard Nixon. When the two young reporters of The Washington Post, Bob Woodward and Carl Bernstein, started investigating the arrest of four men for a burglary at Watergate, the Democratic Party's national headquarters on June 17, 1972, they had no idea that their inquiry would culminate in the resignation of the President. The remarkable thing about their investigation was that it kept to the highest standards of professional journalism. The reporters did not start gunning for Nixon from the beginning. They merely pursued the burglary attempt and only later came up with startling facts linking the White House with it. "We did not go after the President, we went after the story", they explained.

Though the Washington Post stories led to the downfall of President Nixon, the same paper, later in 1980, got involved in the most celebrated case of journalist fraud in modern times-the case of Janet Cooke, already described in this unit. Janet Cooke's case gives a clear warning that every story whether "investigative" or not, should be handled by editors with great care and caution, otherwise, it will bring the newspaper to disrepute. N.J. Herbert Altsehull in his book from Milton to McLuhan (Longman, New York, 1990) states how the Janet Cooke story got into the Washington Post. An internal investigation by the newspaper's Ombudsman, Bill Green, blamed "failure of a system" for not checking up thoroughly on Cook's story. The failure to check was in part, Green said, the result of the fact that Cooke was black and that white editors did not want to be seen as racist. The Cooke's story appeared in the Post on 28 September 1980 and the edition featuring 8 Green's report appeared on 19 April 1981. Cooke was fired from the Post and was forced to return the Pulitzer Prize.

In our country, investigative reporters have brought to high a number of scandals-the Bhagalpur blindings incidents by the police, Kuo oil deal, A.R. Antulay's Private trusts, the securities scam involving Indian and foreign banks and stock brokers, etc. An enterprising reporter once got himself arrested so that he could give a first-hand account of life in Delhi's Tihar jail.

With governments becoming increasingly secretive and corruption spreading its tentacles far and wide, the need for investigative reporting cannot be over emphasized. Yet we must remember that investigative reporting is not everybody's cup of tea. It requires hard and sustained work. The investigative reporter should be combination of a crusader, super detective and blood hound and he should have the necessary time and finance to carry out his work.

In the pursuit of his quarry, the investigative reporter must draw a line between candid reporting and muck-raking, mud-slinging, character assassination or blackmail. He should base his report on incontrovertible facts, not on half-truths and lies. He should be wary of lobbies and lobbyists-political or commercial-trying to misguide him, and he should not behave like a peeping Tom or a prosecutor.

The best king of investigative reporting is that which keeps the public interest in mind. It may highlight an injustice, expose corrupt practices or unmask dishonest politicians and bureaucrats.

Experience has been that unless an investigative reporter or a crusading reporter gets the support of the Judiciary, the executive or the legislative, cannot bring his reports to logical ends. The Bhagalpur blinding report would have ended like any other report if a public interest litigation would not have been filed against the police. In the USA the Watergate stories would not have produced any result if they did not get the support of the legislative which threatened the impeachment of President Richard Nixon.

Crime Reporting

Crime reporting is not separate from the objective, interpretative an investigative form of reporting. Here it is separately dealt with because it is a separate and important beat in all big and medium level daily newspapers.

There is a tremendous public interest in crime stores and no newspaper can afford to ignore them without damage to its circulation and credibility. Attempts made by some newspapers to keep crime out of their columns, proved to be counterproductive and were soon abandoned.

Crime is a part of life and it is a newspaper's duty to inform the readers of what crimes are going on in their city, state or country. However, crime reporting should not aim at satisfying morbid curiosity or sensation mongering.

Although crime reporting is usually assigned to one of the junior reporters in a newspaper, it is a highly responsible and specialised job. The reporter should not only have the ability to shift the grain from the chaff, and the truth from lies, he should also have good contacts in the police and other departments of the administration as well as a working knowledge of the penal codes and law on libel and other relevant matters.

Besides, he must observe a code of honour. He should be as objective as is humanly possible and avoid resorting to sensationalism or cheap gimmicks to catch the attention of the readers. He should not suppress news of public interest. Nor should he seek to settle personal scores with police officers or lawyers or judges. And he must be careful that in the course of this work, he does not unnecessarily, invade a citizen's privacy. There has been much criticism of press reporting of crime and not all of it is baseless. Some reporters have been found quality of unethical standards, thus causing much pain and sorrow to their victims or their families and friends. In the case of the brutal murder of two Bombay nuns, some newspapers published totally baseless allegations conveyed to them by irresponsible police officials that the nuns were in the habit of receiving male visitors. The reports offended all decent citizens, particularly the members of the Christian Community.

A leading newspaper once published a fictitious report about a couple having been waylaid by a gang on the national highway. The report said that the husband was beaten up and the women was molested. The story was subsequently found to be incorrect, the product of the imagination of a reporter anxious his by-line in the paper. Reports glorifying the activities of criminals or making heroes of them should be discouraged as much as a resort to sensationalism. The crime reporter must never violate standards of decency and good taste.

Crime as News : There are several types of crime news-murders, fires, accidents, robberies, burglaries, fraud, blackmail, kidnaping, rape, etc.

Fires : The reporter must get his facts correct about the essential elements of a fire story-the number of persons killed or injured, the extent of damage to property, the loss of valuables, etc. He must also find out if the fire brigade responded in time or was guilty of delaying the fire fighting operations through sheer lethargy or incompetence or a lack of water supply. He should question eye-witnesses about any acts of bravery or cowardice. All these are essential ingredients of a fire story.

The lead in a fire story would normally suggest itself. It, for instance, lives have been lost, it needs highlighting in the lead. Where possible, list the names of the dead and the injured.

A major fire caused extensive damage to New Delhi's Vigyan Bhavan, the premier venue of international and national conferences, on Monday night, a chowkidar on duty received minor burns. According to preliminary investigations, the fire broke out in the kitchen and soon spread to other rooms on the ground floor. The chowkidar raised an alarm which alerted the head clerk on duty who informed the fire brigade and the police. Ten fire tenders soon arrived on the scene. However, their fire fighting operations were hampered by lack of water in the hydrants. By the time water tankers rushed to the site, the fire had engulfed a large area and damaged files, furniture, curtains and ceilings.

The police suspect electric short-circuit as the cause of the fire.

Homicides : In cases of a major murder, the reporter should rush to the scene as soon as possible after receiving a tip and gather all the relevant facts. In nine cases out of ten, crime reporters in, say, Delhi, depend on police information about murders and there is a time lapse before they can begin their investigations.

This often hampers their search for the truth. The reporter must, in any case, exercise great care in how he handles the story. Otherwise he runs the risk of causing offense.

In reporting dowry deaths or alleged dowry deaths, for instance, the reporter should refrain from levelling uncorroborated statements by one party or the other. He must therefore get his facts correct-by talking to the investigating police officer, the girl's in-laws and her parents, and, if possible, the neighbours.

A 25 year old housewife, Renu, died in NN Memorial Hospital on Monday morning from burns received in a kitchen fire. The housewife's parents allege that she was murdered by her in-laws who had been dissatisfied with the dowry she brought at the time of her wedding a year ago.

However, the husband, Kishore, a garment merchant in Chandni Chowk, and his father who were in the house at the time of the accident maintain, that Sushmita's sari caught fire when she was lighting a stove in the kitchen. Since the kitchen door was closed, they did not hear her cries for help.

The police are questioning the women's relatives as well as neighbours and are reluctant to offer an opinion until the investigations are complete. At the insistence of Renu's parents, however, they have registered a case against her in-laws.

Accidents : Most accidents are reported on the basis of police bulletins or information supplied by police spokesmen. However wherever possible the crime reporter must rush to the scene of a major accident to give authenticity to his story.

Three members of a family-husband, wife and daughter-were killed on the spot when a speeding truck remmed into their car on the road to Indira Gandhi International Airport on Sunday morning. A fourth member of the family had a providential escape. According to the police, the truck driver lost control of the vehicle and swerved sharply to the right and hit the car coming from the opposite direction.

Those killed are Ram, a businessman of Agra, his wife, Janki and their daughter, Aasha. The second daughter, Geeta, had a miraculous escape and suffered only minor bruises on her arms and legs. She was treated at the Safdarjung Hospital and allowed to go home.

The truck has been seized by the police but the truck driver, Sasi Singh is absconding.

News in the Making

All copy reaching a newspaper office from different sources is processed at the news desk. The desk is manned by sub-editors and usually a chief sub-editor leads the team and works as copy taster and also as revise editor or slotman. He sits in the very useful slot of the horse shot shaped copy desk facing other sub-editors on the rim. After distributing copy to other subs he also checks their work for any mistakes and passes to on to the composing room.

The sub-editor does some or all these to every story:

- Reads the story for clarity of language and meaning and rewrites where necessary.
- Shortens the story while retaining the essentials and maintaining coherence.
- Combines one story with another, or perhaps combines running reports from several news agencies, correspondents and reporters to produce a single intelligible report from different and sometimes contradictory messages.

- Saves space when verbosity creeps in.
- Corrects the grammar and checks for house style.
- Checks for apparent errors of fact.
- Checks for taste.
- Adds important background facts and provides answers for any implied questions.
- Writes headlines which attract the attention of the reader and also writes sub-headings if necessary.

The chief-sub of revise editor checks the work of sub-editors ensuring accuracy of details. He also becomes the fist reader of the story and sees whether the headline and copy make sense.

Another senior sub-editor or chief sub looks after the work at 'the stone'. He is called 'stone editor' also. Though with change in technology the stone has vanished but the term persists. The job of the composing room where the pages are made up with metal types and picture blocks or with strips of film or bromide. The stone sub can also be called production editor or make up editor. He deals with minor disharmonies. If the text is too long, he cuts it. If the page plan does not work, he changes it. If there is late news, he makes room for it. He checks the galley proofs and page proofs and finally sends them to the press.

Thus a sub-editor has to know all about news writing and how a reporter should write news copy. He is supposed to improve upon the work of the reporter. He should not change something for the sake of change but he must make sure that every correction or change the makes improves the copy.

Bulk from News Agency

The bulk of copy which comes to the news desk is from wire agencies. The teleprinter keeps on creeding information almost all the time during peak news hours of the afternoon and evening. This copy comes in takes the unit of news agency transmission or unit of newswriting.

Foreign news items have their own serial numbers, FG., FS,

FES FTF, PAS and POOL. Whereas FG, FS and FES files carry news items received from Reuter, AFP and UPI and are credited to those agencies, the PTF file is made up of reports received from PTI's own correspondents and stringers abroad. Items taken from the services of agencies like TASS. Xinhua, Antra Bernama, Tangug and other agencies with which PTI has exchange arrangements go under the PAS series. The POOL file is devoted to agencies participating with PTI in the Press Agencies Pool of Non-aligned countries.

Sobhraj-style is slug-an identification tag. Every story even a story consisting of only one take, must carry at the top a suitable slug. Generally the slug is one word which is often the key work in the story. Thus a story about rain would which is often the key work in the story. Thus a story about rain would be slugged "rain" and one about the police firing, "firing". Slugs are nouns and not adjectives pour in from various points, a master slug should be used with sub-slugs for individual story. In the above example Sobhraj is master slug while style is sub-slug.

Play boy of prisons once more outwitted is the headline. This is a new development. Agencies normally are not supported to give headlines but now to lighten the burden of newspaper sub-editors they have also started putting headlines. If the sub-editor. At the newspaper desk likes it he can indicate the type size for the headline.

New Delhi Apr. 7 is dateline and PTI is credit line. It appears just after date line in the fist take of the story and again at the end of each take. All the takes of the story except the last end with More-PTI as in the above example. The last take of the story is closed with PTI. For Spl of Espl services or sometimes for all stories the story can be reopened. In re-opening an item, reference is given to the previous take by its number for instant, "Sobhraj five-New Delhi-re-open Del 33".

RR RT BDS are initials of the reporter, the deskman or deskman processing it and the teleprinter operator punching it on the tape. Each take also carries at the end ,that time at which it is transmitted in the services.

The Lead : In news agency lead is used in the case of developing stories for updating the top, as necessary, in the light of fresh facts as they become available. Examples of such stories could be train or air mishap, a conference or meeting, an election, a state visit by a VIP. Such stories may require one or more leads as the story advances with the day. A lead can also be used to tie up loose ends of dispersed story, or to provide combined top for two or three different items about a single subject or related development.

There can be one or more leads to a story. For example, the leads on an air crash story, slugged "Crash" could be "Lead Crash", "Second Lead Crash", and so on. The final wrap-up story would be "Lead all Crash".

Pick-up: A lead often overhauls a substantial part of a story or even the entire story. Such lead is also called a "round up". Close to deadlines of newspapers roundups are not useful and therefore the lead is in the form of a brief one or two para top, that is, just the new intro. This intro introduces the new element that has emerged in situation. In such cases an appropriate pick-up line is given linking with the part of earlier story specifying the item by number, slug and dateline and giving the location of the point of pick-up.

Kill Note: If an agency wants to withdraw or kill a story which has come on the ticker, it puts out a kill note. The kill note has priority marking 'Kill' and is without a dateline. It gives the number, slug, dateline and subject of the story which it kills and also indicates whether a substitute follows.

Similarly, corrections are also issued specifying the take line and words of the earlier story and then the whole take is re-issued with corrections.

Service Messages: Sometimes service messages which are meant for internal use also reach newspapers. Such messages have the word "service" at the top. Ordinarily a service is addressed to the editor at a particular place. These messages should not be confused with messages and stories sent for use in newspapers.

In order to prevent mistakes the words not, now and nor are

repeated in news agency copy. While editing the copy a sub-editor should delete one of these words.

Sorting : News agencies keep on creeding takes of different stories one after the other, while reporters and correspondents also continue filing copy so that subjects covered by news agencies are also covered by the members of newspaper staff.

If the same story is covered by a member of newspaper staff his copy should get priority over the news agency copy. Additional information given by the news agencies can be added to his copy giving credit to the agency.

News copy coming from different sources is sorted out at the desk and all copy relating to a particular story is kept separate. This helps the sub-editor doing that story to read the whole-copy, analyse it and do justice with it. This sorting helps also in knowing whether the news agency has completed the story or some more takes are likely to follow.

Judging the importance of the story the chief-sub decides the space to be given to it. This has to be in relation to total news fall. The relative importance of the story also determines the page where the story would go. Except developing or running stories, all other stories are edited as soon as it is decided that they are to be used. For running stories the deskmen wait for more information. When they come close to the deadline of the edition they proceed with what they have. When additional information comes, the story is changed again for the next edition.

A word about copy. Good copy, also called clean copy, has the name of the reporter and the date on the top of the first page. At least a third of this page is left blank to allow room for instructions to sub-editor and the printer. Sufficient margin should be left on both sides of the copy-say one and a half inch on the left hand side and one inch on the right hand side of all pages of the copy. At least a two inch space should be left at the top and the bottom of each page. News copy should be typed double space.

Every page of the copy should start and end with a paragraph. I there is a mistake in typing a word, it should be typed again. Corrections should be made above the line.

A reporter should leave underscoring paragraph, indents and all other typographical markings to the sub-editor. Wrong underscoring and paragraph marks make a mess of copy. At the end of each page before the last 'more follows' or MF is essential and the end of the last page should be marked 'End'.

On the copy the sub-editor crosses out certain things and circles others. Neither will be set in type but the distinction is that what nobody needs to see any more is crossed out, but essential service messages are circled. The page and edition where the story will go are written on the top of the story and encircled. For example, P 1/2 would mean page one of the second edition. Sub-editor's name or initials are also written and encircled, if there is a printer's or proof reader's query it can be referred to the sub-editor who has edited the copy. Type size and columns are also indicated and encircled. For example, 8 x 1 would mean that the copy is to be set in 8 point type of the newspaper text print across one column. There is no need to specify the face or to say that it is in roman. The rule in newspaper setting is to specify the unusual and otherwise to keep the copy clean. The fewer the marks the better it is.

Catch line or slug is also essential on edited text takes and headline folio, the operator setting the text sets the catch line and it can be married, with the other folios of the same story. Thus a story may have 'Rajiv' as slug or catchline. Its headline folio will carry 'Rajiv I' and its first text take would have 'Rajiv 2', and so on.

The News Headline : Every headline is written on a separate folio. The headline should be written clearly-in capitals if necessary. The letter which need capitalisation should be double ticked. Edition and page mark go on the top left hand corner and the catchline on top right had corner. It also carries instructions regarding type and the columns over which the headline will be spread and the headline style. For example, '14 CBLCX1 set left' would mean that the headline has to be set left over single column in 14 point century bold type in lower case. If the normal headline style is set left in that case it need not be specified in the instructions.

However, it is essential that the style breaking headlines should be marked with words and symbols.

Spread and Arrangement: The first headlines were single column. Now they can be spread over all the columns in the newspaper. Newspapers today use the opportunities for display by mixing single column and multi-column headlines depending on the importance of the news.

Banner headline should not be in lower case because lower case letters across such a wide measure look straggly. Moreover, headlines should be crisp and lower case headline will be unduly wordy.

There is a wide range of possibilities regarding arrangements of headline. A newspaper may standardise on one form, such as the centered head, or it can mix them between headlines. But much depends on the skill of the page planners and the ideas they try to communicate.

The basic typographic arrangements are flush left, centered, stepped, flush right and hanging indention.

Flush Lelf : Many newspapers have switched to this style. The flush left heading has one or more lines which are set flush to the left. This should not touch the column rule. The flush left headlines look better when each line is indented on the column rule leaving 6 points or half an em space on an 11 cm column.

Centered: In this type of arrangement each line of headline type is centered on the white of the column. The well-constructed, centered heading, whether of a multiline or a multi-deck has its own symmetry and it is neatly framed in white.

The patterns created by this need slightly more attention than the patterns the flush left heading creates, but neither needs as much attention as some other patterns.

If one is writing a multi-deck headlines they should be centered where they look best. The common double column headline is a single deck of two lines with centered headings. The second line should always be shorter than the first at least by two units. One should never try to write headlines in tight caps. They need more white around themselves for legibility.

Stepped: In this arrangement the first line is set flush left and the last flush right and the middle lines centered. Each line has to be about the same length, and they look like steps. To achieve a smooth step requires great care in headline writing. This style is discouraged by modern experts of readability. However, the greatest difficulty is that the stepped style depends too much on a precise count and any failure can lead to ugly results.

Flush Right: Each line is pushed against the righthand margin to create a stepped effect on the left. It has even more limited application than the stepped headline. It may be occasional variant in a paper but it cannot be recommended as a regular style. It is slow to set and difficult to read.

Hanging Indention: The first line is set full out and the others indented, usually to the left. It cannot be a regular style but can be used as an occasional variant.

Quotes: Old school considered that quotes and dashes were full letters. New school thinks it is an ugly habit. No headline should need double quotes: Only simple quotes should do. With flush left headings the flush line should be, the initial letter of each line-not the quote. The quote should be left to hang in the white.

Writing Headline: Writing headline involves half the skill of a good deskman. The difficulty in writing headlines is in conveying in a few attractive words the essence of a complicated set of facts. In half a dozen words the headline has to inform the reader what the story contains.

The headline gives emphasis to a few words in bold types. Hence every word should be weighed. Accuracy, intelligibility and vigour are the requirements and any newspaper which is careless with its headlines is careless about its own purpose and vitality. Wordy and vague headlines leave a newspaper reader confused and irritate him. Where every headline goes to the print with precision or wit, the whole newspaper comes alive.

Headline writing is art and craft at the same time. The art is in imagination and vocabulary and the craft lies in accuracy of content, attractiveness of appearance and practicality.

Counting the Units: A headline must fit in the space available to it. A headline with too many letters to be accommodated in the width and type required is called a "bouncer". It bounces back to the desk from the printer's room and wastes time at various levels. The deskman should always write a headline which should fit. But if there is a superb headline which will not fit in the heading scheme, the scheme can be changed to fit it. A chief-sub may consider this if the merit of the headline so demands.

A sub-editor counts the units in the words he writes for a headline. These units must not exceed the number of units allowed by the size of the type, its style and the number of columns the headline is being allowed to run.

The unit count system begins by giving a unit value to every letter and figure in the alphabet. It is based on a count of one for most letters with adjustments for thinner or fatter letters, and for capitals when they are mixed with lower-case letters. While m and w are counted as 1½ units; i, .1, f and t are counted 1h unit. Other letters are counted as one unit. Where capitals and numerals occur in a headline which is otherwise in lower case, allowance must be made for the extra space the capital letter or numerals will take compared with the lower-case letter. In a headline set u/lc (upper and lower case), count any ordinary capital letter or numeral as an extra 1/2 unit, that is, 1½ units. Exceptions are: M and W which should be counted as two units when in caps and I and J and numeral I should be counted as one unit.

If the headline is in all caps the letters M and W should be counted as 1½ unit while I and numeral 1 should be counted as 1/2 unit. Other letters and numerals will be one unit. The space between the words is counted by some experienced sub-editors as 1/2 unit, while others insist that the space should be counted as full unit. It is better to count it as full unit as if it is in excess it is on the right side and it also simplifies the count.

How does one know the number of units available? In newspapers there is always a list of headline types composed and pasted somewhere for ready reference. It may be available in the style sheet or style book.

If it is not available then the sub-editor should prepare a unit count card which gives the various counts at a glance. Unit count card can be prepared from the type schedule or by counting headlines as published in the newspaper for each style, size and spread. Count a dozen representatives of each headline and average the unit count obtained. Working in this way from published examples the deskman can write headings that fit without the need to count them. Experienced sub-editors resort to a unit count only in case of doubt.

Language: But the real art in headline writing is in using the language to sum up the news item and attract the attention of the reader. Before writing the headline the sub-editor must read the copy carefully and decide on the basic news point. The sub-editor must think hard about the single element in the story which makes it worth its space in the paper. When he finds one or more such points he should write them on a piece of paper.

Some sub-editors prepare to write a headline first and sub the copy later. Their argument is that it concentrates the mind on the subject of they copy and becomes the test for intro. If the basic news point is not in the intro it has to be re-written. So, while the sub-editor tries to look for basic news point for headline he is also evaluating the work of the reporter. However, in many cases headline has to be given later, after a first few takes are composed. But even in such a situation the sub-editor must write down the basic news sentence. Often when edited this basic news sentence yields a good headline.

However, the headline writer should always be cautious about the meaning of the words when they are written in different lines of the same headline. There are a few rules. Never split a hyphenated word, look for another way of saying the same thing without using a hyhen at all; never split compound verbs or compound nouns between lines.

A sub-editor must pretest the headline on himself. He must read it to himself and at the end of each line think if t means what he wants to say. If there is any doubt or awkwardness he must re-write the headline.

When multi-deck headlines are used, there is no point in repeating the same information in several decks. Only the first deck should be completely self-contained. Once the first deck has declared the subject area, other decks can take it for granted and use the space to supplement and elaborate.

The first deck should have the most important news point. The second deck may elaborate this with a significant detail without repeating any word or -it may add a further newsprint. Repetition of a word should be avoided but in no case should it be replaced by a difficult or confusing word. In that case the general rule is to repeat rather than to confuse. Overline, if it is there, should elaborate or supplement the main deck.

Accuracy and impartiality are the basic requirements of a good headline. A news headline expressed the news and not the views of the sub-editor who is writing it. Care should be taken to write headlines of political stories. They should not look as if the paper is supporting some political party's view point while in fact it is just reporting the view point. To avoid such a situation one may use quotes on name the person or, party in the main deck. The headline writer must put his personal views aside. He must remember that his job is to reflect as accurately as possible the content of the story.

Quotes are one of the devices for dealing with strong opinions in headlining speeches or political party resolutions. One may put the name of the speaker or party in the headline. Headlines entirely in quotes are usually weak and should always be avoided. It is better to use single quotes for the part of headline which really needs them. When headline is in decks often the attribution is, given in the second deck, it is a bad practice. A headline with opinion and without quotes cannot be made acceptable by putting an attribution in the second deck. Attributions must be contained in the same deck as assertions, otherwise the statement in the first deck seems to have the authority of the newspaper for it.

But there should be no quotes when the opinion is obviously of the paper or the critic or columnist. It is unnecessary and may mean- that the critic or columnist has relayed gossip. Another word of caution is that the people in the news, particularly in crime stories should not be identified by race, colour, religion or nationality unless such identifications are pertinent in the news context. It is wrong to indulge in puns when the subject is death, injury or religion. Funny headlines should not be given for serious events. The sub-editor should always check whether the meaning of the headline is the same as the content of the story. Normally it is the duty of the chief-sub to check the work of subs as far as copy editing and headlining is concerned. He must also keep all these considerations in the mind, for he is again a person on whom the headline and the copy is pretested for clarity of language and meaning.

Strong Verbs: There should always be a verb in the headline. News is activity and verbs bring activity and life to headline. In a normal headline there should be no room for adjectives. Its colour and spice must come from a rich verb. One should avoid using parts of weak verb 'to be' or 'to have' as the main verb in headline. The verbs 'to be' or 'to have' are not needed even as auxiliaries. For example "Sobhraj arrested" is better than "sobhraj is arrested". There are occasions when the very 'to be' should be omitted even though this seems to leave the headline without a very. This verb is better when implied. Its physical presence in the headline makes it weak.

Passive voice has been major culprint in headline writing. A verb should be used in active voice as far as possible. At least before using the passive voice the sub-editor should himself try the active voice and should explain to himself the reason for not using active voice Passive voice normally breeds extra words and burdens a headline. Usually, rejecting a passive voice construction can lead to a more vivid headline. However, care should be taken to see that the main news point is as close to the beginning of headline as possible.

The headlines have been using the present tense to describe events that have already happened. The arguments in support of this phenomenon is that the present tense is active, it puts the reader in the middle of the action and gives him a feeling of participation. The event described in present tense in the headline may be past, but it is recent past and the reader is learning about it now. He also understands the convention and will imply that in the present tense his morning newspaper's headline is giving the news of yesterday. 'Yesterday' is almost never justified in a morning newspaper headline because in that case almost all items could have yesterday in the headline. The reader takes for granted that it was yesterday unless it is otherwise specified.

There is an added advantage in using present tense. It is invariable shorter. It gives the feel of recency to the news below the headline.

Subject is an essential part of a sentence like verb and headline is really a truncated but still meaningful sentence that the reader understands. It should be in the headline either as such or as understood. It may be possible to write a headline without a subject in many circumstances but one should remember a headline with a subject tells more about the story than one without it.

The rule regarding the use of subject in a headline is to give the name if it is well known or the title if he is not well known. One must headline a name in case of obituary even if a person is not so well known.

The weakest form of subject in a headline is 'he' or 'she.'. It is not an identification. But it will be at times good to use 'he' or 'she' headline on a human interest story with a picture of the subject.

'Man' or 'woman' are weak identifications of subject but at times they are unevitable. 'Wife, husband, father, mother's are better because they narrow the field. But they should not be taken as another name for man or woman. 'Husband banned at club' will suggest that he cannot go while wife is allowed. Thus it is better to be more specific about the subject but it should be ensured that there is no distortion. Don't say "child" in headline if the child is not yet two. Better use 'baby' or say boy or girl and give age.

Headlines should be as specific as possible not only in identification of the subject but also in other matters as well. One should be specific about the main newsprint and a headline should tell as much as possible. It does not however I mean that 'where' of the story should always be included. One should test by examining the headline whether the addition of a place name adds significance. It is sufficient to say 'Barnala condemned terrorism at a Chandigarh press conference.' Further place name comes the first thing after the headline as a part of dateline. But in stories where place is important it must be there in a headline. For example, 'Earthquake rocks Simla'.

The language of headline should be positive. Some stories must be negative but the headline writer should avoid using 'no' or 'not' and try to express the same thing in different words. Short and simple words should be used for longer ones. For example, talks can be used for 'negotiations' and 'goods' for 'commodities'.

Headline should express a single thought to ensure clarity. It is difficult to communicate, a single idea in limited space; if more than one idea is involved it becomes almost impossible. Therefore the most important idea or thought or event should be identified to be put in headline. The deskman has to decide what the news really is and then he should express it with verbs and nouns using positive, simple and short words. This is the rule If the circumstances need the rule can be broken but the sub-editor should know that he is breaking a rule and should be careful about clarity and content of the headline.

15

Technical Aspects

The history of typography has shown that the type which is easy to read is better than any fancy type and the Italian humanist lettering now called Roman ousted Caxton's Germamic Gothic in England and everywhere else because people found it easier to read.

Different Types

Types bear many eighteenth century names of pioneers who cut type. William Caslon of London cut his famous type in 1720. John Baskerville of Birmingham and Giambattista Bodoni who made his fame from 1786 in the printing office of the Duke of Parma. But these types were originally designed as small-sized types for books. When the type manufacturers had to meet the demand for display faces for posters, shops, advertisement and newspapers, they produced strengthened versions of the book faces and later wholly new designs of their own.

Though there is today a vast range of display type, a newspaper must select from a limited range. Speed of production requires that headline type in general use in the newspaper shall come as metal from a key boarded machines of linotype and intertype or the semi-mechanized Ludlow system, or as film set characters from these and other manufacturers. An attractive hand set type from a founder can only be used for larger sizes at wide measure when hand-setting will be as fast as machine because type setter will be setting just a few characters.

In hot-metal process the Ludlow system of slug casting from hand-set matrices is most popular for headlines as the key board machines do not set above 36 pt in upper and lower case.

There is no need to leave extra-white between letters and words. It normally spoils the visual impact of the headline. Spacing in the headline should always be judged visually. If it looks wrong it is wrong without any doubt.

Use of underscoring, bucket, hood or curtain and box should be avoided in headline particularly when it is spread over single or double column. It indicates failure to choose right type size and only therefore one needs column rules to separate this headline from the rest.

While using reverse block one should always choose an open bold face without fine serifs Open sans or a slab serif is ideal.

Punctuations: Full point is not used in headlines. The last word is the end of a thought and therefore no need to put full stop. When two thoughts are joined together in a deck (though one should avoid this) they should be separated by colon. The use of semi-colon should be avoided for simplicity and typographic neatness for easy reading. Exclamation and question marks should be rarely used. Comma should be used to separate clauses and sometimes used to indicate the omission of 'and'. While using comma care should be taken to ensure right meaning. Quotation marks are used to indicate external authority for a statement and also to indicate doubt about an assertion.

New technology of type setting: For many years the only kind of type setting was that done by hand and therefore the production of newspapers was necessarily slow. The invention and adoption of line-casting type-setting machines 'linotypes' enabled publishers to greatly speed up the production of newspapers. The Linotype continued to be the most widely used technique of setting type until about 1966 when a number of typesetting inventions began to be accepted and adopted by many newspapers throughout the world. The type is now set photographically and with the aid of computers and some related inventions revolutionised the speed of newspaper production. The video display terminal (VDT) allows the reporter to not only type his original story and a have the words show up on a video display screen but he can also correct and edit that story without touching a piece of paper and operate the phototypesetter on a push of button.

The optical character reader (OCR) enables the reporter to type his story on a special electric typewriter, edit it on the same machine and then feed his written story to the OCR to 'read' the words on the paper and operate the phototypesetter subsequently.

Hand-set and machine-set type were best adopted to letter-press printing which consists of printing from raised letters, directly on paper. Phototypesetting is better with offset printing method in which after a printing plate is coated with ink and water it first prints on a rubber sheet (called a blanket) and then from the blanket onto paper.

Photoprints, when used with offset, are pasted directly on a page format along with screened pictures. Then the entire page is photographed as a single entity, converted into a negative and finally into a printing plate.

The basic phototype setting technique consists of placing a film negative of each letter in a sentence in front of a light source and then shining light through the negative onto light-sensitive photographic paper. The result is a picture of letters assembled into lines. Once enough lines have been set photographically they can be pasted on to a page form photographed and converted into a printing plate.

The first generation of phototypesetters were really a

modification of hot typesetting machines where each letter of the alphabet was first made in the form of a mold (called a mat). Hot lead was poured into the molds thereby producing a line of metal type. These mat were modified by replacing the molds with a film negative of each letter. After the first line was set, the photographic paper would be advanced ready to receive a new line of letters. Thus, the first generation phototypesetters were really photo-mechanical in nature and therefore relatively slow. The fastest could set twenty lines a minute depending upon the versatility of the operator.

The second generation of phototypesetters could set type faster and the method of photographing the letters was different. At least four different modes of negatives were developed by various competitors. All the letters of the alphabet, numbers and punctuation marks were prepared on a single film negative surface such as a disc, a drum, a film strip or a rectangular grid. It was possible to move these letters more quickly than older machines. This generation increased the speed of setting to about 150 lines a minute.

The third generation phototypesetting machine are almost totally electronic. They use a cathode ray tube (CRT) as a scanning device and throw light through a lens and then through each of the letters in a sentence on the negative surface. A photoelectric cell behind the negative picks up the light and delivers it to another cathode ray tube which eventually prints the letters originally scanned on photographic paper. This third generation typesetter can set upto 500 lines a minute.

The fourth generation typesetter has also emerged. The distinguished feature of this typesetter is that it uses laser beam in the setting process and has no photographic negative to shine light through. Instead a laser beam generates letters from a memory control, electronically through a series of strokes and build letters somewhat like that of CRT machine but without a master negative. Fonts of type are stored in the memory unit of this machine and can be called forth by pressing a button. This machine can set

1000 lines per minute. It is also possible to generate line art and halftones in the laser typesetters. This will enable the user to make up all of the elements of a page on a video display tube. When the page is made up, it may be printed on photographic paper ready for conversion to an offset printing plate.

Most photosetters installed in newspaper plants are operated in conjunction with either a VDT or an OCR in addition to a computer. Assembly of these various operating machines wired to each other is called a system.

In this system the reporter types copy on VDT key board. He then corrects and edits it. When he is satisfied he sends the story to computer for storage. Other stories are also in storage. Sub-editor or chief sub can retrieve it from the storage for checking and can do editing using the VDT. He can also write headlines, specifying the kind of type, size and width and returns the story to computer for storage. If he feels he should edit it fully or rewrite it he can have it printed on paper at 360 lines a minute speed. Then he can edit it on paper and later on VDT and return it to computer for storage.

When the news editor is reading to dummy page, he can ask computer to print all sluglines on VDT and decide what stories he wants. After this decision he calls up each story on VDT, determines its length and begins to dummy the page. After this he presses a button and sends body copy and headlines to be set on a phototypesetter which delivers a photoprint. Story now goes to the printer for paste up.

Photographs

Good pictures speak for themselves. While making selection of news pictures the prime consideration should be context in which the picture is being used. The picture should have information related to the story with which it is to be used.

A good news photograph should reflect the feelings and

responses of the people photographed. Even routine events yield good photographs if the people are caught by the camera in action and their feelings and emotions are expressed on the faces. Animation is one of the prime quality of a good news photograph.

Photograph should reflect the mood of the moment. Even selecting from file pictures care should be taken to select a photograph which depicts the right mood. When a person is sacked a picture depicting him in a happy mood will be a misfit.

Like words pictures also have meaning. There are occasions when symbolism could be effective to impact meaning. Sometimes comparison provide meaning to pictures.

Looking at certain photographs one is surprised what little eyes can see when the event is taking place. Action photographs particularly come in this category. In sports events and cultural events action photographs depicting the climax of a movement if captured by camera becomes an exciting picture.

A photographer must reach on a scheduled event a few minutes before the time and look for key moment while shooting. Camera is very much similar to the notebook of a trained reporter. It should catch the key moments of the event that are most relevant to the news event. News photographer should have news sense and it should be sharpened by selection of his most newsy pictures by the photo-editor.

Only a photographer with a keen news sense will be able to catch decisive moments of history with is camera. In every event there is sequence of action of which only a few moments are at the climax and only one of them is really decisive. Nearer the photograph is to that moment the better news photograph it is.

The photograph once selected has to be edited for size, shape and story content. The basic determining factor is the story content because it determines the size and shape of the photograph or whether the photograph should be used at all.

It is debated whether a photograph should be cropped. Many photographers of international repute argue that a good photograph should never undergo cropping. But it may be true of only excellent news photographs capturing decisive moments. Most of the photographs can be improved by cropping. While cropping the emphasis should be on the story and what is in the picture. One may remove irrelevant portion of a picture and emphasis could be added to the relevant portion of the picture. Shape of picture is also decided by the story content.

While determining the size of a picture emphasis should be on legibility and impact. It is pointless to give a photograph if it is printed so small that the relevant detail is lost. Legibility determines the minimum size of the picture and maximum has to determined by the availability of space, competition from other news pictures or stories. It should also be seen whether giving a bigger size justifies the expense of space by increase in the impact. Space should be used with discrimination to ensure that the photograph which really needs it should get it.

Cropping is a creative job. Looking at the above factors one has to identify the key image in the photograph and enlarge it to give maximum information or impact. The words with the picture should match. The reader must be told what, where, when and why of the photograph. If explanation improves the understanding the key factor it should be given.

Design and Layout: It is essential to realise that newspaper design is part of journalism. It is not decoration ut communication. Newspaper communicates news and ideas and design is an integral part of the process.

A sub-editor begins with a blank sheet of newsprint and wants to communicate several ideas and the day's news. It is the function of newspaper design to present that mosaic in an organised and comprehensive way by using text type, display type, photograph, line work, white space and a sequence of pages in the most fitting combination.

The Layout

Newspaper design has to care for the audience too. Researchers find out the readership habits and give, it due consideration. For example, the broadsheet format of a serious newspaper will not suit a metropolitan evening daily which is produced for commuters on crowded trains or buses. Ideal format for such a newspaper will be tabaloid for ease in handling. Front and back page of such a newspaper should have the widest possible range of appeal.

There are other considerations of utility. A family newspaper should not publish women's column on sports page or on the other side of sports page. Magazine sections are separate from news sections of the newspaper. Such elementary consideration form the framework of newspaper design.

There is an important role in newspapers for artists and designers but they must be closely involved with journalists and journalism. They must share the idea of communication and the audience. A designer should not think that a day's news can fit in his preconceived patterns. The design cannot be left to the artist alone. If he produces something which is more useful in communication of an idea it should be used. Any refinement which interferes with function should not be allowed. There should be a balance between form and function where function is the priority. There is need for continuous dialogue between journalist, designer and the researcher to achieve a better balance between the form and function of newspaper design.

Organising the Content: Editorial content can be divided into two groups: (i) Unpredictable-Spot news in words and pictures which can be divided into local, national, foreign, and so on. (ii) Predictable: Stock-market prices, weather forecast, TV and radio programmes, film, art criticism, letters to editor, editorial, crossword puzzles, bridge column, etc.

Predictable content should be in predictable positions. Television and radio programmes, share prices, weather, etc., should be anchored in the same place day after day.

When the unpredictable news is organised in departments foreign, sport, business, etc., these should appear in approximately the same position in the newspaper every day. The space will vary according to the news and the size of the paper but the page should not be changed from day to day. Page sequence should be logical and consideration of reader habits should determine it. For example, right hand side pages particularly at the beginning of the newspaper get more reader attention so they should have material in which maximum readership is interested.

The Front Page: It is the most important page of a newspaper. It induces the reader to pick up the paper and read it. It establishes the identify and character of the paper and also introduces freshness by its display and content. According to function visualised for the front page it could be:

Signal and Text Front Page: It is typical modern front page where a selection of the most important news items is signaled by headlining and positioning on a clear scale of priorities and supported with text. Less important items go to inside pages. Most broadsheet newspaper follow this style with exceptions like Punjab Kesari, Jagbani, Akali Patrika. Efforts should be made to give the full text of an item on the front page. If the text does turn to another page it may be because of more items that deserve the signal treatment on front page.

Posterfront Page: It contains all the important news items on front page-just one or two paragraphs of each indicating the page on which details appear. Even as late as 1965 designers recommended this type for The Times, London. However, it was not accepted.

Many newspapers use variations and combinations of the two styles. Part of front page of signal and text front page can be used everyday to encapsulate the main news (and features) presented inside. The Times of India used this combination type front page.

Feature Front Page: Punjab Kesari, Jagbani and Akali Patrika give features on front page. Front page has normally nothing to do with news in these newspapers. This kind of front page has established in Punjab and it was regarded that change in this style may lead to fall in circulation. However, Ajit has changed from feature front page to signal-and-text front page an the circulation actually did not go down but increased.

Page Layout: make-up or layout of the page is determined by -the format of the page-the number of columns in -which the page is divided

Eight columns of 11 or 11½ picas each is the standard for broadsheets partly dictated by advertising standards of 11 picas. Layouts can vary in this format and number of display positions are available if the nature of newspaper is serious.

However there are nine or ten column papers. This format provides excess of display portion. It is difficult to manage typography and make such a page attractive. Readability of such papers is poor.

There is a A6 column format also. The standard 11 pica measure is retained for six columns and the seventh column is equal to 1½ column and the remaining half column is distributed as white space in the gutters. Many papers use this format which is attractive and convenient and also provides variety.

Six-column is regarded 'optimum format' because it takes optimum text line for easy reading (about 15 picas). However, the display positions are less than the eight column pages. In this format long stories can be handled with extra ease.

Five column format is also used by some papers. Some papers use this 14.6 picas grid for editorials or long analytical articles requiring long text.

For tabloids five and four column layouts are convenient and widely used. However, this format may vary from page to page and even on the same page. The varying format is most justified when it signals a distinct change of content. For example, editorial comment from general news content.

The column grid is part of basic format of the paper and is more or less a fixed element of newspaper design. Layout or make up occurs in this format.

Layout means arrangement of headlines, text, artwork and white space on a page or pages.

Layout could be static or dynamic. If one can predict the layout of tomorrow's page today because it has been similar with minor variations day after day the layout is called static. In such layout one can predict that the first lead story will be on say left hand side. There will be pictures and then there will be the second lead. There will be a third major story below the picture. The Times of India and Statesman provide good examples of such layout.

But layout is dynamic when no body can predict what it will be-the lead may be on left or right and if there is a striking picture headlines will be submerged to make room for it. Here designer is attempting to respond dynamically to the news. The Telegraph and Jansatta are god examples.

Layout, whether static or dynamic, could be modular or irregular. Modular layout breaks the page into series of rectangles-headline and related text form a four sided rectangular unit.

Irregular layout breaks the page into series of interlocking shapes. Most or all headlines themselves are irregular in shape and most or all headline-text units on a page form irregular shapes.

Vertical vs Horizontal: Vertical layout gives the simplest page organisation. Headlines are set in the width of basic single-column grid and the text runs single column. This oldest layout style has limited range of news value expression. Though it is visually depressing, maximum number of stories can be given above the fold.

When headlines side by side are the same size and style the result if called 'tombstoning'. This is a major problem of vertical layout. It can be overcome with alteration of colour along horizontal line. Colour here means blocks, greys and white and with modern display type adjacent heads can be varied to express different news values or tone. The headings can be set left in the white to avoid clash of headlines.

Another way is to vary the width of the headline grid. For example, a two column head is used to express more important news. The width of text setting can also vary to avoid monotony of tombstoning.

Horizontal Layout: This is another simple layout but with more capacity for emphasis. It is modular with text squared up under multi-columns heads to create a horizontal unit. Page is then made up of a series of these units lying flat on each other.

In this layout a long story seems shorter. Complete stories can be read with page folded at the natural midpage fold and without the reader having to shuffle the paper up and down, headlines are separated from each other by text and thus each headline retains its emphasis. In horizontal layout full use of the width of the page is possible for display. However, there are only a few stories above the midfold which can be seen at retail outlets.

Quadrant Layout: It envisages the page as four separate sections divided by a line at the fold and a line down the middle of the page. Each unit has a strong display item consisting of either multi-column headlines and picture or panel. This formula reminds that there is more to a page than its top half. But this formula if followed with geometric rigidity may lead to display of news item disproportionate to news value.

Diagonal Layout: Here the designer places headlines along two imaginary diagonal lines, which divide the page and cross each other. It reminds that headlines can be distributed anywhere on the paper. But it is difficult to coordinate display with the news values.

France Layout: The columns one and eight on an eight column paper should be solid text so that beneath the paper's title and eight-column banner heads the frame, the content of the page. It is more a gimmick than a formula for layout. After all, newspaper page is not a picture to be framed and put on the wall.

Brace Layout: In brace layout headlines are arranged in steps so that the one higher in the page is supported by another running parallel. In such a layout the headlines compete for attention with each other and lose emphasis. It also forces text away from the headlines. Headlines can actually stand on their own. They do not need each other's support as is provided in this type of layout.

Circus Layout: In circus layout emphasis is on variety contrasts and movement but not on order or news value. There are many points of attraction, not necessarily related to news values. The reader is to be distracted and entertained. The mast head of the paper may appear in any position above the fold.

Symmetrical Layout: This layout attempts to produce an equal balance of eight around an axis, classically the optical centre of the page. Each side of the optical centre should be a mirror image of the other. Optical centre, the pivotal point, is a point one-third of the distance from the top where the horizontal forces are in equilibrium with the vertical forces and is the point of perfect balance.

Symmetrical layout need not be static. The essence of axial symmetry is balance at the centre and this can be achieved in dynamic layout.

Symmetrical layout has a powerful appeal for serious papers as it appears to organise the heterogeneous content rationally and satisfies the human mind's natural demand for -balance. It is of little use to the newspapers that thrive on excitement. Even in serious newspapers the symmetrical balance threatens display in relation to news values. It is also difficult to produce a perfectly symmetrical page, particularly a newspage. Further, perfect balance may be boring also.

Asymmetrical Layout: This layout is dynamic and excludes any axial symmetry, any predetermined point of balance. Here 'artistic balance' or 'informal balance' is achieved by a balance of unequal forces at unequal distances from the centre.

Asymmetrical layouts have a balance which is subtle. It enables the page to satisfy our natural desire for order, organisation and balance while providing emphasis and movement. Balance is there but it is not a mechanical balance and it does not force the news to conform to set pattern. This assists functional relationship of content and display.

The newspaper design and layout must be functional. There should be organisation and rational coordination of heterogeneous material but the news values should get priority in deciding the display. It should give emphasis to the most important news to attract the reader. There should be order, but the prime importance should be given to news values.

16

Reporting on Scientific Matters

Technical writing is a term that can be applied to many subjects. Thus, it can deal with physics, chemistry, biology, microbiology, engineering, architecture, in fact, with anything that has a bearing on the mechanics of structure, whether of molecules, cells or cantilevers. This calls for a great deal of knowledge of scientific and technical subjects. A good writer would have a basic degree in science and engineering, a willingness to apply his mind to subjects related to his own discipline and above all a penchant for accuracy. One can get away with a description of a flower show but not with a description of the flower. The latter has to be specific and accurate. To say that a rose is a rose is a rose may be new literature but to confuse one variety of rose with another would be sacrilege.

Technical Reporting

Technical writing, unfortunately, is at a low stage of development in India which lacks sufficient number of technical and scientific journals to make technical writing attractive as a means of livelihood. Much of the technical writing is done by engineers or men and women specialising in a particular discipline. These writers would be knowledgeable but not necessarily readable. If a technical writer is writing solely for technicians, use of technical jargon may be understandable, though not necessarily wise. What, for example, would a non-technician understand in the following paragraph?

The lowest and most used mode of oscillations in a co-axial cable is that in which the electric vector is radial from the centre conductor to the outer conductor.

Co-axial lines carrying this mode are the only one discussed in this text. In some places reference will be made to the fact that more difficulty is encountered in achieving the desired result with large-sized lines. This is because other modes can be propagated in a co-axial line if the diameter exceeds a certain limit.

Microwave techniques

MIT Radiation Laboratory

There are words and phrases above that are intelligible to none but to the expert in microwave techniques. Mode of Oscillation. Co-axial cable. Outer Conductor. Large-sized Lines. Radial. This is a kind of writing that may be germane to a specialised journal but would be out of place in an article intended for the layman. The layman wants everything to be explained to him in language that he can readily understand. In technical writing, therefore, the writer should first ask himself the basic question: for whom am I writing?

If this is first cleared, then the rest is easily worked out. If the writing is intended for the knowledgeable, it should be apparent that the writer need not necessarily strain at trying to explain each and every technical word. He knows in advance that the "jargon" he uses will be comprehended, though even an expert would appreciate the writing more if it is precise, uncluttered and simple.

But if the writer is writing for the layman or for a broader audience, it is self-evident that jargon simply will not do. Every technical term would then have to be defined.

Take two examples of science reporting, for example, taken from *Science Today* (June 1980).

There are also increased numbers of hypothenar and second interdigital patterns on palms of thalassemia patients. In this severe defect of hemoglobin synthesis, there is a compensatory mechanism of rapid formation of blood cells and this may enlarge bone marrow and influence the bones of the limbs. Dermatoglyphic variations in this case are not of as much diagnostic value as in skeletal deformities, but results from other countries do suggest that dermatoglyphics could be used in future also for the genetic screening of this widely occurring hereditary anemia. . . .

Supernova Remnant : Stars are mortal. A good number of the stars we see today will blow up at the end of their 'life'. The blowing up of a star is called a supernova event (SNE). To a distant observer, such an event appears as the waxing of a star or even appearance of a new star. An SNE could outshine Venus in the sky and may even be visible during daytime for 10 to 20 days. Then the brightness wanes and the star is lost into oblivion. Chinese astronomers, a few thousand years ago, referred to these events as the appearance of 'guest stars'.

An SNE involves the release of enormous energy, most of which is transferred to the debris of the star (referred to as supernova remnant or SNR).

In the first example, scientific words are used that make no meaning or sense to the casual layman. The article from which the paragraph has been excerpted is evidently intended for the writer's peer group, which may be small. In the second example, excerpted from the same magazine, an attempt is made to explain terms, What is an SNE? What is an SNR? An average reader with not much knowledge of how the universe functions can still understand what a supernova is and what happens when a star dissolves or comes to the end of its natural life. Simple writing is what good writing is all about.

Sound Knowledge : The technical (or science) writer must, in the first place, have a sound grasp of his subject. In any writing of this sort, this is most important. A writer who knows very little of his subject can hardly do justice to it. And he is quickly found out. Indeed, in this regard, a little knowledge can be a dangerous thing. In the circumstances, a technical writer would do one of two things: get guidance from a knowledgeable source or have his writing checked out by an expert. It is bad journalism and worse pedagogy to pretend to know where knowledge is absent. In such a situation it can truly be said that where ignorance is bliss, 'tis folly to be wise.

But no single person can possibly know all about biology, aeronautics, computer science or hydrodynamics. Knowledge is vast and the time for any single individual to amass it is limited, though that does not mean that he should not try. What the technical writer should remember is that his can only be a full-time job. This is definitely not for the dilettante.

Up-to-date with the Latest Developments : A good technical writer is well advised to build an adequate library of technical and scientific books of his own for ready reference. In the absence of such a library he will get access to such books elsewhere, whether at a college, a technical institute or a university. He will also stay in touch with professional engineers, scientists, technologists so that he is up-date on newest developments. If he is a serious writer, he will also subscribe to technical and science journals to see how others go about their job. In this field, more than in any other, humility is a virtue. The technical writer should never be ashamed to ask. Engineers, scientists and their compeers are human and while they may enjoy feeling superior to their lay fellow men, most are also willing to explain their particular expertise to one who approaches them with the necessary humility. The writer who goes to interview a scientist must do so to seek enlightenment, not an argument.

In writing a technical article, the following questions assume relevance:

What is the market for the article?

Who has the necessary expertise on the subject on which the article is required?

What is the wordage needed?

Is diagrammatic explanation possible?

The writer will then seek the expert, explain his mission, get him to clarify complex areas of information, do a preliminary draft and have it finally cleared by the expert. That completes the cycle.

Ordinary science reporting that does not involve great expertise is the stuff that daily journalism is made of. Consider this report from *The Times:*

***High Energy Frustrations* :** For the second time in a decade, pressure on the American science budget is facing United States high energy physicists with the prospect of a lengthy pause in the construction of new particle accelerators, the machines used to investigate the elementary properties of matter.

The initial pause came in the early 1970's when the physics budget dropped for the first time since the Second World War. But this has been followed by a period of renewed growth, with a new electron-proton collider being completed at the Stanford Linear Accelerator Centre (SLAC) in California, for example.

Under construction are large machines using superconducting magnets to reduce energy consumption at the other two national accelerator centres. One will collide pairs of protons at energies of 400 gev (thousand million electron volts) at the Brookhaven National Laboratory on Long Island, the other will hurl protons on to fixed targets at 1,000 gev at Fermilab, near Chicago. . ..

The restraints are particularly frustrating to physicists because they come at a time when the experimental discoveries of the past decade are beginning to fit together into a broad pattern for understanding nature's building blocks. But the large amounts of energy needed to 'smash' atoms and their constituent particles makes high energy physics expensive, and hence an attractive target for budget-cutting. ...

For the time being, physicists have agreed that the construction of the accelerators at Brookhaven and Fermilab should remain top priority, even if research funds have to be sacrificed. Both accelerators will be world leaders capable of entering hitherto unexploded regions of physics.

But this is something of a gamble. Both were conceived in the early 1970's when the most promising avenue for physics appeared to be the disintegration of protons at ever higher energies. Since then, however, theoretical developments and in particular the unified theory of weak and electro-magnetic interactions for which Steven Weinberg and Abdus Salam last year shared the Nobel Prize for physics with Sheldon Glashon— have suggested that another direction may be more fruitful: the collision of electrons and their anti-matter equivalent, positrons (electrons with positive charge).

A particular new goal is the study of such collisions at an energy level of about 100 gev since the unified field theory predicts that this should produce a particle known as the neutral intermediate vector boson—or ZO, (Z to the zero degree)—which would be the heaviest elementary particle yet discovered.

European physicists hope to explore the world of the ZO with a giant new accelerator which Cern (European Centre for Nuclear Research) is being asked to build in the second half of the 1980's. United States physicists, rising to the challenge, are putting forward their own proposals for investigating the same collisions.

One, the most advanced at present, would be to pass bunches of electrons and positrons in tandemn down the linear accelerator at SLAC, then send them down in opposite directions around a ring at the end to collide on the other side.

Another would be to upgrade electron storage rings which recently began operation at Cornell University.

Both projects have caught the imagination of physicists ....

It is evident from this report that the reporter had consulted physicists to explain to him what was involved in America's cutting down the budget for scientific research and what was being planned. The result is a succinct and understandable account of one aspect of molecular research.

A series of minor, if useful, changes to Alfa Romeo's Alfasud give the excuse to praise again arguably the best small car of the past decade. It led the field when it first appeared in 1972 and is still up with the best today... .

The latest changes include the fitting of a front spoiler (not that from a handling point of view, the car needed one), new bumpers and light clusters, side strips to protect the bodywork and liberal use of matt black as a scratch proof finish on the door handles, radiator grill and so on. There are new front seats, giving better support, and more space has been created in the back by giving the rear seat an extra tilt.

The essence of the Alfasud is that it drives like a sports car and yet has none of the traditional sports car vices such as boneshaking ride, raucous and cramped seating. On the contrary, it has the space, comfort, and refinement to make it just acceptable to the family motorist as to the enthusiast who likes to open the throttle and tear round corners.

In its design, the Alfasud combines flair with plenty of commonsense. Under the latter heading it must be said that few cars of such compact overall dimensions (less than 13 ft long) manage to offer so much passenger and luggage space. The car is a genuine four-to-five seater and has a generous boot. The boot opening is on the small side but leaves no awkward lip to negotiate.

There is common sense, too, in the power unit. The horizontally opposed cylinder layout was chosen by the Alfasud's Austrian designer, Rudi Hrusha, for its tidy shape, quiet running and low vibration rather than for the sake of being different. It is an engine that never sounds bad-tempered, however provoked, and will run sweetly all day at 70 mph even if it is turning over at 4,000 rpm in top gear.

It is also a very lively unit. On the 1.5 model it comes in 1490 cc form, developing 84 bhp, takes the car from rest to 60 mph in just over 11 seconds, gives excellent flexibility and provides a top speed of about 100 mph. Such figures put the Alfasud among the quickest in its class. Performance is not achieved at the expense of fuel economy: I returned 28 mpg in town and upto 40 mpg, using the fifth gear which is standard on this model on the open road.

The outstanding characteristic of the Alfasud is, however, its handling. I cannot think of another small car that is so responsive in everything that it does—steering, brakes, cornering—all give the driver the feeling of tautness, of being totally in control. The road-holding is superb. Enjoyment of driving is enhanced by crisp gear-changes, although until the box warms up reverse can be difficult to engage.

The ride is firm and does not soak up the bumps .. . the modified seats are well padded and give good thigh and side support, while their range of adjustments, together with a height adjustable steering column, mean that most drivers should find an ideal position ....

It is clear from the above that the reporter knows all about cars, has driven many in all sorts of situations and has carefully recorded his impressions. He has credibility. The language is nontechnical as far as that is possible and can be understood by the average owner of a car. The most important thing in such a case is the extent to which the reporter has established his credibility. He is making value judgements, in addition to narrating straight facts. There is the possibility that he may be challenged in which eventually, he should be in a position to defend himself with ease. Note the style. *It is an engine that never sounds bad-tempered, however provoked, and will run sweetly all day. . . .* Such reporting carries the day.

It will be seen that the reporter has not only given us the facts about the Alfasud but has further provided us with interpretation. *Performance is not achieved at the expense of fuel economy.* This is interpretation of the fact that followed, namely, that the car gave 28 mpg in town and upto 40 mpg on the open road.

The Processing

Technical writing is concerned not only with writing about mechanical things (cars, aeroplanes, ships, engines of all sorts) but with the art of processing as well. How, for instance, would a technical writer deal with the processing of tobacco from harvesting the crop to selling the final product?

Consult experts. The first step, as in all cases of feature writing, is to consult experts in the field. From them, the technical writer may learn the various steps involved in the processing, which he would then use for an outline for a first draft, somewhat as follows:

I. *Harvesting the crop.*

1.a. Harvest season.

1. b. Methods of cutting.

l.b.l Individual leaf.

l.b.2 Whole plant.

II. *Curing the leaves.*

1.a. Air-curing.

1. b. Flue-curing.

1. c. Fire-curing.

III. *Sorting the leaves.*

1.a. Size

1.b. Quality

1. c. Colour.

IV. *Packaging the tobacco.*

l. a. Cases.

1. b. Bales.

1. c. Hogsheads.

The method would be the same whether one is dealing with processing of tobacco, or manufacture of cheese. The important point to remember is that the writer must think through his topic, gather and organise his material, break his available information under meaningful heads and finally link them to make a coherent and readable story.

The second point to remember is not to leave technical words undefined. The average reader would not know what is meant by "flue-curing" or a "hogshead". That will have to be explained to him.

A third point to remember is making effective use of statistics. Often a writer makes a point clear and vivid by drawing a comparison to something else.

And finally, a story can be strengthened by using quotes. Here is an example' of how a good technical story can be written (*Fortune,* March 24, 1980):

Fiber Optics : The wondrous technology heralded as the replacement for copper wire in communications systems has come out of the labs at last. But some potential customers haven't got the message yet.

For nearly two decades, the promise of transmitting information with bursts of light through glass fibres hovered like a tantalising mirage on the horizon of telecommunications. The practical application of fiber optics, as this *wondrous technology* is called, advanced very slowly. By 1978, all the installed fiberoptic cables in the world *added up to a mere 600 miles.*

This maddeningly sluggish pace turned impatient enthusiasts into cynics. "Every year that I've been to fiber optics" recalls William Caton, a consultant to I.T.T's Cannon Electric Division in Santa Ana, California, "people have been predicting that next year it was just going to explode. Many companies have been burned, and many people have been burned in their personal careers in the sense that they oversold fiber optics to their bosses".

There is news at last to cheer even the most despondent. Thanks to steady improvements in technology, fiber optics has finally become competitive with conventional copper cable in some applications. ...

A major reason is that the fibers save space. A skinny fiber cable can carry many more messages than a much-thicker copper-wire cable. This means that telephone companies can stuff additional message-carrying capacity into existing underground ducts; there's no need to dig up streets to lay new conduits

The total sales of fiber-optics cable and associated equipment are still miniscule—and estimated $ 40 million a year. But the principal manufacturers—Corning Glass Works, I.T.T. and A.T. & T's Western Electric—expect the business to grow to several hundred million dollars a year by 1985 ....

Note how fiber optics is defined as "transmitting information with bursts of light through glass fibers". The definition comes quite early in the story so that the reader does not have to seek what the writer wants to convey. Note also how statistics is used to give a feel of what the position is today and what it can grow into in the years to come. Note, too, how skillfully a quote is used and the person quoted fully identified to give it verisimilitude. The story follows a brief introduction in which what follows is neatly summarised. The headline promises hope as against despair. Fiber Optics Finally Sees the Light of Day. There is a definitiveness about the word "finally". It indicates that a lot has gone before and the story deals with the *culmination* and *fruition* of a long process. The reader's interest is thus aroused. He would want to know how it happened. Suspense is in-built in the first two paragraphs.

Research Reports : Many editors would like to have not merely long articles on a given subject (Fiber Optics, in the case of *Fortune* magazine) but frequently a round-up of research in a particular area of inquiry and sometimes just short notes on research in science or latest developments therein. Here is an example of how research is reported *(Science Today,* June 1980).

Missing Neutrinos : Neutrinos are once again in the news. They seem to be changing their identity during their travel. Experiments by F. Reines, H.W. Sobel and E. Pasierb of the University of California at Irvine, seem to imply that nearly half of the neutrino population at a nuclear reactor changes its identity by the time it travels a few meters from the reactor core.

Nuclear reactors are excellent sources of neutrinos because many of the radio-active nuclei created during fission eventually beta-decay, releasing an electron and an attendant neutrino. Physicists call this neutrino from the reactor, for the purpose of book-keeping, the 'anti-neutrino of the electron-type'. So far—although three types of neutrinos have ' been discovered (e-type, mu-type and tau-type, which has yet to be confirmed) in the experiments with accelerators—there has been no evidence that a neutrino of one type changes into another type. The results of the reactor experiment to be published shortly in *Physical Review Letters* suggest a mixing among the neutrino types.

Neutrinos are notoriously elusive and detecting them requires extraordinary skill and patience. To detect a neutrino, it must somehow interact with matter, and that almost never happens. Neutrinos interact with matter by the so-called 'weak' forces—the kind which created them originally in the beta-decay. A momentous discovery of the past decade was that neutrinos interact with matter by another variety of weak force called the 'neutral' variety, so named because under its influence the electric charge of the participants does not change. In the forces that control the beta-decay, however, the electric chape jumps from one participant to the other. This kind of force was later named the 'charged' variety of weak force.

Reines and co-workers exploited this ambi-dexterous property of the neutrino. Their experiment consisted of figuring out the break-up of a deuteron in the heavy water by both varieties of weak forces. The 'neutral' variety causes a single neutron to come out, while the 'charged' variety causes the release of two neutrons along with a positron. So they undertook to 'count' the neutrons by counters immersed in a 268-kg pool of heavy water exposed to neutrinos from the 2,000 megawatt Savannah River Reactor located at a distance of 11.2 meters. They found that the ratio of the number of deutron break-ups by the weak forces of the 'charged' variety to those by the 'neutral' variety, was about half of what was expected.

This result is understandable in a simple way if we suppose that during the 11-meter travel to the apparatus, about half of the reactor neutrinos got changed to neutrinos of another type which cannot break up the deuteron by the charged weak forces, whereas the break-up of deuteron by the neutral weak force is 'indifferent' to the type of neutrino. These changes among the neutrino types, called neutrino oscillations, can occur back and forth, many times over.

The extremely fascinating concept of neutrino oscillations was conceived originally by the Japanese team, Z. Maki, M. Nakagawa and S. Sakata in 1962 and by B. Pontecorvo in Russia in 1968 ....

The recent experiment implies that at least one of the masses of the two underlying waves (Reines called them 'neutrettos') must be more than about an electron-volt. That may not sound big compared to the electron mass of 51 1,003 electron-volts; but even the small mass is exciting since neutrinos are commonly believed to have no mass at all.

There are several interesting puzzles—big and small—which will start clearing up if there are no neutrino oscillations. A very interesting one refers to the 'Kolar events'. In 1975, an Indo-Japanese team of physicists from the Tata Institute of Fundamental Research, Bombay, and the University of Osaka, working at the Kolar Gold mines in Karnataka reported some puzzling events produced by the atmospheric neutrinos. Other experimental groups using neutrinos from particle accelerators have not been able to confirm these observations.

Why was the round-up of research on missing neutrinos relevant? The author claims that this is because "neutrinos are once again in the news". That is good enough reason. Identified are the scientists engaged in experimentation, the place where experiments were carried out, the nature of the experiments, the extent of success and the manner in which they were conducted. Neutrinos are clearly defined, so are areas of disagreement among scientists. Among scientists it is not enough if one group comes to certain conclusions. These conclusions must be confirmed by experimentation by other groups *independently*. Which is why any survey of research must take into account work done by various scientists simultaneously engaged in similar activity.

Short Write-ups

Short notes on science are intended more to inform and educate than to define the full extent of research done. A round-up is comprehensive in its approach and detailed in its analysis. A short note is less pretentious. Here is an example from *Science Today* (June 1980):

The Hard Link : Some years ago, it was found that the incidence of cardiovascular deaths was 50 per cent higher in soft water areas than in hard water areas. Scientists had then attributed the higher death rate to the corrosiveness and the capacity of soft water to dissolve heavy metals, especially Cadmium.

Following this finding a few English towns had even begun hardening their water with calcium and magnesium. Well, they had done the right thing. According to P.D.M.V. Turlapaty and B.M. Altura of the State University of New York Down-state Medical Centre, Brooklyn, USA, it is the lower levels of magnesium that caused the deaths.

The researchers incubated isolated dog arteries in a solution and exposed them to various concentrations of magnesium. Earlier studies had shown that heart muscles of sudden death victims contained lower than normal levels of magnesium increased the artery tone, whereas high levels decreased the tone.

Also, a lowered magnesium level made the artery more responsive to body chemicals. Thus mypomagnesemia, they conclude, could produce vaso-constriction resulting in coronary arterial spasm leading to sudden death.

Microbes to Dissolve Clots : Blood clots are a problem for heart patients; they can choke a vital blood vessel and cause death. The clots can be dissolved by an enzyme called urokinase. Urokinase, at present, is extracted either from human urine, or cultured human kidney cells. The method using cultured cells, beside being expensive, is complicated. The enzyme is formed along with other proteins from which it has to be isolated.

Now scientists at an American pharmaceutical company have used genetic engineering techniques to synthesize the enzyme. They extracted messenger RNA from human kidney cells using an enzyme called reverse transcriptase. From this they built up the DNA which contains the gene that codes for urokinase and introduced it into *Escherichia coli.* The bacterium churned out the alien protein.

The genetic engineers are now planning to induce the bug to make more of the enzyme and in a purer form.

Writings on Medicine

From writing short notes on science subjects to writing medical copy for drugs and Pharmaceuticals is a major jump. In the latter case, there is a set style for writing that should be scrupulously followed. It is presumed that the writer, in the first instance, knows all that needs to be known about the drug, its effects and after-effects, not to mention likely side-effects and is as accurate as possible. Below are examples of medical copy that are inserted in drug packages:

For the use of registered medical practitioners or a hospital or a laboratory

Triominic Syrup

Syrup of Phenylpropanolamine,

Pheniramine and Mepyramine

Oral Nasal Decongestant, Antihistaminic

Composition: Each teaspoonful (5 ml) of the syrup contains:

Phenylpropanolamine hydrochloride NF	12.5 mg
Pheniramine maleate I.P.	6.25 mg
Mepyramine maleate I.P.	6.25 mg

Properties: Triominic Syrup is a balanced combination of three ingredients carefully selected to provide reliable and prompt relief of nasal congestion. Since the drugs are taken orally and act through the blood stream, they can reach areas of nasal and respiratory mucosae which a locally applied drug may not reach. This results in a wider and more complete decongesting effect. Oral administration is also free from the risk of rebound congestion or injury to the sensitive mucosa due to indiscriminate local application.

Phenylpropanolamine is a potent vasoconstrictor with little effect on the central nervous or cardiovascular systems. By constricting the blood vessels, Phenylpropanolamine diminishes excessive secretions from the nasal and respiratory mucosae.

Pheniramine and Mepyramine are both antihistamines which relieve the allergic component in colds and other respiratory infections. They also diminish secretions by preventing the increase of capillary permeability due to histamine. Use of two antihistamines instead of one reduces the dose of these drugs and hence minimises the side effects.

TRIOMINIC SYRUP has a pleasant taste and flavour and is easy to administer to children.

Indications: Prompt and prolonged relief from such symptoms as nasal congestion, profuse nasal discharge, and post-nasal drip associated with colds, nasal allergies, sinusitis and rhinitis. Rapid decongestion facilitates free breathing and permits easier flow of secreted material, thus reducing the dangers of sinus and middle ear infection.

Dosage: Infants between 3-6 months: 1/4 teaspoonful 3 times a day.

Infants below 3 months: at the doctor's discretion.

Adults: 1 to 2 teaspoonfuls 4 times a day.

Children between 6-12 years: ½ to 1 teaspoonful 4 times a day.

Children from 6 months to 6 years ¼ to ½ teaspoonful 4 times a day.

Side-effects: TRIOMINIC SYRUP is generally well-tolerated. Very occasionally the following side-effects may be noticed: drowsiness, slight blurring of vision, palpitation, flushing, dizziness, nervousness and gastrointestinal upsets.

Precautions: If drowsiness occurs, patients should not drive a car or operate dangerous machines. Use with caution in patients with hypertension, heart disease, diabetes or thyrotoxicosis.

Presentation: 100 ml bottles with a spoon.

Manufactured by

WANDER LIMITED

Shivsagar 'A',

Dr. Annie Besant Road, Bombay 400 018

Under License from:

WANDER LIMITED, Berne, Switzerland.

Some medical literature use terms in vogue in medical science. Instead of speaking of "properties", the word "pharmacology" may be used. Some other will simplify the language, as for instance, copy for SIQUIL manufactured by Sarabhai Chemicals.

For the use only of registered medical practitioners or a hospital or a laboratory.

SIQUIL

Triflupromazine Hydrochloride

What is It?

SIQUIL (Triflupromazine Hydrochloride) is designated

chemically as 10- (3- dimethylaminopropyl) -2- (trifiuoromethyl) phenothiazine hydrochloride. It is a new phenothiazine compound improved chemically and pharmacologically through fluoridation of the basic phenothiazine structure.

What does it do?

In all cases where SIQUIL has been used, it has demonstrated a marked ability to control excessive abnormal agitation without producing marked sedation or drowsiness ....

What are the indications?

Nausea and vomiting: SIQUIL is effective in the control and prevention of nausea and vomiting....

Pre-and post-operative sedation: SIQUIL has been used with great success for pre-operative sedation particularly when used with local anaesthesia. Post-operatively SIQUIL controls or prevents emergence delirium and ensures easier management of the patient.

What are the contra-indications and precautions?

SIQUIL should not be given to patients receiving large doses of hypnotics and in comatose states.

Agranulocytosis and leukopenia have been observed with phenothiazine derivatives. If blood count confirms these complications, the drug should be discontinued and appropriate treatment, including intensive antibiotic therapy should be instituted immediately.

What are the Advantages?

SIQUIL is more potent and effective than many similar drugs with fewer and milder undesirable reactions on the patient.. .

Administration and Aosage

The parental administration of drugs like SIQUIL may sometimes cause postural hypertension....

Overdosage : The principal symptoms of intentional or

accidental over-dosage reflect circulatory or extrapyramidal involvement, . .

What is the Supply?

Oral tablets—10 mg (white press-coated).

Bottles of 25's.

Foil packs of 10 and 100 (10 n 10's).

25 mg (yellow press-coated).

Bottles of 25's.

Parenteral Solution:

10 ml multiple dose vial (10 mg/ml).

5 ml multiple dose vial (20 mg/ml).

1 ml single dose ampoule (10 mg/ml) box of 5 amps.

1 ml single dose ampoule (3 mg/ml) box of 5 amps.

Storage : Solutions of SIQUIL should be protected against exposure to light. A slight discolouration resulting from mild exposure does not indicate any change that would prevent the drug from being used, but when definite colour changes occur due to improper storage, the preparation should not be used.

R represents the Registered Trademark of E.R. Squibb & Sons Inc., of which Sarabhai Chemicals are the licensed users.

Procedures in Outlining Medical Literature : From the examples cited above, the following procedure appears to be essential in outlining medical literature for the guidance of physicians and other qualified authorities:

First, it must be clearly stated that the product is strictly for the use of registered medical practitioners or a hospital or a laboratory so that a medical prescription would be needed for a patient to get it. This warning is intended against indiscriminate use of the product.

Second, the manufacturer must state the exact composition of the product and not just its trade name. It must also be stated whether the standards followed are American (U.S. Pharmacopoeia—USP), British (B.P.) or Indian (I.P.).

Third, information must be provided about what the drug will *do* for the cure of the ailment specified.

Fourth, it must mention what the drug or product is for in considerable detail.

Fifth, it must state the dosage, age-wise.

Sixth, it must state under what conditions the product should *not* be used, and, if inadvertently used, what steps should be taken to contract the likely ill-effects.

Seventh, information should also be provided as to what needs to be done in case of *overdosage.*

Eighth, the likely side-effects of the use of the product should be mentioned to caution both doctor and patient what to expect in odd cases.

Ninth, the physician should know the nature and strength of the product as well as of the package, whether it comes as a tablet, an injectible, an ointment or a tonic and how it is available (in bottles, foil packets, tubes or ampoules).

Tenth, where necessary warning should be given as to how to store the product. Is it to be refrigerated, kept at room temperature or away from sunlight?

Eleventh, the manufacturer's address must be given in full and information further given on whether the product has been made indigenously or under license from a foreign manufacturer.

Some manufacturers take the additional trouble of providing references to research literature on the product offered for the information of the physicians who may want to know more about its pharmacology.

It is also customary to indicate on the label the date of manufacture of the product and the batch number as well for identification purposes. In many cases, the retail price is stated so customers do not feel cheated by the retailer. In case the product is a Scheduled drug, it is clearly mentioned that the product is to be sold by retail on the prescription of a registered medical practitioner only.

In most developed nations the rules governing the detailing of a drug are so strict that penalties accompany their non-observance.

Surfeit of Facts : Technical or scientific writing invariably involves facts and figures. These are important to the development of the story. In the case of detailing drugs one can even say that there cannot be any surfeit of facts since we are dealing with matters of life and death. The truth about a drug must be fully and totally revealed.

Some companies apparently do not believe in telling the whole truth about the products they manufacture. A writer, Atul B. Vaidya, pointed this out in an article entitled *'Drugging' The Third World (The Illustrated Weekly of India,* May 4, 1980).

Four hundred Iraqis died in 1972 and 5,000 were hospitalised after eating food made out of 8,000 tons of wheat and barley coated with an organic mercuric fungicide, the use of which was, of course, banned in the US. Grain shipments to Pakistan were also similarly contaminated, causing many ill-effects a few years ago.

Then there is a case of pesticide called leptophos, manufactured by Chicago's Velsicol Chemical Corporation under the brand name of Phosvel. It is an organophosphate nerve toxin that attacks the human body like the snake venom. A few years ago, over a thousand water buffaloes died in Egypt after being exposed to Phosvel . . .

Pesticide DRCP, an acronym for 1, 2-Dibromo-3-Chloropropane, was banned in California in August 1977, because it causes sterility and cancer. But to this day, it has not stopped the Amvac Chemical Corporation in Los Angeles from shipping it to banana republics in Latin America ....

Responsible corporations prefer to give all valid information to suppressing inconvenient facts.

Brevity—a Virtue in Writing? Brevity is often regarded as a virtue in writing, but where technical writing is concerned it is better to use an extra word, if thereby the meaning is made clear. The sin of wordiness and the virtue of supplying sufficient detail, as an American writer has said, are completely different. Generally speaking, the ratio of words in a first draft to those in the final draft is reckoned to be often something like 7 to 5. In other words, a reporter writing a 500-word story should probably have a first draft of 700-words which he can then hone to perfection, eliminating unnecessary words and replacing a set of words with fewer, but more appropriate ones. But there are exceptions to the rule. A technical report can be taut—but understandable to a limited number of readers. The science reporter of a daily newspaper is writing not for the experts, but for the layman. Tautness is commendable, but clarity is desirable. And a few additional words in the interests of clarity need not be spurned.

Facts not Opinions : The reporter, in summarising long technical reports must remember that these deal with facts, not opinions. A politician's speech is more easily summarised than a Ph.D. thesis in chemistry. The first objective of a science reporter must be *accuracy*. This, of course, is true of all reporting, but where science reporting is concerned, this assumes an additional shade of meaning. The second objective must be *completeness*. Science reporting which leaves loose threads hanging around can be maddening. The third objective surely is *coherence*. Much science reporting goes completely over the reader's head because the writer is incoherent. He is vainly trying to be clever and is out to impress the reader with his grasp of the subject. The objective must always be to clarify. Knowledge must lie lightly on the writer's shoulders. The writing must be effortless, to the point that the reader should be able to exclaim: "Why, now I know all about Relativity!"

Reporter's Credibility

Finally, science reporting must be *authentic*. There is, however, a general belief that to sound authentic, a writer must be dull and stick to the facts. This erroneous notion has been responsible for some of the dullest writing on science and technology. Science is one of the most exciting of subjects. There was no science writer around when man first discovered how to make fire, but one can well imagine the former's excitement at his discovery. We do not know either what man said when he discovered the wheel and literate as our Vedic seers were there is no record of what was said when the Hindu mathematician conceived zero as an arithmetical value. We know what Archimedes said when he discovered the principle now named after him and today, the meanest discovery quickly has a ready scribe to record it—and make it sound exciting. And if not very exciting, at least interesting.

Take this example from *Time,* quoted by Crosby and Estey, in their delightful book *Just Rhetoric:*

In the basement of Harvard's School of Dental Medicine, biochemist James H. Shaw and his assistants worked for more than ten years with cages full of white rats and cotton rats, with sugar-rich and sugar-free chow, with test tubes and dissecting boards. The twofold aim: to find out how certain sugars promote tooth decay, then find a way to forestall it. The Sugar Research Foundation, Inc., set up by the sugar industry, bankrolled the project for a total of $ 57,000. Now in the *Journal of the American Dental Association,* Dr. Shaw reports his findings.

Tooth decay is caused only by food remaining in the mouth—proved by feeding rats through stomach tubes. Even sugar, fed this way, causes no decay.

Sugar, in solution, causes little decay: granulated sugar (as sprinkled on fruits and cereals) causes much more.

Of the various kinds of sugar, fructose (from most fruit), glucose (from grapes and starch foods), sucrose (table sugar from cane or beets), lactose (from milk) and maltose (from beer) are all precipitators of decay. So is a high-starch diet, even when relatively low in sugar. It does no good to substitute raw for refined sugar, but blackstrap molassescause a marked reduction in cavities.

Saliva is a good tooth protector. Removal of successive salivary glands gave a progressive increase in decay. Penicillin and chlorotetracycline (Aureomycin) are effective anti-decay agents, as are urea and dibasic ammonium carbonate; other antibiotics and chemicals tested (among them, many of those now commonly blended into toothpastes) do little or no good.

Dr. Shaw's conclusion: "We should cut down on sugar consumption, particularly candy. We should be careful about sugar in forms that remain in the mouth because of their physical properties." Along with his findings, Dr. Shaw also reported that his work has stopped. Reason: the Sugar Research Foundation withdrew its support.

Building Up a Story : *Time* magazine never wastes space on stories that are irrelevant or uninteresting. Then what is it about this story that attracted *Time's* attention? The opening sentence makes plain that the problem of tooth decay caused by sugar consumption is important enough for some men to work *ten* years on it. This is the story's appeal.

The writer moves on to answer two questions: What causes decay? How can it be prevented? This arouses curiosity.

Inevitably, the reader is moved to keep reading and his curiosity is satisfied by providing the answers, which constitute the body of the report.

But there has to be a summing up without which the story is incomplete. This is provided in the last paragraph, but with just the right kind of twist. In this instance, the report ends with the statement that the sugar industry apparently believing that the findings could hurt sales, discontinued support to further research. And this suggests a controversy, which is the meat of much good reporting.

But notice how the reporter defines the words *granulated, sucrose, maltose, glucose* and *lactose*. These add to our understanding of the story all the more. Also note how well the conclusion blends with the rest of the story. In fact, a conclusion should:

* Arise naturally out of what has been said.
* Relate smoothly to the body of the report.

* Bring out the main point or points that have been made.
* Make a strong impression on the reader, sufficiently to cause him to remember the whole story.
* Agree in tone with the main structure of the report.

Conclusion to be Effective : There are various ways of making a conclusion effective. The ending could be unusual or unexpected, or it could raise a rhetorical question or be a strong statement of intent or belief. Where none of these is possible, the writer can vary the length or rhythm of his sentences, but none of these will really work unless the conclusion as a whole fulfills the five basic requirements listed above.

While it is true that technical and science reporting is not for the uninitiated, a good reporter can find the right kind of story if only he is of an inquiring bent of mind. He has to look for stories in unexpected places. Take this report, for instance, from *Popular Science* (March 1970):

Science Builds a Guitar with the New Sound Taking the vibration out of copters helped design a new 'well-rounded" guitar By Paul Wahl.

Guitars and helicopters have a common problem—the control of vibration. Guitars need quality vibration to make music. In helicopters, vibration makes trouble. The Kaman Corp. spent years and millions taking vibrations out of whirlybirds. Recently Charles H. Kaman, president of the firm and an accomplished amateur guitarist, reasoned that they might use their hard-won know-how to design a better guitar.

Not much has been done to change the acoustic (non-electric) guitar since about 1550. After extensive accoustical testing and comparison of almost every kind of antique and contemporary guitar plus more than 70 of their own original designs, Kaman engineers decided that the most efficient shape for a guitar sounding box is actually a semi-parabolic bowl, something like an orchestra shell.

The rounded bowl reflects sound better than the flat back of conventional guitars. Roundback sound is measurably fuller, richer, deeper and more constant from top to bottom of the seals.

Having found the ideal shape, the engineers next had to find the ideal Material. Wood wouldn't do. Made thin enough to vibrate at its best, the wood of a bowl would be impracticably fragile, even with undesirable sound-baffling internal braces and re-inforcing members. After many trials, they invented 'Lyrachord'.

Related to other lightweight laminar substances Kaman had perfected for copter rotors and other aerospace components, Lyrachord is an omnidirectional silicone fiber bounded with resins. Virtually indestructable, it can be precision-moulded to any shape. Lyrachord has a smooth, highly sound-reflectant surface with uniform vibrating characteristics. Its molecular structure can be precisely tuned chemically and thermally to the desired resonance.

Thus imaginative application of today's aerospace technology to the age-old craft of the luthier has built a better guitar— the first really new acoustic design of this sort in more than 400 years.

It will be noticed that there are hardly any difficulty to understand technical words. The writer uses the "parallelism" technique to draw attention. The very first line attracts curiosity: *Guitars and helicopters have a common problem.* Guitars and helicopters? Who wouldn't want to read further? A point to remember in regard to technical writing is how much a report's essence is enhanced by use of suitable pictures or diagrams. *Popular Science* has, in fact, raised the matching of report with illustration to perfection, as, of course, *Popular Mechanics.*

Easy Way to the Editor's Heart : In technical writing, an easy way to the editor's heart is to suggest a series of how-to-do-it-yourself gimmics. How to fix your cycle. How to repair a sewing machine. How to wire your lamp etc. This does not call for a particularly high level of knowledge. What one needs to know is how to express oneself in clear sentences. Take this example from *Popular Mechanics:*

Bicycle brakes aren't really complicated, but they do need correct adjustment for maximum braking efficiency. Basically, there are two types of bicycle brakes in popular use today: the old-fashioned 'coaster brakes' which may or may not be combined with a three-speed rear hub, and call per brakes. Because coaster brakes seldom require maintenance and many bikes now have caliper brakes, let's concentrate on the latter ....

Technical Writing not Fearsome: Technical writing is not as fearsome as one would think, not need it be. If it was so, magazines like *Popular Mechanics* or *Popular Science* would not have the kind of sale they enjoy. In fact these magazines can easily give themselves the sub-title: Technology Without Tears. Most technology lends itself to simple language. The trick is to know the trade. And knowledge comes from reading.

The Jupiter Effect **:** Both technical and science writing can be made entertaining with some effort. This is how Dr. V. S. Venkatavaradan dealt with the Jupiter Effect in the *Free Press Journal* (July 7, 1980):

Jupiter is the biggest planet in the Solar System with a mass about 300 times that of the earth. In fact the mass of Jupiter is more than the combined mass of all other planets in the Solar System. Can Jupiter affect the earth in any significant way due to its massive size? Some scientists believe that Jupiter affects even the Sun. The variation of Solar activity—which is evident from the variation of the number of Sun Spots—is believed to be governed by the Planet Jupiter to some extent. Space missions to Jupiter like Pioneers and Voyagers have found that energy particles emitted by Jupiter are received by the earth. These particles can, to some extent, affect the earth's weather.

The *Jupiter Effect*, as it is called, is supposed to be dominant when all the planets including Jupiter align themselves on the same side of the Sun. Such an alignment will add to the force of Jupiter against the Sun. Normally the planets occur randomly in the sky—some will be on one side of the Sun and others on the other side. In such a situation the effect of Jupiter is believed to be scanty. When the planets align on the same side with Jupiter, they add to the force of Jupiter.

Today, Jupiter is seen in the constellation Leo along with planets Mars and Saturn. Planets Mercury and Venus (the interior planets) are in the constellation Gemini. In general, the planets may occupy any one of the twelve zodiacal constellations. Sometimes more than one planet may be in a constellation and at other times there may be none.

In astrology, the twelve heavenly constellations are transformed into twelve houses of the horoscope. The horoscope is a transformation of the positions of the Sun, Moon and other planets in the sky, in the form of a chart. Astrologically, the planets are believed to be influencing the earthlings. But can the planets, including Jupiter, affect the earth in an astronomical way?

The alignment of planets, will take place sometime during 1982. Such an alignment takes place once in about 180 years. This alignment of the planets is expected to give rise to some unusual tidal forces. It is predicted that some major earthquakes and volcano eruptions may occur during this period. It is also interesting to note that the solar activity (i. e. the number of Sun Spots on the face of the sun) is at a maximum during this time. Earth's climate is affected in a significant way during solar maximum with severe summers and very cold winters. Increase in rainfall and intense cyclonic activity also occur during the period of solar maximum. Jupiter Effect, it is believed, may add to the situation and one can expect a very unusual climate during that time.

The Jupiter Effect is not a well understood scientific theory but is only based on some empirical data. One does not also under stand well about the sun spot correlation with earth's weather. So the predicted effects form the alignment of the planets on one side of sun belongs to speculative astronomy which borders on astrology.

In astrology, the conjunction of certain planets appear to have some significant effects on the destiny of man and even a country. Probably astrology must have developed by observing the occurrence of some significant events during the conjunction of planets. For instance, today, the three major planets Jupiter, Saturn and Mars are in the same zodiacal sign and about a month ago Jupiter, Mars and a star Regulus were in a straight line. A few months ago planet Venus which was very bright was seen very near to the crescent Moon and in fact many thought that Venus was some strange object.

Such occurrences are easily recognised in view of their rarity and if any event of major significance occur on earth during these astronomical events, the mind tries to correlate astronomical events with earthly happenings.

At this time it is interesting to recall the story concerning Indrajit, son of Ravana. When Indrajit was born, Ravana wanted to make sure that all the planets were in the 11th house which was supposed to bring good luck to and make Indrajit omnipotent. Devas, who were afraid of such an eventuality, requested Saturn to stretch his leg to the 12th house and Saturn obliged. Saturn in 12th house brings bad luck and gave uncontrollable pride to Indrajit which resulted in his destruction. When Ravana knew of Saturn's trick, he cut off his leg and that is why Saturn is called a lame planet. Today man-made spacecrafts have landed on many planets and have seen a number of them at close distance. Yet the human mind wants to speculate on the happenings of some events during the alignment of planets in 1982.

The Jupiter Effect may be a myth but it shows the deep rooted feelings and evolution of astrological and astronomical thoughts over many centuries.

The Applicability

Science and technology are vast subjects that encompass a variety of human knowledge. If one approaches them with humility and a desire to understand, reporting on them becomes a pleasure. What is needed is *application,* whether one writes about pure science, applied science or popular science. Assimilation of information comes first. Science writing is not a hasty affair. A reporter can file a crime story or a political report without much hassle, but a science story is something else. It calls for a good deal of study, especially where writing is concerned with pure science. Not only must one know what is the core and pith of the mass of material available, but one must also be able to assess its significance. Every Ph.D. thesis does not make news, but the discovery of penicillin or cortisone did. When Venkaravaradan wrote about the Jupiter Effect he knew he would catch the reader's attention because in a country where people are astrologically-minded, a story on the movement of planets would have a built-in readership. And in the final analysis, that is what science reporting is all about. Effective and meaningful communication.

17

Reporting on Economic Matters

Economic and commercial reporting is probably one of the least understood or appreciated aspects of reporting in India. Commercial editors are seldom heard of though it is on them that the large, influential and powerful business community depends.

Model Reports

Bulls, Bears and other Animals : What do we mean when we say that the market is bearish? Where is Dalal Street and what does it signify? What does Hapur Market refer to? What is understood by the headline "Equities Decline on Profit—Booking?" Or by the headline "Bullish Tendency Well Sustained?" What, in other words, go into a commercial and finance Page?

The Times' of India has a column called *Company News. The Sunday Standard* runs the same information under *Corporate News*. The object of the column is to report on how companies and corporations are faring. The information is based on company reports provided to the public.

We will take note of two columns published on June 8, 1980 by both *The Times of India* and *The Sunday Standard* to see how the two papers have dealt with the same information available and how, in the second place, company notes are written:

This from *The Times of India:*

Arlem Breweries Pay more : *Bombay, June 7:* The preliminary statement from Arlem Breweries on its working results for the year ended March 1980 shows a marked improvement over the previous year. Sales and profits are substantially higher than the previous year but the margins are under pressure. Dividend has been raised from 12 per cent to 15 per cent. Turnover has gone up by 52.7 per cent from Rs. 190.77 lakhs in 1978-79 to Rs. 301.70 lakhs and the gross profit is up by about 33.8 per cent from Rs. 28.12 lakhs to Rs. 37.70 lakhs. The ratio of gross profit to sales has gone down from 14.7 per cent to 12.2 per cent.

After providing Rs. 9.74 lakhs (Rs. 9.06 lakhs) for depreciation and Rs. 1.85 lakhs (nil) for taxation and making some adjustments, there is a surplus of Rs. 26.14 lakhs against Rs. 19.06 lakhs. A sum of Rs. 8.26 lakhs (Rs. 0.55 lakhs) has been transferred to general reserve. The proposed dividend will absorb Rs. 12 lakhs (Rs. 9.60 lakhs).

Graphite India : Graphite India which announced a bonus issue of one equity share for every two shares and a dividend of 16 per cent for 1979 had to stagger the expansion programme at Bangalore due to severe power cut. Unit II of the company has gone into production in June 1979 increasing the existing annual capacity by 3,000 tonnes. Installation of Unit III is in progress and when commissioned, this would increase the capacity by further 2,450 tonnes per annum. The company's application for expansion of the renewal of the Durgapur plant's annual capacity from 5,400 tonnes to 10,000 tonnes is yet to be approved by the government.

Now consider how the same two company news has been dealt by *The Sunday Standard:*

Arlem Breweries Steps up : Arlem Breweries has produced improved results for the year 1979 and the Directors have raised the equity dividend by three per cent to 15 per cent which will absorb Rs. 12 lakhs (Rs. 9.60 lakhs).

According to the preliminary statement, sales have risen from

Rs. 1.91 crores to Rs. 3.02 crores and the gross profit from Rs. 28.13 lakhs to Rs. 37.71 lakhs.

After providing for depreciation at Rs. 9.75 lakhs (Rs. 9.06 lakhs) and for taxation Rs. 1.85 lakhs (nil), there remains a net profit of Rs. 26.11 lakhs as compared to Rs. 19.07 lakhs last year.

Better Performance : Despite labour unrest at its Durgapur Plant, raw material shortages and severe power cut at Bangalore Plant, Graphite India has reported better performance during 1979.

Sales during the year were higher at Rs. 18.54 crores as compared to Rs. 14.74 crores on 1978. Production of graphite electrodes, anodes and miscellaneous graphite products was higher at 7,214 tonnes (7086 tonnes) and that of carbon pastes at 4,264 tonnes (2,346 tonnes). Exports were substantially higher at Rs. 98.69 lakhs as against Rs. 20.61 lakhs on F.O.B. basis.

Lots of achievements were made in updating graphite technology and developing new products in the research and development division. The Directors hope that this division would have substantial contribution during the forthcoming years.

Due to critical power situation at Bangalore, the expansion programme had to be staggered. The Unit No. II had gone into production in June 1979, increasing the installed capacity , by 3,000 tonnes. Installation of Unit No. III is in progress and when commissioned would increase the annual capacity by 2,450 tonnes.

The application for expansion of Durgapur Plant's capacity from 5,400 tonnes to 10,000 tonnes is yet to be approved by the government.

As earlier announced, the company has recommended a higher equity dividend of 16 per cent for 1979 as compared to 14 per cent in 1978 and has also proposed to issue bonus shares in the ratio of 1: 2 by capitalising a sum of Rs. 140.25 lakhs. The management has recorded its intention to pay 15 per cent dividend on the expanding capital following bonus issue.

Company Notes : Company notes inform the shareholders and the public at large as to how corporations have fared in the year under review. Did a company lose or make profits? If so what was the loss or profit and how do these figures compare with last year's? Is the company contemplating expansion? If not why not? What were the constraints under which the company has been operating? What affected the company for a loss to be reported? If there have been profits, what dividend have the Directors declared? Company notes provide the information in brief.

Take another example, this one from the *Free Press Journal* (June 5,1980):

Mahindra Spicer Ltd. has suffered a setback in its working for the year ended 31st January 1980. Despite small rise in turnover from Rs. 6.81 crores to Rs. 9.40 crores, the gross profit slumped to Rs. 40.72 lakhs from Rs. 58.92 lakhs in 1978-79.

The Board has declared an unchanged dividend of 10 per cent for the year. The proposed dividend will absorb up to Rs. 12.50 lakhs.

Depreciation took care of Rs. 25.99 lakhs (Rs. 11.08 lakhs). No provision has been made for taxation. Investment allowance reserve gets nil (Rs. 20 lakhs). A sum of Rs. 38.65 lakhs (Rs. 21.40 lakhs) has been carried to the balance sheet.

Sandoz Sales Move Up : Sales by Sandoz (India) Ltd. in the first five months (Jan-May) of the current year are higher by about 42 per cent at Rs. 19.70 crores as compared to Rs. 13.89 crores in the corresponding period of 1979 and Rs. 15.05 crores in the same period of 1978. This was disclosed by Dr. J.N. Banerjee, Managing Director, at the Company's annual general meeting.

Dr. Banerjee pointed out that a comparison of sales in the first five months of 1980 with the disturbed corresponding period last year would not be meaningful. Although turnover was substantially higher, it did not measure up to expectations with regard to two of the Divisions whose operations are not necessarily linked to factors like adequate rains and avilability of power and raw materials. . .. However, in the textile and leather markets—on which Dyes and Chemicals Division is dependent—sluggish conditions continue to cause concern. Sales of Pharmaceuticals specialities have been encouraging, despite shortages of certain important products.

Stock Exchanges : Another important part of a city page or commercial page is the reporting on stock exchanges. A stock exchange is a place where stocks and shares are sold and bought. In Bombay the Stock Exchange is situated at Dalai Street and it has about the same connotation as Wall Street in New York. Consider this report in the *Free Press Journal* (June 5, 1980):

Bullish-tendency Well Sustained : Despite end-account considerations, select scrips forged ahead on the stock exchange on Wednesday following strong speculative support. Prospects of good monsoon and reports of sizeable export inquiries for many items from Iran boosted the sentiment. Sellers were reserved in Century and Cent Enka on expectations of backwardation charges in these scrips at the turn of settlement on Friday. Business was quite heavy.

Both Century and Century Enka scored small gains on professional support. Gujarat Fertilisers moved narrowly before closing shade lower.

Great Eastern Shipping advanced further on fresh purchases to the tune of 15,000 shares on rumours of interim dividend. Scindia also improved.

Standard reacted modestly.

Tata Steel and TELCO quietened down in the absence of follow-up support at higher levels.

Indian Dyestuff and NOCIL ruled firm.

Cheerful conditions continued to prevail in the cash section. Mah Ugine, Mah and Mah, Ingersoll, Hind-Dorr, Asea and Sandvik meet with keen investment inquiries. W.I. Erectors lost Rs. 2 at Rs. 62.

Delhi : Hardening tendency continued to persist in the Delhi Stock Exchange on Wednesday on fair support. Business was moderate.

Swadeshi Polytex, Southern Petro-Chemical and Rasoi Vanaspati rose sharply to Rs 17.81, Rs 13.25 and Rs 21.25 respectively at close on encouraging corporate news.

In the cleared section Modi Spinning recovered 18 paise at Rs 45.31 and East India Hotel 25 paise at Rs 21.25.

Prices of shares can rise or fall for a variety of reasons: heavy profits or sharp losses, hopes of regaining the market, a good monsoon, drought, prospects of new markets and exports, loss of overseas markets, government's taxation policies, improvement of management and a host of other factors which register on the sensitive stock exchange. Indeed, the stock exchange is rightly known as the barometer of a country's economy.

Pre-Budget Report : Commercial editors watch the stock market carefully just before the presentation of the Union budget, as did The Times of India's man on June 16, 1980 two days before the event. The Market Round-Up for the day ran as follows:

Dalai Street Rules Firm on the Eve of Budget : The stock exchange has shown distinct signs of firmness on the eve of the Union budget scheduled to be presented on Wednesday, June 18. Last week, several popular counters scored handsome gains in fair turnover.

The marketmen's optimism seems to be based on expectations that the Union Finance Minister Mr. R. Venkatraman is likely to offer incentives to revive the economy through increased savings and investment and that in any case he is unlikely to resort to any fiscal measures which will hurt the corporate sector.

In this connection, they have taken note of the statement in the pre-budget economic survey presented to the Parliament on Friday last that there is 'limited scope' for additional resource mobilisation through taxation in view of the lack of growth in the economy and the substantial burden imposed by the large oil price increase, and that there is need for a greater effort to realise the full potential of the existing system through better administration. . ..

It is agreed that the Finance Minister faces contradictory challenges because of the poor performance of the economy last year and the many challenges and difficulties it faces in the current year. In this situation, it is pointed out, that he will be obliged to resort to fiscal and monetary discipline in order to control inflation. Moreover, how Mr. Venkatraman is able to contain the deficit financing within "tolerance limits of the economy" in view of the difficult resources position and the need for a larger developmental outlay would have to be watched.

However, it is generally felt in market circles that he will not take the risk of deflating the economy by raising higher personal and corporate taxes. If at all, he may resort to deficit tax concessions and even a modest reduction in tax rates to provide a psychological boost. How far these expectations materialise remains to be seen. The future course of the market will depend largely on this and the progress of the monsoon. ...

How did the market react after the budget was introduced? Note, first, how the pre-budget report was phrased. "The market-men's optimism seems to be based..."; "In this connection they have taken note of. . .", "It is agreed that the Finance Minister faces . . .", "It is pointed out that he will be obliged. . .". "However, it is generally felt.. .". Nobody specifically has been quoted. The report was based (a) or the reporter's discussions with stockbrokers, industrialists and businessmen in general and (b) on his own understanding and appreciation of the issues involved, the shape of the economy and some intelligent guesswork based on political realitics. *The Times of India* (June 19, 1980) said:

By and large, the business community reacted favourably to the Union budget, its only regret being that the Finance Minister has not gone the whole hog in revitalising the economy through sufficiently strong incentives to industry, particularly the Corporate Sector.

If it has been somewhat reserved in its response, it is mainly because the budget has come close on the heels of the severe jolt caused by the Rs. 2,100 crore hike in the price of petroleum products and the stiff increase in rail fares and freights.

Considering the burden that the government has already imposed, most businessmen had been fervently hoping that the budget would not penalise industry and trade further, and they were, indeed, satisfied that the Finance Minister has touched them lightly and even made modest gestures in respect of the depreciation on new machinery installed, the relaxation of the convertibility clause and the reduction in personal taxation.

Reflecting the quiet satisfaction caused by the budget, the share market contented itself with a marked rise in Century, the market leader, the closing quotation at Rs 850 showing net gain of Rs 19 against the pre-budget level. Indian Rayon, Colgate Palmolive and Atlas Cycle were other bright features. The manufacturers of sophisticated consumer products were happy at what they regarded to be a shift back in favour of the urban consumer as reflected in the reduction of the burden of duty on electric bulbs, cheaper soaps, TV sets, radios, tooth paste and paper and boards. The abolition of duty on sewing machines, bicycles and controlled cloth was also warmly appreciated by them.

There are several factors that went into the correspondent's thinking when he wrote the pre-budget report. The Janata Government had come down very heavily on the urban consumer. There had been a good deal of resentment among the consumers that prices of even such items as soaps and radios had shot up as a result. The fact that soap, especially the cheaper variety was also used fairly extensively by the rural consumer, must have weighed very heavily on the Congress Finance Minister, one of whose tasks, surely, was to introduce a budget that would be hailed by all sections of the community. His, in the circumstances, would have been a political decision, as well as an economic decision. Most commercial editors therefore felt reasonably assured that the Congress Finance Minister would be more considerate and in this their judgement was borne out. The *Free Press Journal's* city page said:

> Wide swings in equities marked the post-Budget trading on Dalal Street on Wednesday evening (the day the budget was introduced). The market opened on a buoyant tone in the absence of a heavy dose of taxation in the budget.

The rank and file of the traders welcomed relief in personal taxation, reduction in surcharge on Income Tax, extension of tax holiday for new companies from five years to seven years and increase in depreciation allowance.

Century continued to be in limelight and scored a fresh gain of Rs 19 at Rs 8.50. About 15,000 shares changed hands. A leading firm of brokers which is bull in the scrip purchased about 7,000 shares. Gwalior Kayon after a firm start reacted sharply on Calcutta offerings to the tune of 50,000 shares.

Century Enka touched a new high of Rs 584 on nervous short covering. It, however, came down sharply to close at Rs 567 on sizeable profit-taking . . .

Other Commodities : The commercial (city) page also features the fortunes of other commodities such as bullion (gold and silver), groundnut oil, cotton. The quotations are usually obtained from prominent dealers in the commodities and reported with comments. Thus, *The Free Press Journal* of June 5, 1980:

Sharp Setback in Gold : A sharp setback in gold was the feature of Wednesday's trading in the local bullion market. Silver continued to rule easy.

Gold tumbled down by Rs 20 per 10 gms to Rs 1310 in the wake of a marked rise in offerings. This, in turn, was prompted by distinctly easy advices from the overseas markets, especially London.

The white metal fell further by Rs 17 to Rs 2350 following weak advices from New York.

Silver 996 (per kg) moved at Rs 2340, 2350 and standard gold at 1325, 1310.

	Tuesday	*Wednesday*
Silver (996)	2367	2350
Silver (916)	2367	2351
Standard gold	1330	1310
22 Ct gold	1219	1201

Groundnut Oil Firms Up : The easy trend in groundnut oil was reversed in the oilseeds exchange on Wednesday. The commodity firmed up on reduced offerings followed by strong advices from Gujarat. Groundnuts ruled fully steady.

Sesame oil was a bearish feature. Its nose dived by Rs 12 per 10 kg to Rs 118 on very poor demand at the peak levels.

Among industrial oils, linseed oil reacted on poor enquiries. Castor oils were quiet.

There are several varieties of cotton and the price of each varies from the other and these prices can be obtained from important dealers. In Bombay the cotton market is at a place called Sewri.

Cotton Steady : Steady conditions persisted in the Sewri cotton market on Wednesday. Turnover was poor and the inquiries were restricted mainly to S4, 797 and Wagad varieties.

Other commodities frequently quoted are foodgrains, gur, viscose and nylon yarn, sugar, spices and metals.

How prices can be affected by political events can be gauged from the following report in *The Sunday Standard* (June 8, 1980):

Gold Prices Reaching 600 Dollar Mark : London, June 7: Gold prices approached the 600-dollar an ounce barrier in Europe yesterday with dealers reporting a bullish surge for the metal after three months of reduced demand.

Gold's latest burst began on rumours unconfirmed that American hostages had been shot in Iran. Prices surged 25 dollars in a day breaking out of the stagnant 500-530 dollar range ....

Seeking to explain gold's advance, the London *Daily Telegraph* said on Friday that there is speculation that Saudi Arabia has contracted to buy up to 200 tonnes a year of Soviet-produced gold at 600 dollars an ounce. . . .

Racial unrest in South Africa is another reason cited for gold's recovery.

"Fuelling the advance are the increasing hostility between Iraq and Iran, the attacks on the Iranian Embassy in Kuwait and the ever deeper morass in Afghanistan into which the Kremlin has staggered" the *Telegraph* said.

Gold is a precious commodity. It is the difference between security and insecurity for many countries. If there is political tension or upheaval in any part of the world involving the Super Powers, the bullion market can react sharply and prices may shoot up, as the *Telegraph* tried to explain.

achievements of a department or its plans for further development. Development in this sense means the whole range of economic and social change and therefore development reporting involves the social conscience of the reporter.

Development is much more than just the passage from poor to rich, from a traditional rural economy to a sophisticated urban one. It carries with it, not only the idea of economic betterment but also of great human dignity, security, justice and equality.

There is a difference between economic growth and development. Growth is a quantitative process involving mainly the extension of an already established structure of production, where as development suggests a qualitative change for a better human life.

Therefore, the development reporting has to cover the whole complex and interlocking web of economic activity, catalytic forces unleashed by technology and industrialisation, the tides and undercurrents of social change, the momentum of urbanisation, and its impact on politics, society and religion. Development reporting has to include these larger and more relevant areas of reality and not the traditional concept of "bad news is good news".

Development reporting calls for an honest collection, intelligent processing and interesting presentation and interpretation of information. Interpretation here means making the report relevant to the readers, situating it in the daily experience of the reader, the creation of a traditionally recognised meaning by giving voice to thoughts of the people and also the creation of new meanings that affect all our lives. A development reporter has to take ideas to the people and the people to ideas.

No Propaganda

Development reporting should not be one sided or propagandist. It should not be superficial. It should have depth. Devoting a couple of paragraphs to the inaugural speech of a minister is not development reporting.

18

Reports on Development

Development reporting is a relatively new concept which has emerged in the post-colonial era after World War II when a number of countries became independent. It was observed in these countries that the western media were not interested in the massive development process which had been launched after independence. It looked as if the media always looked at the darker side of life—assassinations, coups, disasters or wars.

These events certainly have their place in news, but the concept of news should not be restricted to these events. Most of the countries of the third world are today witnessing a tremendous upsurge in the developmental activity which should not be ignored by newsmen.

Critics of developmental reporting say that it is "hand out" journalism—the replication of the flattering half-truths put out by official information agencies. It is equated with the reporting only of "positive" news, to the exclusion of the negative or unflattering news.

However, development reporting does not mean governmental publicity in the old-fashioned sense of publishing the

Since development is a multi-dimensional phenomenon its reporting calls for new approaches and responsibilities on the part of a reporter. It is a relatively new and a varied field and therefore provides unlimited scope for innovations. It will thus entail more background reading, more leg work, and often greater understanding than conventional reporting of political goings-on in the capital of a country or in the metropolitan centres of the world.

Failures and shortfalls give a development reporter scope for investigative and interpretative reporting. Success stories could be of human interest. A development reporter has to work hard to get his facts and needs skill to present them interestingly and in logical order. He has to be especially careful while dealing with the social aspects of development. When a development project is finalised or financial arrangement for the project is made a straight report with little interpretation here and there serves the purpose. When loans from international agencies are finalised for development projects, background, plans to utilise such loans and the estimated benefit should be included in the story. Let us have a look at the following example:

India to Use $331m Credit for Agriculture
Hindustan Times Correspondent

New Delhi, March 24. India will use two loans totalling $331 million from the World Bank and a credit of SDR 127. 5 million ($140-million) from the International Development Association (IDA) to help finance projects in the agricultural sector and in the cement industry.

The agricultural project is aimed at raising farm production and income through the expansion of irrigated areas and the efficient use of water supplies at existing irrigation sites. The cement industry project will help increase the production of cement while reducing the consumption of fuel.

The $475. 8 million Andhra Pradesh irrigation project is a combination of new irrigation works and those currently in progress in the State.

World Bank is supporting the project with a loan of $131 million. While IDA—the Bank's concessionary lending arm—will provide assistance with a credit of SDR 127. 5 million ($140 million).

Under the project, the command areas of the Sriramasagar (SRS) and Srisailam Right Branch Canal (SRBC) will be expanded and developed through irrigation network in about 165,000 hectares (ha) in SRS will be modernised and completed, and irrigation will be provided to a further 163,000 ha. Funds will be provided to develop about 65,000 ha of the estimated 77,000 ha that comprise the SRBC. The project is expected to benefit some 101,000 farm families and to create some 47,800 farm jobs and about 12,200 associated jobs. The annual value of crop production is expected to increase by about $127 million.

The cement project, which is designed to increase the production of cement while consuming less fuel, will be supported by a World Bank loan of $200 million. The Project will support the Government's further liberalising of cement prices and production and the introduction of a technology that is energy efficient. To achieve this, six cement plants in the private sector and one in the public sector will be converted from the less efficient wet-process technology to a modern dry-process technology. Investments to rehabilitate and modernise other cement plants will be made. Systems of marketing and distribution will be improved. Training and technical assistance will be upgraded.

The total cost of the project is $469. 8 million. Additional funding will be provided by the Industrial Credit and Investment Corporation of India Limited, Industrial Development Bank of India and other agencies ($140 million) and the Government of India ($129. 1 million).

This story involves two separate projects-one irrigation project and the other related to the cement industry. Both have nothing in common except that the finance ministry must have announced that the loans have been arranged for the projects. The headline is also misleading as it does not refer to the other project which accounts for almost half of the story. The figure mentioned in the headline is also wrong. It should have been $271 million ($131 million + $140 million) as given in the fourth paragraph of the story. The headline writer thought that the two World Bank loans totalling $331 million were for agriculture while as we see later in the story (para 7) a $200 million loan was for the cement project. The moral is that while dealing with development, one has to work hard and be more careful.

After a project is announced development reporter should keep track of its progress. If there is a delay or shortfall it should be pointed out and effort should be made to find out the reasons. The development reporter should also look for social changes in the project area.

An eye for human interest is a must for development reporting. Individual or collective efforts to get over difficulties should not be ignored. Such efforts can make good development reports.

Narmada Farmers' Novel Method
To Meet Water Needs

Indore, March 29 (UNI). Farmers living on the banks of the Narmada river in Khargone district are using a novel method to meet their drinking water needs.

Without waiting for rains or the help from the Government the farmers of Kasravad tehsil of the district have installed pumps which are fitted on carts and can be moved up or down to a water source in the river bed.

Newsmen who visited the dry Kasarvad, Maheshwar and Mandleshwar towns were told by the Kasarvad Janpad Panchayat President Bhan Singh Mandloi that the installation of pumps had made it possible to irrigate and grow wheat in a large area which would have otherwise remained barren due to lack of the rains and the ground level of the water receding to a depth of more than 100 metres.

Mr. Mandloi said that this method of drawing water for

irrigation was much cheaper. Inspired by the farmers, Khargone District Collector Mohan Gupta had drawn up a scheme for enhancing the irrigational potential of the district which has only five per cent of irrigated area.

The scheme, which has been called the Water Arrangement through River Irrigation (WARI) Project, might raise the irrigation percentage of the district to more than 30 per cent-equal to the national average, Mr. Gupta told newsmen.

He said he would make efforts to get WARI included in the Seventh Five Year Plan, its total cost might be Rs 100 crore.

Mr. Gupta said the available water from the Narmada would be lifted with the help of the pumps and piped through hundreds of kilometres of DNG pipelines by the Government. The outlets to the farmers would be provided through PVC pipes which would remain underground, he added.

Opening of projects, exhibitions, etc., provides opportunity for development reports. Efforts should be made to use such opportunities by giving proper background and diversity to the story by giving all possible angles. Here is an example from *The Times of India.*

Alternative Energy Techniques Display

By a Staff Reporter

New Delhi, April 23. An energy park depicting various modes of utilising solar radiation was opened today at a village on the outskirts of the Capital.

The park has been set up by the Delhi Energy Development Agency at a cost of Rs 10 lakhs. It displays the various ways in which people can save conventional fossil fuels and use new and renewable sources of energy.

The park, located in Kanganheri in the Najafgarh Block was inaugurated by the chief executive councillor, Mr. Jag Parvesh Chandra, today. It exhibits technologies based on various non-conventional sources of energy like solar cookers, solar hot water systems, solar air heaters, wind generator, windmill and a biogas plant.

Taking a press party round the park, Mr. Chandra said they were determined to develop Delhi as a model for the use of non-conventional energy sources and in this context, the Delhi administration had decided to establish five energy parks in the five blocks of Delhi. He said 100 acres of land had been acquired for this project and three energy parks had almost been completed while work on the other two was in progress.

The energy park, he pointed out, is a pilot project attempt to use non-conventional sources of energy in an integrated mannerpiped cooking gas, electricity for street lighting through photovoltaic cells and windpower for water pumping and supply to the villagers.

In Kanganheri 50 families out of a 100 odd have accepted the alternative energy source. According to the village pradhan this has reduced the drudgery of conventional cooking and given the village a sense of pride.

Mr. Chandra said the non-conventional energy scheme was three years old in rural areas and two years old in urban areas. In 1985-86, the Delhi Energy Development Agency had spent Rs 2. 60 crores on the implementation of various schemes and had managed to save 16 megawatts of electricity in the last two years, he added.

It was also pointed out that more than 5,000 solar cookers had been sold last year and the demand for them was growing continually which the agency was unable to meet.

Mr. C.S. Khairwal, agency director, said the gas supply from the sanitary landfill at Timarpur was being supplied to Balakram Hospital and about 100 homes in the vicinity.

Mr. D.C. Misra, development commissioner pointed out that 100 battery-operated buses would be in operation by the year-end. Thirty-two such buses have been plying in the congested walled city areas on different routes for the past six months.

The only non-official referred to in this story is the village pradhan. The reporter could have added flavour to the story by talking to actual users and those who have not opted for the new energy sources.

Development reporting is not always positive. Bad planning and improper implementation many a time result in shortfalls leading to difficulties. Such situations must be utilised by development reporters. Background and interpretation is an essential part of such a story and it requires much more leg work than a routine story. An example:

Orissa Power Crisis May Worsen
The Times of India News Service

Bhubaneswar, April 16—Orissa, which was surplus in power till the seventies, is sliding slowly but surely into a position where its peak shortfall in generation will mount from the present 500 MW to over 1,000 MW by 1990. And, worse, there is no sliver lining in sight.

The shortfall may, in fact, turn out to be still higher unless the five ongoing projects Rengali-I and II, Upper Kolab-1, Hirakud-I state-III and the Pteru Small Hydro—together accounting for only 204 MW, go on stream as per the revised schedules.

The projects, originally, scheduled to have been commissioned in phases between 1981-86 are now likely to go on stream between 1987 and mid-1988. Besides, the 600 MW Indravati project was started in 1971 for being commissioned before 1984 (first unit) and 1986 (second unit).

Shortfall : The ongoing projects, except Indravati and the existing ones, will account for 769 MW of power by the end of the seventh plan period against a peak demand for 1,785 MW and an average demand of (at 75 per cent load factor) 1,339 MW. While the peak shortfall is thus estimated at 1,016 MW, the average shortfall works out to 570 MW by the end of 1990.

Shortage of power in the state was indicated by the Central Energy Agency as early as 1979 in its annual load survey reports, when the Orissa electrical engineering service association too drew the attention of the authorities to the developing situation.

Between June and November 1985, there was a statutory power cut of 75 per cent for heavy and power-intensive industries. Some willing industries were however permitted to draw power at a higher tariff, purchased from outside the state by the Orissa State Electricity Board (OSEB).

Supply from AP : In December last the situation worsened as Andhra Pradesh stopped exporting power to the Orissa grid and the OSEB imposed a four-hour power cut on domestic consumers from January 1 last in addition to the 75 per cent cut enforced for industries. Power cut for ten to 12 hours during daytime was imposed on rural areas and for four to five hours on urban areas from February 1. The situation is likely to aggravate on depletion of water in the Hirakud and Balimela reservoirs.

Orissa is the only state where no new power project was started during the sixth plan period despite an investment of about Rs. 15,000 crores on power projects in the country. At the beginning of the seventh plan period, the power generation position was reviewed by a working group set up by the Union Ministry of power which recommended in February 1984, a national investment of Rs 1,420. 46 crores on generation. The amount was subsequently reduced to Rs 873 crores in view of the constraint of resources.

In December 1984 the working group further recommended an investment of Rs. 263.39 crores on new projects, the benefits of which could be expected to accrue during the seventh plan period. The Planning Commission approved Rs. 40.39 crores for "new projects" in Orissa during the seventh Plan period. Thus the expansion of only the Rengali project is possible during the plan period as a "new project".

Talcher Complex : Of the five existing power projects—Hirakud (120 MW), Balimela (135 MW), Machkund (40 MW), Talcher thermal power station-I (105 MW) and TIPS-II (114 MW)—the last two account for a firm power of 229 MW which will be expanded to 240 MW by 1990.

But the availability of power from Talcher is 180 MW on an average and 200 MW at the peak level. By all accounts, the failure of the Talcher complex has been largely responsible for the present power crisis in the state. Lack of training in operation and maintenance, deficiency in management strategy, poor material management and improper monitoring are still reportedly continuing in TTPS.

In June 1970 OSEB took over the management of the plant from the government when the power demand in the state was substantially low compared with the availability of electricity. Since hydel stations were able to meet the load demand in the state, inadequate attention was paid to TTPS by the board.

In the above story the reporter has used data from various sources and carefully interpreted it with background where necessary. The result of this analysis appears in the headline and the intro.

A development reporter has to be more careful while reporting social change. Look at the following story:

Dubey Concession to Kolhan Tribals
The Times of India News Service

Patna, May 8. The Bihar government has dropped the idea of annulling Wilkinson's rules guiding the administration of civil justice in the Kolhan region. This has been done following stiff opposition by some tribal Congress MLAs, informed sources said here yesterday.

The proposal to scrap these rules framed by a British official Capt. T. Wilkinson in 1934, had been prepared by the advocate general of Bihar at the instance of the government, which suddenly discovered that the rules had never been approved by the British authorities.

"There is no document to show that such approval was accorded by the authorities. To crown all these facts, the original Wilkinson's rules remain untraced. They could not be traced even in the national libraries of the country," the advocate-general said.

The revenue minister, Mr. Ramjaipal Singh Yadav, had called a meeting of some tribal Congress legislators here last week to finalise annulment of the rules. The meeting was attended by Mr. Devendra Nath Champia and Mr. Radhe Munda both MLAs from Singhbhum district, which covered the Kolhan region, and senior officials of the revenue department.

Mr. Champia and Mr. Munda expressed their strong opposition to the proposal and asserted that Wilkinson's rules had formed one of the basic guidelines for the British administrations during the colonial days. They were accepted as guidelines by the district administration even after independence. When the minister pointed out that the Congress MP, Mr. Bagun Sumbrai, had approved of the annulment of the rules, the two MLAs said that the latter probably did not understand the draft prepared by the advocate general.

The meeting had not gone for more than half an hour when the minister declared that the rules would not be scrapped.

The dropping of the proposal for annulment of Wilkinson's rules is seen here as another major concession granted by the Dubey ministry to the tribals. There is a strong demand for making Chotanagpur and Santhal Parganas into a Union territory. Mr. Champia has, in recent months, emerged as the central figure of the movement for formation of a Union territory. He has led a team of 50 MPs and MLAs to give a memorandum to the President and the Union Home Minister when they visited Patna some months ago.

Here, the reporter has failed to explain Wilkinson's rules. The story also fails to explain the reasons on the basis of which the two tribal MLAs supported these rules. The reporter has interpreted that by retaining these rules the government has given concessions to Kolhan tribals. But without telling anything about what these rules are and how they differ from normal rules, the story does not make any sense and thus just wastes valuable space.

Development journalism thus deals with a wide variety of

situations. It covers individual projects, the entire planning process and its implementation, difficulties faced by people and efforts made to remove them, economic and social change in rural and urban areas, impact of development efforts in backward and tribal areas and various aspects of development and its socio-economic impact.

There are endless possibilities of innovations. The *Hindustan Times* made history in rural reporting by taking up a village, Chhatera, at the outskirts of Delhi and periodically describing the economic and social changes taking place there. Similarly, *Punjabi Tribune* launched a column, "Pinda Vicho Pind Sunida" in which socio-economic conditions of villages were described. In this column, some reports were excellent covering all aspects of village life while some were very superficial just presenting some statistical data. Hard work and imagination is essential to enliven such reports.

While reporting on a village the reporter should meet members of all the strata of rural society. He should not hesitate in using interpreters where necessary. He should also keep an eye on implementation of various rural development schemes and must try to evaluate the import of these schemes on the various strata of society. Patience and understanding are basic requirements for rural reporting. Rural reporter has to watch for self-glorification and self-pity and must cross-check the facts where necessary.

While reporting on tribal areas it is necessary to understand the customs of the people and their way of life. One has to look for possible socio-economic changes and how these changes affect the routine life of the tribal population. Rural and tribal areas are very fertile for human interest stories related to development.

Thus development reporting is not as simple as its critics in the West think. This is a very complex area of reporting because it does not involve events but socio-economic processes that are much more complex than an assassination or a coup.

Bibliography

Altschull, J.H.: *Agents of Power: the Role of the News Media in Human Affairs,* Longman, New York, 1984.

Baker, R.K., and Ball, SJ.: *Mass Media and Violence, Report to the National Commission on the Causes and Prevention of Violence,* 1969.

Bell, D.V.J.: *Power, Influence and Authority,* Oxford University Press, London, 1975.

Berelson, B.: *Content Analysis in Communication Research,* Free Press, Glencoe, Illinois, 1952.

Bhattacharya, Bhabani: *Gandhi the Writer,* National Book Trust, New Delhi, 1969.

Blumer, J.G.: 'The Political Effect of Television' in Halloran, J.D., *The Effect of Mass Communication,* Leicester University Press, Leicester, 1970.

Carey, James W.: *Communication as Culture: Essays on Media and Society,* Routledge, New York, 1992.

Chaffee, S.H. and Berger, C.R. : *Handbook of Communication Science,* Sage Publications, Beverly Hills, London, 1987.

Chaney, D.: *Processes of Mass Communication,* Macmillan, London, 1972.

Cohen, S. and Young, J. : *The Manufacture of News,* Constable, London, 1973.

Czitrom, Daniel J.: *Media and the American Mind: From Morse to McLuhan,* University of North Corolina Press, Chapel Hill.

Davis, Howard and Walton, Paul : *Language, Image, Media*, Basil Blackwell, Oxford, 1983.

Davison, W.P.: *Mass Gommunication and Conflict Resolution*, Praeger, New York, 1974.

De Fleur, M.: *Theories of Mass Communication*, David Mckay, New York, 1970.

Deutsch, K.V.: *Nationalism and Social Communication*, MIT Press, Cambridge, 1966.

Dexter, L. A. and White, D.M. : *People, Society and Mass Communication*, Free Press, New York, 1964.

Fiske, J.: *Introduction to Communication Studies*, Methuen, London, 1982.

Gerbner, G. : *Mass Media Policies in Changing Cultures*, Wiley, New York, 1977.

Gurvitch, M., Bennet, T. and Woollacott, J. : *Culture, Society and Mass Media*, Methuen, London, 1982.

Hopkins, M. W.: *Mass Media in the Soviet Union*, Pegasus, 1970.

Innis, Harold Adams: *Empire and Communication*, University of Toronto Press, Toronto, 1972.

Katz, E. and Szecsko, T. : *Mass Media and Social Change*, Sage Publications, Beverly Hills and London, 1981.

Kraus, S., and Davis, D.K.: *The Effect of Mass Communication on Political Behaviour*, Pennsylvania State University Press, University Park, 1976.

McLuhan, M.: *Understanding Media*, Routledge and Kegan Paul, London, 1964.

Mendelbaum, S.J.: *Community and Communicating*, Norton, New York, 1972.

Seymour-Ure, C: *The Political Impact of Mass Media*, Constable, New York, 1973.

Szalai, A. : *The United Nations and the News Media*, UNITAR, New York, 1972.